Marriage

THE MICROCOSMIC
DANCE OF CREATION

Based on the teachings of

Rav Dovber Pinson

IYYUN PUBLISHING

Published by IYYUN Publishing
650 Sackett Street
Brooklyn, NY 11217

http:/www.iyyun.com

Iyyun Publishing books may be purchased for educational, business or sales promotional use. For information please
contact: contact@IYYUN.com

Editor: R. Pinson

Editor: Reb Eden Pearlstein

Cover and book design: RP Design and Development

pb ISBN 979-8-9919640-3-6

Pinson, DovBer 1971–
MARRIAGE : The Microcosmic Dance of Creation

ב"ה

Marriage

THE MICROCOSMIC
DANCE OF CREATION

Based on the teachings of

Rav Dovber Pinson

Sam & Ashley Levinson שיחיו

May your next chapters together be rich with
wonder, growth and blessings.
May your home continue to be a place
of sweetness, where the Divine is felt
in every laugh,
every story,
and every act of kindness.

Opening

Part One

Part Two

Appendix

Note:

This text marks a departure in both tone and content from what is usually shared. These are delicate matters, ideally explored in the sacred space between spouses; quietly, privately, and with dignity (*Chagigah*, 11b). Yet, the heartbreaking reality is that there are rising divorce rates amongst all communities, with many couples struggling to find true joy in their marriages. This doesn't only affect the marriages in question, but when the bond between spouses falters, its ripple often extends into every aspect of life. There was a time when perhaps many of the truths expressed in this book would have been regarded as self-evident, woven into the natural rhythm of loving, healthy relationships and exemplified in the marriages of parents and grandparents, but in our present age, such clarity has been obscured, and what was once intuitive now often requires conscious remembrance. This conscious effort to sustain and nourish marriage is lifegiving for all of creation. It is taught that when peace and love flourish between spouses, the Shechinah, the Divine Presence, comes to dwell within them, resting upon their union and, by extension, radiating blessing and harmony throughout the entire world.

Opening

IN THE BEGINNING

Marriage, at its essence, is an act of creation. In the moment two people join together in matrimony, something entirely new is born—not merely two individuals standing side by side—but a shared being, a living bond, a home that never existed before. Yet marriage is not a single moment of creation; it is a continuous unfolding. It calls us to keep shaping and reshaping the inner life we build together; to grow, to refine, and to co-create not only our shared world, but the world around us.

Before exploring marriage more deeply, it's worth pausing to reflect on the nature of creativity itself.

Creativity is not merely an attribute we possess it is the very core of our being, the essence of who we are.

Like all living things, we need to absorb food, oxygen, experiences, impressions, and inspiration. We are recipients of the world around us and of the Creator of all life. Yet, being fashioned in the Divine image, we are not 'receivers' only. We carry within us an echo of cosmic creativity, that luminous spark through which the world emerged from nothingness. Within us burns an innate drive to self-express, to give, to build, and to contribute. While receiving is 'natural', creating is 'transcendent'; it is an expression of our deepest Divine essence. While receiving sustains us, creating elevates us. By creating, we express our essence and fulfill our role as co-creators in the continuous unfolding of the world.

Genuine creativity does not arise from a place of lack or deficiency within oneself. Creativity is not born from something missing, but from an overflow, a fullness that longs to be expressed. Creativity is not a compensation for emptiness rather, it is the essence of who we are desiring to be communicated. It is the sacred impulse to give form and expression to the richness within, to make visible the ineffable depths of our being.

In the same way, Creation was and is not created from a place of need or absence within the Divine. Being infinite and whole, the Creator lacks nothing. In absolute perfection there is no room for necessity. A need implies something missing, but that which is truly complete is free of needs. Thus, the act of Creation did not emerge from a primordial void, but from the fullness of Divine desire, a yearning to express and share, to reveal the Infinite within the finite, to manifest the Indivisible Divine Self in and through a 'world'.

Every act of true human creativity mirrors that original impulse to Self-express. To create is not to fill a gap, but to overflow, to give voice to the silent music within, to share our inner self simply because it must be shared.

BEING A CREATOR

Our need to create is not limited to bringing new life into the world, though that is its most literal expression of our innate creative drive. To live fully and authentically, we must embrace creativity in all aspects of life.

Moreover, creativity is not limited to tangible expressions alone, such as music, art, or technological innovation. Creativity is, rather, unfolding within every thought, word, and action, interwoven seamlessly into every breath, every heartbeat, and every sparkling moment of existence. In each passing instant, we stand at a crossroads, faced with a profound choice: to remain passive recipients, drifting through life as if victims of circumstance, or to boldly embrace our power as creators. When we claim our role as co-creators of reality, we own our power of choice, and can shape our lives into unique works of art, transforming ordinary moments into opportunities for growth, meaning, and renewal.

The truth is, each one of us is already inherently a creator, continuously sculpting our reality, at times with intention and consciously, yet more often without even realizing our agency. Every moment of our existence is a subtle act of creation, as we are instilling meaning into the ceaseless flow of sensations, perceptions, and emotions that pour through our awareness. We continuously process and contextualize the streams of sensory stimuli, and with every breath and every heartbeat, we silently craft the narrative of our lives, seeing the world not only as it presents itself to us, but as we *choose* to see it, and shape it.

Whether awake or asleep, we are absorbing the world around us, what we see, hear, smell, taste, and touch. But we do not merely 'receive'; we filter, interpret, and imbue these experiences into the fabric of our inner world. In doing so, we construct the lens through which we perceive and engage with life, and then project this 'inner' world upon our 'outer' world.

Although we are often unaware of it, we are always gathering sights, sounds, and sensations and interpreting them. We do not simply 'receive' data we form these fragments into patterns that fit our conditioning and expectations. We may tell ourselves that life happens *to* ,us, as if there is a purely objective world 'out there' affecting a separate subjective world 'in here.' But this is essentially an illusion. We do not just perceive the 'external' world, rather we also 'co-create' this world, moment by moment, within us. In this sense, the observed and the observer are one.

Additionally, as we shape our worldview, we influence how the world responds to us. If I interpret the people around me as friendly, I will react to them positively, and this will draw out from them deeper levels of friendliness.

All of this means that we need to take an active role in the co-creation of our world and our relationships. As beings with a potential for free choice, we need to develop our capacity to consciously choose how we are shaping our lives, rather than passively allowing life to shape us. Although we are mere 'created' beings, the drive to 'create' is inseparable from our being. Creativity is our Divine birthright, an essential part of our humanity, and it is ours to awaken within us.

Within each of us lies an innate need, a deep instinctual desire, to create. Whether it is expressed in the words we use and the imaginative ideas we develop, or the innumerable acts of nurturing and raising a child, this impulse is embedded in our very essence. Our ability to create, to give rise to something new, is a reflection of the Infinite and boundless creative power of the Creator. Miraculously, we finite creations house a spark of this infinite Divine power, an echo of the very force that brought the world into being.

All living organisms desire to procreate, and the drive to create new life is a basic thread woven into human existence. One of the most profound expressions of this creative drive is found in our relationships, especially in the sacred bond of marriage. Here, creativity is realized not only in bearing new biological life, but also in birthing shared meaning and growth, and building a beautiful edifice of generosity and service to others.

Every relationship is an act of 'formation', but marriage is a 'new creation' in its own right, a living, evolving entity that is made moment by moment, shaped by the love, effort, and intention that is poured into it.

YOU ARE THE CREATOR
OF YOUR EXPERIENCES

Our existence is a canvas, and we are its painters, coloring our own perception of life with every brushstroke, every thought, word, and action. Nowhere is this more true than in our relationships. True, it is easy to mar our canvas with dark streaks of blame and resentment, to see ourselves as victims of circumstance and claim that our emotions are our spouse's fault. But we can always start cultivating the choice to live authentically and take full responsibility for the tones of our own experience. We have the power to paint our canvas with the graceful shades of patience and emotional intelligence that we wish to see.

We need to recognize that the 'steering wheel' of our life is our own choices and actions. To thrive, we need to acknowledge our own role in 'steering' our reality toward what we want it to be.

True growth begins when we stop shifting the blame for our experience, and start recognizing that it is about us, not 'them'. We are the architect of our happiness. The moment we embrace this truth, we reclaim our power, stepping into the role of active builders rather than passive recipients of life.

Put bluntly, we need to cease blaming others and start living with the knowledge that our happiness and satisfaction are ultimately in *our* hands. We stop shifting the responsibility. *We* create our experience, and no one else; not our parents nor our boss, nor our spouse, is responsible for the way we experience life. How we live and how we see and experience our circumstances is *our* choice.

Every moment, whether consciously or not, we make choices that guide us on a specific path. We hold the power to progress in the direction we want to go, to make intentional decisions that reflect our deepest values, desires, and soul-guidance. Our specific destination may not be in our hands, but we can always take the 'higher road', determining not only how we experience the world, but also influencing how the world responds to us.

Owning your life means embracing your responsibilities, stepping into your creative power, and continuously growing in the present. It is always about *you*. When you take control in this way, when you create with purpose, you unlock the limitless potential that is already within you.

The moment you stop consciously creating, stop actively shaping your life and choosing how to respond to events and stimuli, you slip into autopilot, living mechanically and reactively. When this happens, the present becomes a mere echo of the past; you begin to hypnotically live out past conditioning or ineffective patterns lodged in your subconscious mind. Life then feels like a monotonous cycle and you may begin to feel that you might as well give up on having what you want and need.

At times, when the darkness of stagnation or even depression sets in, you might even consider making drastic changes, such as moving or finding a new job, in order to bring you a sense of renewal. But in reality, all you need is to reconnect with your creative essence, which is always fresh and new. When you make the decision to live creatively in the present, moment by moment, you begin to reclaim your life and transform it from the inside out.

In relationships, when people stop owning their reactions and responses to the other person, when they begin to see themselves as victims, they fall into a rut. They lose sight of meaning and purpose, feeling disconnected from passion and fulfillment. Gradually, this sense of stagnation can lead them to consider that they must make drastic changes in their lives, such as divorce, in order to feel alive again. But in truth, what is needed for a 'fresh start' is not a dramatic or radical outer change, rather a simple return to creativity and a commitment to engaging mindfully in the work of nurturing the relationship.

When people decisively turn to creativity and intention, they will no longer feel like victims. When they reclaim their creative instinct, they will take charge of their happiness. They will breathe new life into all aspects of their life — their marriage included — and rediscover the original purpose and passion that fueled it.

If someone refuses to accept that they are a creator of their domestic happiness, and they tenaciously hold onto a sense of entitlement, being married can seem like an insurmountable chore. As they believe that they should be the 'receiver' of domestic happiness, instead of embracing the work required to create it, when a challenge arises, it seems unmanageable and they may feel the urge to simply opt out. However, this escape strategy only brings an increased sense of victimization and burden, leaving them even more unfulfilled and resentful. Sadly, the escape itself becomes a prison, as subsequent relationships eventually follow the same pattern as the preceding one. One remains passive, stuck in a cycle.

Marriage calls for effort, devotion, courage, and creativity. It may seem 'easier' to walk away from its challenges, but the profundity of this bond is only discovered when one leans into the challenges, and chooses to actively nurture and reimagine. We are given innumerable opportunities to infuse our relationship with new vitality, deeper love, and evolving connection. A marriage is not delivered to our door, assembled and with a charged battery rather, it is continually created and recreated, day to day and moment to moment.

Sadly, those living in more westernized or open societies are highly vulnerable to a multi-billion-dollar industry that subtly, and at times not at all subtly, encourages divorce. Advertising media, entertainment and cultural messaging display seeming incentives in disposing of an older relationship and acquiring a new one, or simply remaining single. A vast web of lawyers and other service professionals and corporations is activated well before spouses are given the tools to heal, grow, rediscover one another, and rescue their marriage. While this phenomenon is particularly prevalent in more secular environments, still, the 'culture virus' of divorce, and the huge profit machine fed by it, has infiltrated nearly all communities. No one is entirely immune.

EXTERNAL AND INTERNAL CREATIVITY

Interestingly, some of the most artistically creative individuals today are not married or are refraining from physical procreation. Every person, being created in the Divine image, carries an innate drive to create and be like the Creator. When the drive to create is not channeled into a relationship or parenting, it will find other means of expression.

Yet, the deepest of all forms of creativity occurs within a healthy marriage relationship. When two individuals choose to make a sacred covenant and live with each other, they mirror the Divine act of creation itself, reflecting the Creator's intention to create a world and thereby relate to 'another' in a sacred bond. The ability to literally create new life, to bring children into the world, is an expression of creativity. But equally significant is the creative energy that flows within the relationship itself, as two individual people commit to growing together. Indeed, within this dynamic, we experience the most profound creative potential within ourselves.

In the very act of becoming married, one co-creates a brand new entity: there is now a new couple, a new home in the world. Being married also gives us the continuous opportunity to evolve, to be the creators of our own inner life and, by extension, the creators of the world around us.

MARRIAGE AS A MIRROR

Marriage is the ultimate and proverbial mirror, constantly reflecting back to you who you truly are, revealing whether you are living up to your full physical, mental, emotional, and spiritual potential. Every day, in each moment, marriage shows where you stand in your growth, whether you are becoming more kind, thoughtful, patient, and spiritually aligned with your purpose in this world.

While a person may project a certain self-image to the outside world, their true self is revealed in marriage. The one person who can truly see you as you are, and understand where you are in your journey, is your spouse.

Marriage serves as the greatest measure of our honesty and sincerity, offering a clear reflection of where we stand in relation to who we really are, and where we are holding in our personal development.

Marriage is not merely about choosing one's spouse in the privacy of the heart, but also about choosing them again and again, in public, in moments of pressure, and in the tests that life inevitably brings. It is within the sacred crucible of marriage that some of the deepest *Tikunim* / rectifications and corrections of self-character are revealed and achieved.

A purpose of marriage is to help our spouse, through kindness, love, and gentle support, to fulfill their Tikun, guiding and nurturing their journey toward spiritual and emotional healing and wholeness.

Often, people marry someone who reflects the traits of a parent with whom they had challenges, and in doing so, they are presented with the opportunity to heal and break outdated patterns—to do things differently this time. Each spouse holds the potential to nurture the other's growth, helping to heal their wounds. Within the sacred bond of marriage, one has the power to reawaken in their spouse the life-giving spirituality of being a human being, in a way that brings them healing, renewal, and restoration.

Our *Tikun* / soul elevation and correction, is to bring deep creativity to such life experiences, and to be intentional in each moment, avoiding slipping into automatic, autopilot living. We need to avoid repeating negative patterns, or clinging to a victim mentality, no matter our circumstances. We are called to choose life and be dynamic, mindful creators of wholeness. Each moment offers the opportunity to create something new, to break free from ineffective ways of relating to people, and to choose a different path. In doing so, we not only heal ourselves but bring healing and Tikunim to our spouse, transforming our life and theirs as well.

DESIRE WITHIN CONTINUED COMMITMENT

Marriage includes passion, desire, excitement, creativity, and vibrancy, within the boundaries and structure of order, commitment, dedication, and devotion. The prophet Hoshea writes that Hashem (G-d) tells us, "I will betroth you forever." Often our relationship with the Creator is referred to in terms of marriage, but here it is precisely the idea of engagement which gives us a 'forever.'

Betrothal is a season of wonder, a delicate dance of anticipation, passion, and unfolding discovery. Every situation feels electric, every word charged with possibility. Nothing compares to the poetry of beginning, the quiet thrill of finding one's soul revealed in another. Marriage, in its maturity, does bring a new kind of blessing, a deep sense of stability, safety, and often the quiet regularity and rhythm of shared life. While this is valuable, there is a risk as a marriage matures: that the fire may be lulled into a gentle, predictable flicker.

The Creator's eternal promise, "I will betroth you to Me forever," speaks of a love that never dulls, a bond that defies time. It informs us that a true and living covenant is not meant to fade into habit and expectation, but to continually renew itself, pulsing with the vitality of that first connection. The secret to enduring love lies in preserving the spirit of 'engagement'.

To remain 'engaged' in marriage is to never stop looking at your spouse with eyes of wonder, gratitude, and curiosity. Curiosity means being open to the unfolding mystery of the other, never presuming to fully know them, always ready to be pleasantly surprised. The moment curiosity ceases, wonder withers, and when wonder withers, life itself begins to lose its color, becoming predictable, stagnant, stale, and unimaginative. But when we stay awake to each other, when we greet our spouse with openness, as if meeting them for the first time, we breathe life into the relationship. Real passion is not found in time-bound novelty nor in high emotions; it is found in a deepening capacity to see our spouse anew. In profound curiosity, there is a well of passion and love that never runs dry.

The relationship between ourselves and the Creator serves as the ultimate paradigm of marriage. For example, we have an eternal covenant, we are in a sense like old spouses, and yet, we are constantly reminded to view our connection to the Source of all Life as fresh and new, as if we are right now standing at the foot of Mount Sinai, on our metaphorical wedding day. Our human marriage covenant is also eternal, and yet it needs to be continually reinvigorated, combining the security of commitment and obligation with the thrill of discovery.

Sadly, many people long to live with passion, vibrancy, and creativity, yet they feel that they must do so at the *expense* of their true integrity and commitment, and even their fidelity. They believe that in order to tap into a flow of freshness and creative freedom, they must escape the constraints of commitment. However, much like a painter needs a canvas or a musician needs an instrument to express their art, we need a context and container in which to live out our creativity. Marriage provides this context, and it is only within the container of this profound bond that a person can channel the full passion of their heart and liberate their creative energy. Whether 'creating' and raising children, sculpting a solid relationship, or composing new passageways for healing and Tikun, a healthy marriage is the *Kli* / implement with which one can flourish in the art of life.

ATTENTIVENESS TO YOUR INNER HURT AND THE HURT WITHIN YOUR SPOUSE

Just as there are people who live consciously and people who do not yet live consciously, there are conscious marriages and unconscious ones. When one is not fully present and mindful in their marriage, frustration and resentment quietly begin to accumulate and then take root. Without realizing it, spouses become entrapped in replaying their old habits, unconscious patterns, and unresolved traumas. Conversations grow reactive, interactions become mechanical, and the space between them gradually fills with tension and distance.

Unhealed emotional wounds, especially those rooted in childhood, have a way of resurfacing, often in unexpected moments. A word, gesture, or even a few seconds of silence, can reawaken hidden pain lingering beneath the surface of a person's consciousness.

When one does not acknowledge or tend to their own long-repressed emotion, hurt, or fear, its pent-up energy eventually begins to break through and create a behavioral rut or loop, contaminating the present with the past. Say, for some reason, one's buried childhood sense of defensiveness erupts, and, misplaced, it is directed at one's spouse. In an uncannily precise way, this triggers their spouse's buried sense of insecurity and anxiety, calling forth in them an instinct to retreat and shut down. Unfortunately, seeing them shut down exacerbates the first spouse's defensiveness, and a vicious cycle is established. In due time, such a dynamic casts a dark shadow over the relationship, and both parties begin to view their once joyful bond as a source of suffering, anger, and distance.

To cultivate a thriving marriage, we must choose to be conscious and creative, just as in any other area of our life. Only by recognizing our own unconscious reactivity, and returning to intentionality, can we break free from habitual words and behaviors that do not serve us, and form new, effective responses. Only then can we create a partnership that is awake, alive, and on the path of healing and Tikun.

So many people are open to hold the pain of others, precisely when those others are strangers or distant from our immediate orbit. Yet, the most important person in your world is your spouse. That is the one who needs you most to hold their pain. And when you hold your spouse fully, with presence, tenderness, and care, you open yourself to hold the fullness of life itself, with all its joy, sorrow, depth, and beauty.

CHESED & GEVURAH / EXPANSION, CREATIVITY & MAINTENANCE, SECURITY

There are, broadly speaking, two fundamental forces that flow through the universe. One is the force of *Chesed* / creative, expansive generosity and the impulse to give. The other is the force of *Gevurah* / restraint, discipline, the power to hold back or contain. These opposing energies complement each other as they shape the dynamic aliveness of existence.*

When the Creator brought Creation into being, it began to expand without restraint or boundaries. It was only when the Divine voice declared, *Dai* / "Enough; stop!" that this expansion was contained and given form.** This interplay between boundless growth and deliberate limitation lies at the heart of all sustainable creativity. Giving without boundaries spirals into chaos. Restriction without any expansiveness suffocates potential and stifles structural integrity before it can emerge. Even if a stage of structural integrity has an opportunity to emerge, unchecked restriction leads to stagnation and collapse. Only through the perfect balance of the forces of giving and holding back can the existence of Creation endure.

---

* They are also called *Rachamim* and *Din*. These two forces are also the *Chomer* and *Tzurah* / substance and form, as the Tzemach Tzedek explains: *Ohr HaTorah*, Chanukah.

** *Chagigah*, 12a.

This means that within all of Creation, two forces are always at play: the expansive, evolutionary energy of giving and growth, the force that furthers and nurtures life, and the restrictive, disciplined energy of boundaries and restraint, the force that preserves and sustains life.

Similarly, as beings created in the Divine image, we possess two intrinsic forces within us: the drive to create, perpetuate, and advance life, and the urge to maintain, preserve, and safeguard what we already have and value. These two dominant forces guide us, one propelling us to procreate and further life, and the other to preserve and extend our life.

In the Garden of Eden, humanity was charged with two intertwined tasks: "to work and to protect"; to be productive and creative, and to maintain and safeguard Creation. The very first Mitzvah, the first Divine command, given to us was "create and multiply." This summons us to participate in the Divine act of creation itself: to generate life, to cultivate growth, and to further existence. This is a call to embody creativity, expansion, and the forward movement of life. Yet immediately, the Torah adds, "and master it." We are tasked not only with creating and expanding, but also with guiding, and disciplining our creative urge. From the very beginning, our purpose lies in the integration of both forces.

"To work" and "to protect" are inherent in all people. While some individuals excel at maintaining value and others shine in creating value, some are more artistic and innovative, while others are adept at managing, organizing, and instilling order, all have capacities for both giving and holding back.

The need for these dual forces is deeply embedded in every human relationship, and especially marriage. Our sages say, "Any man without a woman... dwells without a wall of protection." A healthy marriage not only brings a person stability and security, but also a context to expansively express their creativity, from having children to engaging in ongoing spiritual, psychological and relational growth and renewal. Hence, "a man without a woman... is left without *Beracha* / blessing." Beracha is generative; it means a continuously increasing creation of benefit.*

Indeed, at the heart of a good marriage lies the dynamic balance of Chesed and Gevurah, of giving and holding back. Marriage requires both the inspiring practices of creativity and renewal, and the steadying practices of responsibility and stabilization. A healthy union thrives on the interplay of exciting change and the reassurance of a dependable status quo. While a relationship needs a container of routine and an anchor of consistency, it also needs constant reinvention and shared explorations of new perspectives and experiences. This balance is essential.

LOVE IS THE ESSENCE OF CREATION

The archetype of marriage is woven into the very fabric of Creation itself. Creation mirrors the deep yearning of the soul, and our relationships are microcosmic reflections of that primordial act of Divine love. Love is not merely an ornament within Creation rather it is the hidden force from which creation was birthed.

---

* *Yevamos*, 62b. 'Blessing' means something that increases, especially on its own: *Kidushin*, 17a, Rashi. Rambam, *Hilchos Avadim*, 3:14.

Love is the foundation of all that exists: *Olam Chesed Yibaneh* / "The world is built upon kindness."* The root of every soul, beneath every joy and sorrow, harbors a secret, eternal longing: to love and to be loved.

Even before the first Divine Word shattered the stillness and summoned worlds into being, Infinite Love filled the Infinite Light, yearning, as it were, to give of Itself to *another*, to express Itself to and within someone 'other than Itself.' From that original Divine longing our world unfolded; and from that love, each soul, a spark of purest essence, was formed as a vessel to receive, and to give, love. Love is who we are.

An act of love makes space for the 'other' to fully become, emerge and flower in their uniqueness. A primal example of this is a parent who loves their child and makes space for the child to exist, to become who they are called to be, in this world.

Love is not a mere emotion it is the cosmic force animating all things. Torah urges us, "Love your fellow as yourself; *I Am* the Infinite Source of Existence (Hashem)." The two halves of this imperative are not separate. To love another person *is* to awaken to the Divine 'I Am', and to touch the infinite source of our own existence.

If you feel or imagine that you 'know G-d', but struggle to love people, know that you do not yet know G-d. Conversely, if you believe you feel and understand love, and yet you cannot find your way to G-d, know that you do not yet understand love.

---

* *Tehilim*, 89:3.

We are drawn to love, for in love we find our origin. And it is to that Endless 'I Am', the Source of Love, that we will, inevitably, return. Indeed, true love is the most powerful and tangible revelation of Divine Be-ing in this world. When we encounter authentic love, we are tasting the very radiance of the Creator woven into Creation. Love *is* the Infinite Light: fierce yet tender, the sheer brilliance of the Timeless and Spaceless One revealing Its Presence within the realm of time, space, and human interactions.

As we experience love, we experience a 'taste' of that Light. This is why, when spouses are giving each other true love and honor, the *Shechinah* / Divine Presence rests between them in a tangible way. The Hebrew word for love, אהבה / *Ahavah,* is an acronym for *Ohr HaKadosh Baruch Hu* / "the Light of the Holy Blessed One." When love flows freely between spouses, the Light of the Creator illuminates their hearts and spills outward, transforming their home into a sanctuary of warmth, love, and holiness.

Sometimes you can simply walk into a home and feel the unmistakable presence of something unseen yet profoundly real. You can sense if a house is heavy with strife or filled with an invisible, shimmering Presence.

When we live in harmony with this love, when we align our lives with this sacred and creative Light from which we were fashioned, this light radiates outward, transforming not only our homes but everything and everyone around us.

Part One

THE COSMIC TEMPLATE
OF MARRIAGE

The most profound way to understand the dynamics of healthy relationships is to explore how the Torah describes the birth of humanity, the very 'genesis' of all relationships.

In these primal moments lie the keys not only to our interpersonal bonds, but also to the cosmic relationship between the Creator and Creation, the *Above* is mirrored in the world *below*, and the *below* reflects the *Above*. By studying these origins, we uncover the deeper design of connection; within ourselves, with each other, and connection with the Divine.*

---

* In general, marital issues are a delicate matter, and best explored in private. *Chagigah*, 11b. Beyond the issue of 'modesty', which unfortunately is widely misunderstood, another reason not to speak about such sensitive issues in public is

THE WAY THE TORAH DESCRIBES
THE CREATION OF MANKIND

The Torah presents a majestic progression of creation, unfolding in purposeful stages. On the "fifth day," the world comes alive with movement and breath, as creatures of the sea and birds of the sky are brought into being, each according to its kind, filling the waters and the heavens with vibrant life. Then, on the "sixth day," the animal kingdom is formed: beasts, cattle, and creeping things, each emerging from the earth, and completing the diversity of earthly life. Only then, as the crown of Creation, does humanity appear. Man and woman are fashioned last, emerging after all else.

Yet, there are seemingly two different ways the Torah describes the creation of the human being, with the prototype of human beings, Adam and Chava / Eve.

In Chapter One of *Bereishis*, the Torah relates how Adam and Chava are created with one body, half male and half female: "And Elokim (a Name of G-d connoting the Divine Light as manifest

---

also because there is no one-size-fits-all form of advice; no two relationships are the same, and there are many different types of relationship that can work, each with different strengths, needs and pitfalls. While there are different paradigms of marriage that fit different cultures and communities, there are also unique dynamics brought by the specific upbringing, conditioning and past experiences of each partner. All of these factors modulate a person's expectations and experience of marriage. Since there is no one model of marriage, there is arguably very little *human* advice or guidance that will be relevant and acceptable cross-culturally, in every place and situation. However, teachings about marriage are effective when they emanate from the Divine paradigm of Torah, universal higher wisdom that can be integrated by anyone and in any circumstance. That said, this does not negate the importance of seeking professional help when needed.

in the natural world and in human experience) created the human in His image*; in the image of Elokim He created him; male and female He created *them*."**

This means that the male and female dimensions of the human being were created 'back-to-back', as a singular body with two opposite 'faces' or sides. The human being, Adam, is thus presented as a unified, androgynous being, a creation containing both masculine and feminine aspects within a single form. This is a depiction of an *Achor b'Achor* / 'back-to back' relationship, as will be explored.***

In Chapter Two of Bereishis, there is a seemingly contradictory story.**** Here, the Creator says, "It is not good for Adam to be alone; I shall make him a helpmate opposite him." But wasn't male and female already created? What does it mean that Adam was "alone"? Besides, "It is not good for Adam to be alone," seems to suggest that Adam was 'male', however we just learned that "male and female He created them," meaning that the 'original' human was in some way a plurality, both male and female.*****

Either way, noticing 'his' loneliness, the Torah continues, "and

---

* Hebrew is a gendered language, and when the Torah speaks of G-d as Creator, the masculine pronouns are used.

** *Bereishis*, 1:27.

*** *Eiruvin*, 18a-b. *Berachos*, 61a. *Medrash Rabbah*, Bereishis, 8:1.

**** There are no actual 'chapters' in the Torah, as evidenced in the Torah scroll itself. Yet, the 'academic' overlay of chapters has been universally adopted for easy reference.

***** The *Zohar* (1, 55b) teaches that there is a difference between *Adam* / man, which is the complete human being, both male and female (5:1-2). Whereas *HaAdam* / the man (2:18), is the incomplete human, a male without a female counterpart.

so Hashem Elokim cast a deep sleep upon 'the Adam', and while he slept, He took one of his ribs (or 'sides') and closed up the flesh at that spot. And Hashem Elokim fashioned the side that He had taken from 'the man' into a woman; and He brought her to the man." Here, it clearly appears that Chava was created out of a 'part' of Adam, yet in Chapter One, they were already referred to as "them," with the understanding that Adam and Chava were different parts of a single human being.

In Chapter One, 'Adam-Chava' is created as one being, by Elokim, the Divine Power that creates nature and vests itself in nature. Hence, in this unfolding of the story, Adam and Chava are part of each other, and part of their surrounding environment, almost like an unselfconscious animal, or like a plant with two opposite-facing blossoms.

In Chapter Two, there is a completely different story of their creation, as if the first story had not even happened: "And Hashem Elokim formed man of dust from the ground, and He breathed into his nostrils the soul of life, and man became a living soul."* In this scenario, Adam and Chava are created as fully 'human', birthed with the soul of life, which means with the ability to speak and communicate. Thus, at the outset, they are invested with 'soul', something that sets them apart from their natural environment. As their souls come from the Divine "breath," this part of them is otherworldly, not part of the natural Creation. Furthermore, the Name Hashem, connoting the Transcendent dimension of Divinity, is used in this version of their creation, not merely the Name Elokim, as in Chapter One:

---

* *Bereishis,* 2:7.

"And *Elokim* said, 'Let us make man in Our image, after Our likeness, and they shall rule over the fish of the sea and over the fowl of the heaven and over the animals and over all the earth and over all the creeping things that creep upon the earth.' And *Elokim* created man in His image; in the image of *Elokim* He created him; male and female He created them.'"*

In Chapter Two, "Hashem Elokim" blows into Adam's nostrils a breath of life. The Name Hashem, sometimes called 'the Tetragrammaton', is made up of four Hebrew letters: Yud, Hei, Vav, and Hei. These four letters can be rearranged and permuted to spell the words *Hayah* / it was, *Hoveh* / it is, *Yihyeh* / it will be. They can also be read as Yud-HoVeH. *Hoveh* / 'is' means 'the present', and the Yud transforms that meaning into a 'continuous act'.** In this way, Yud-HoVeH means 'Eternally Present'. This is the attribute of the breath transmitted from the 'inside' of the Creator, as it were, as "He who blows, blows from within him." The Creator exhaled Eternal Presence from the innermost Divine essence into the innermost being of humanity, giving us the ability to return to conscious presence in the 'now', and to 'begin again' at any moment.

"In (or 'with') the beginning, Elokim created...." In this, the first Pasuk, verse in the Torah, 'Elokim' created the world in the *past tense*. Yet, 'Hashem' is the Creator in the *present tense*, as in many of the blessings we recite, for example, *Borei Pri haGafen* / "(Blessed is Hashem...who) *creates* the fruit of the vine."***

---

* *Bereishis*, 1:26-27.
** Rashi, *Iyov*, 1:5. *Tanya*, Sha'ar Yichud v'haEmunah, 4.
*** See *Kedushas Levi*, Bereishis: ולכן אנו אומרים יוצר אור ... ולא יצר אור ...רק יוצר בלשון
.הוה, כי בכל רגע הוא יוצר שבכל רגע הוא משפיע רגע חיות לכל חי

Conscious presence is only available in the paradigm of 'the Name Hashem', as distinct from 'the paradigm of 'the Name Elokim'. Free choice and the possibility to change at any moment, the idea of Teshuvah, is only possible in a context of the Name Hashem. If we have deviated from who we are and what we are meant to be doing in this world, we can return to presence and begin again, because our origin as humans is the breath of the Eternally Present One.

By contrast, in the context of 'Elokim', everything is absolute and linear. In a world bound by measure and consequence, each effect follows its cause without deviation. Animals and plants do not wield free choice. They are created in a mode of cause and effect. Their existence is shaped by instinct and nature's laws, not by the freedom to choose or to change.

Originally, Adam and Chava were created as one, *Achor b'Achor* / back-to-back. They were attached or merged with each other, but did not encounter each other as complete in their own right. Wherever one moved, the other moved as well. Theirs was always a 'one-sided discussion' or relationship. It was a *Zivug Temidi* / 'constant (and thus unappreciated) connection', as well as a *Zivug Chitzoni* / superficial relationship, as there was no real, genuine encounter with the 'other' in their uniqueness.

Adam and Chava's back-to-back state mirrored the status of Creation as a whole, which was created and nourished by the Name Elokim. *Elokim* refers to the attribute of judgment. A judge dispensing judgment is a one-sided conversation. There is no conscious or 'face-to-face' quality in it, no real relationship. In the world of Elokim, the Divine Judge and Ruler imposes Its will upon Creation, and all of Creation does exactly as told: a lion hunts to eat and a gazelle grazes. At all times, nature choicelessly performs the will and patterns set by its Creator. This is the paradigm of the Creator as the *Moshel* / Master of the Universe.

As Creation was birthed via the Name Elokim, we relate to the Creator as the powerful Giver of Life. We are the humble receivers of life, following the causal laws of the Judge. In this stage of development, we are not yet full 'human beings' with free choice; if we stray from our path, our lifeforce can become severed. Nor can we choose to do Teshuvah / 'returning' our past to the Creator in order to start over and retroactively change the course of our lives. Like an animal or plant, we are simply what we are, marching forward through natural, linear time. There is no becoming, only being. In such a back-to-back relationship, we cannot truly love or enjoy conscious closeness with the Creator.

The relationship between Adam and Chava mirrors the same fixed, automatic, and unconscious dynamic. Without the presence of free will on either side, their bond is not one of longing for one another, nor of choosing one another. There is no 'romantic' dance of opposites, no magnetic pull between 'I and other', for in such a state, there is no 'other'. Yearning can only arise between distinct people, and when there is a possibility of bridging the distance between them and uniting.

This is why 'Hashem' (not 'Elokim') says, "It is not good for Adam to be alone; I shall make him a helpmate *opposite* him" (2:18). On the surface, Adam is not alone, for Chava stands beside him. Nor is Chava alone, as Adam is always physically present. Yet, as they awaken to their humanity, and become aware that they are merely extensions of each other, a deeper realization dawns: they are, in truth, profoundly alone. Perhaps they are not physically alone, but they are emotionally, intellectually, spiritually, and existentially alone. Though merged and 'attached at the hip,' so to speak, there is no other person there for them to encounter, no distinct presence to meet and get to know. Their very closeness is profoundly isolating. Without the possibility of 'choosing someone', there is an absence of the tension from which a real relationship is born.

The essence of a fully realized human being is the capacity to enter into a conscious, face-to-face relationship with another on all aspects of soul and personal character. In such a relationship, the individuals are not just participants, but Creators, shaping, choosing, and giving rise to the relationship anew in every moment. After being created, Adam and Chava begin to awaken to the fact that they are not plants or reptiles, beings which do not need to gaze lovingly into another's eyes. They are human beings who have a drive to face and know another person. Upon realizing this, they both feel a deep inner void, an absence of conscious encounter. Initially, they had no helpmate opposite them, no mirror and mystery, no counterpart and contrast. When they receive the Divine breath of life, a spark of their Creator, they suddenly yearn to meet each other and become creators and givers, no longer mere receivers.

FROM PRE-PERSONAL TO TRANSPERSONAL

Even before that full realization, Hashem puts Adam, who at this point embodies both male and female, to sleep. While Adam is under this 'general anesthesia', Hashem surgically 'severs' the feminine side from the masculine side. "And Adam gave names to all the cattle and to the birds of the sky and to all the wild beasts; but no fitting counterpart (עזר כנגדו / helper that was *Kenegdo* / against him) for Adam was found. So Hashem cast a deep sleep upon Adam, and while he slept, took one of his sides and closed up the flesh at that site. And Hashem fashioned the side that had been taken from Adam into a woman, bringing her to Adam. Then Adam said, "This one, at last, is bone of my bones, and flesh of my flesh... And therefore, a man leaves his father and mother and clings to his wife, so that they become one flesh.'"*

Like in any surgery, Adam's sleep is essential for survival. Yet, on a deeper level, he is put 'under' not simply to rest or to avoid the pain of surgery; he is put to sleep so that he can dream of *becoming*. In this state, the unified Adam-Chava is gently parted and disentwined. This separation is not a rupture, but a purposeful unfolding. From the oneness emerges twoness; distinct beings who can now turn and face one another. Thus is born the possibility of *Kenegdo*, a counterpart "against him", meaning *Keneged* / 'in front of' him, as an equal yet opposite, a true other. Their ability to consciously face one another creates the sacred tension from which their relationship, love, and transformation can flourish. The ultimate purpose of this Divine choreography is, "Therefore, a man shall leave his father and mother and cleave to his wife, and they

---

* *Bereishis*, 2:20-24.

shall become one flesh." They emerge from a cocoon of unity into a world of separation, and then reveal a full metamorphosis: their separation becomes the setting for a higher unity. They do not dissolve back into sameness, nor lose themselves in the other, but unite in a mode of harmony. Two beings who once were one, now meet again, not as halves, but as whole souls choosing to rejoin, not in an unconscious fusion, but a conscious union.

BY HAVING A CHILD TOGETHER, SPOUSES BECOME "ONE FLESH"

Parenthetically, the ultimate union is to "become one flesh." "And therefore, a man leaves his father and mother and clings to his wife, so that they become one flesh." On one level, this refers to the child born of their union, a literal embodiment of "one flesh," a being formed from both the father and the mother. But on a deeper level, the Torah is pointing to the fact that spouses themselves, through their union, become one, not just emotionally or spiritually, but physically and biologically.

Modern science now reveals what Torah has always hinted at in mystery and metaphor. During pregnancy, a small number of fetal cells, containing the child's DNA, a blend of both parents, can cross the placenta and enter the mother's body. These cells, known as fetal microchimerism, can embed themselves in her organs and tissues, including the brain, heart, and liver, and may remain there for decades. In this way, the mother literally carries within her traces of the child, and by extension, of the father as well.

It is a stunning realization that through conception, pregnancy, and birth, the couple does not merely symbolically become one flesh they actually become interwoven at the cellular level. Their love is not only emotional or covenantal, but etched into the physical fabric of each other's bodies through the life they create together.

This is the deeper truth of "and clings to his wife," a union so intimate, so foundational, that it transcends the boundaries between two individuals. In the child, in the shared cells, in the ongoing influence they have on each other's bodies and souls, they are no longer just spouses they become, in a very real sense, part of one another.

This is why, in the holy love poem of *Shir HaShirim* / Song of Songs, the beloved is called, "My sister, my beloved, my dove, my perfect one."* It is not mere romantic language; it reflects a profound truth. One's spouse is not only one's 'beloved', he or she is like family, like a brother or "sister."

Your marriage partner is not just your 'soulmate', united above in a single root soul, while separate from you below. When you become married, you are from that moment "as one flesh." This is not only a spiritual reunion, rather one that takes place on every level, including mental, emotional and biological. Marriage transforms two into one, and not only through love and covenant, but through physiology. In marriage, your beloved becomes an actual part of your essence: "Bone of my bone, flesh of my flesh…"

---

* *Shir HaShirim*, 5:2.

THREE STAGES OF EVOLUTION

Essentially, there are three stages of evolution in life:

1) Pre-individuation; pre-personal self

2) Individuation; personal self

3) Trans-individuation; transpersonal or post-personal self

These stages correspond to three states of relationship: unconscious fusion, separation, and conscious unity.

Once the initial state of pre-individuation is severed and there are two separate beings, a full Adam and a full Chava, then a level of unity much higher than 'fusion' can be attained: one that is consciously chosen by individuals. Thus, 'one' becomes 'two' in order to become 'One': "Therefore a man shall leave his father and mother, and cleave to his wife, and become as one flesh." This command and prediction, "therefore a man...as one flesh," pertains to both men and women.*

'Leaving the home of your parents (and/or detaching from any inner and outer dependencies upon them) and cleaving to your soulmate', is a transition from a natural, inherited bond to one forged through longing, choice, and encounter. Parental love, and love toward one's parents, can be deep and essential, yet it is often calm, steady, and sometimes taken for granted. This is called *Ahavah KaMayim* / love like water — nourishing, life-giving, and flowing in quiet channels. For much of one's early life, one may

* *Sanhedrin,* 57b.

even feel like an extension of their parents, bound more to one's origins than to one's individual existence. This relationship echoes the state of Adam and Chava before the Nesira, before the 'severing' that created space between them. In that pre-separation state, there is closeness, but no face-to-face encounters. There is proximity but not presence.

As a child matures and goes through adolescence, the process of individuation begins to unfold more rapidly. Ideally, when the youngster is ready to "leave" their father and mother, he or she is ready and capable of entering true face-to-face relationships. Ultimately, this is achieved with a spouse, here one meets not sameness, but otherness, not fusion, but the mystery of difference. Now, two souls can learn to behold one another fully, to truly encounter each other and see the other for who they are.

In the primordial, archetypal narrative of Adam and Chava, Adam must awaken, not merely from physical sleep, but from an inner slumber of self-enclosure. He must come to yearn for someone beyond himself. To truly cleave to another as an 'other', he must open his eyes and see his unconscious habits of dominance and blurring boundaries. He must be willing to evolve so that his ache of separation can become a desire to encounter, to behold and to connect, with reverence and sensitivity.

True union can only arise when there is first individuation. And so, Chava too must step forward and emerge as her own person, not as an appendage, shadow, or passive reflection, not merely as 'Adam's side', in the language of our Sages. Chava needs to attain her own voice, vision, and vitality. To become a 'partner', she needs to become distinct, and an equal. Only then can she become *Ezer Kenegdo* / a help 'opposite him', meaning one who stands in profound tension with Adam, strong in her own essence, using her power not to control but to uplift and empower her husband.

The sleepiness of conventional roles—who leads and who follows—dissolves, and in its place arises a dynamic of mutuality, a living relationship that demands presence, nuance, and reverence. Only in this *Panim El Panim* / face-to-face posture, can Adam truly see Chava, and in that seeing, recognize her not as part of himself, but as her own being, whole in her own right. "Then the man said, 'This one, at last, is bone of my bones and flesh of my flesh…'" This moment marks a shift in consciousness. Adam is now awake, not just in body, but in soul. He beholds Chava not with ownership, but with awe, and in that profound recognition, a new level of unity is born, no longer fusion and dependency, but communion.

Together, masculine and feminine step into a higher union, one that is greater than its 'parts', amplifying one another's creativity, intelligence, and power to act, beyond the potential of any individual. Through the act of separation and reunion, they birth not only a family, but an era and a *Binyan Olam* / eternal structure. In their conscious collaboration, the seeds of redemption are sown.

THE MICROCOSMIC REFLECTS THE MACROCOSMIC

This unfolding takes place not only within the intimacy of personal, inner worlds, it is also mirrored on a cosmic scale. The dynamic of individuation, separation, and reunion is not only the story of healthy human relationships, but the very blueprint of Creation. The microcosm reflects the macrocosm, and "As Above, so below." Human beings awaken to themselves and to one another through a dance of differentiation and longing, and the cosmos emerges into being with the same choreography.

Until the close of Chapter One of Bereishis, there is only one voice, one will — that of the Creator. Creation, at this point, is still a one-sided act, unilateral and absolute. Yet, from the outset, the Creator's intention was never to remain the sole actor on the stage of existence. The Divine longing was to bring forth a sacred other, a conscious being who could stand face-to-face, and enter into a relationship with the Infinite. The Creator 'craved' for a co-creator, a 'partner' who would not be fused into Unity, but dance with it.

At first, there was only the *Ohr Ein Sof* / the Infinite Light. In this primordial condition, the Ein Sof was, so to speak, *Elent*, a yiddish term for 'lonely', and 'yearned' for the perception of otherness to arise.

Before the *Tzimtzum* / contraction of the Infinite Light, only Infinity was revealed, and the *Koach haGevul* / Power of Limitations, of finite boundaries was included but unexpressed within the Ein Sof, the Infinite Light, as if in an 'unconscious' back-to-back relationship. In other words, there was a Divine Power of Limitation (Chava, the feminine and the receiver, in the human metaphor) within the Creator, but before the Tzimtzum of the Infinite Light, this finite Light was completely subsumed and overwhelmed within the Infinite Light, like a child subsumed within the will and desires of her parents, with no separate, revealed will of her own.

The Tzimtzum was a *'Nesira'* / severing, a separation between the *Koach haGevul* / Power of Limitation and the *Koach haBilti Gevul* / Power of No Limitation. In other words, the Infinite Creator created a perceptual withdrawal of Its own Infinity. This was the moment the Power of Limitation began to emerge, as it was no longer hidden, 'fused' within Infinity. A space was carved out for limitation, boundaries, form, and otherness, and finally, an 'independent' Creation, seemingly separate from its Creator. Due to this, the possibility for a 'face-to-face' relationship with HaKadosh Baruch Hu, the Holy Blessed One, arose, fulfilling the desire that initiated the creation process in the first place.

Decades ago, when my beloved son Mendel was four years old, he was sitting quietly in the back seat of the car, whispering a profound and luminous, yet simple truth. We overheard him say, to no one in particular, "When I was with Hashem, I was very sad, and it was very dark. So I decided to make my family. Now I am happy." After a moment of silence, he added: "I love the world." When I heard those words, I knew one day they would be written in a book of mine. And here is where it goes.

THE THREE STAGES OF THE COSMIC STORY

Cosmically, the *pre-individuation* stage is an 'era' before any distinctions are created, when all is merged within the *Ohr Ein Sof* / Infinite Light. Here, the *Koach HaGevul* / the Power of Limitation and boundaries, exists only in potential, utterly subsumed within the boundlessness of the Infinite Light. This is the level of *Yachid* / simple Singularity.

Individuation occurs through *Tzimtzum* / a contraction of the Infinite Light leaving an 'empty space'. From this space emerges *Gevul* / Finitude, boundaries, time and space, self and other. Here, consciousness begins to awaken in the cosmos. The soul begins to sense itself, to know its edges. This is the stage of recognizing otherness and feeling separation and longing. It is the stage that my son Mendel expressed so accurately: "When I was with Hashem, I was very sad, and it was very dark...."

Trans-Individuation begins when a limited ray of the Infinite Light re-enters the empty space, creating worlds in which both individuality and oneness can co-exist, described by little Mendel's utterance, "I decided to make my family." This stage culminates when, from within the experience of multiplicity and duality, the soul is able to perceive that all is, in truth, One. This oneness is not a dissolution back into sameness, but an 'inclusive transcendence'. It is not a return to Yachid, but an arrival at Echad, unity born through harmony, relationship, mutual recognition, love. Here, multiple entities unify even while remaining distinct. As Mendel concluded, "Now I am happy...I love the world."

THREE STAGES OF THE HUMAN STORY

We all begin as one soul, a spark within the Great Soul of Adam, the original, all-encompassing, undivided 'Yachid' soul. Then we are gently severed and divided into distinct personal souls. Each of these fragments of the Great Soul is sent into this world, clothed in a unique body, bearing its own path, personality, Tikkun, and purpose. Yet, with this individuation comes an inevitable ache, a quiet sense of loneliness, and whether conscious or subconscious, a subtle sense of sadness or 'darkness'.

Having these sensations is not a flaw, but a calling, stirring within us the longing for connection. And so we begin to seek our soulmate. Hopefully, the search is not driven by an existential lack or desperation, for such grasping only drives away the very one we yearn to draw close to. Our longing for our soulmate can arise instead from the deeper inner knowing that even while we are whole and complete in ourselves, there is still something incomplete about us, something that whispers of a deeper wholeness we have yet to touch.

At the appointed time, the two souls encounter one another. They meet, not in order to become one in 'sameness', nor to dissolve into each other, but to enter into a higher unity, a harmony born of embracing differences, a union that honors the sacred space between self and other. As such, for this unity to be true and lasting, it must begin with reverence for the otherness of the other, their individuality and autonomy, and their unique inner world. Only when we truly see the one before us as distinct, as a full representation of the Divine image in their own right, can real unity emerge.

This is the secret of love: do not merge into 'sameness' with your soulmate, nor try to make your soulmate conform to your personality. Rather, meet in the fullness of each of your beings, with your differences. In this harmony, you will merit to create something greater than either of you could alone, and this, too, will increase your love.

AN ESSENTIAL INGREDIENT FOR MARRIAGE IS RECOGNIZING THE OTHERNESS OF OUR SPOUSE

A true and lasting bond is built upon a simple yet profound truth, the recognition of the otherness of the other.

Each soul is unique, distinct, a world unto itself. Your spouse is not your reflection, nor your shadow or 'side'. They are not an extension of your being, but a universe with their own rhythm; a mind that thinks in their own patterns, a heart that beats to their own melody, a spirit that journeys on their own path. To love someone is to honor this uniqueness, to cherish the individuality, to celebrate the beautiful idiosyncrasies that make them who they are.

True unity is not found in erasing oneself or one's spouse to form a back-to-back relationship. It is found in the sacred dance of two souls standing proudly, and yet in awe and honor, in a face-to-face-encounter.

A healthy marriage is not a singularity, where one is lost within the other, nor is it a distant coexistence, where souls drift apart. It is symmetry or harmony. There are two souls, distinct yet entwined, dancing as one. The two do not think the same way, but through this dance, they can reach the same conclusion and dream the same dreams. They do not erase their differences, but allow their differences to illuminate their bond, together becoming something greater than any individual.

A healthy marriage is where two souls intertwine, not by mirroring each other, but by complementing; not by losing themselves, but by finding a space of togetherness. They are bound by common values, kindred ambitions, and dreams that echo in both hearts, yet each one sees, thinks, and feels in their own way. Sameness does not forge true unity, but a harmonization of differences, two voices singing a single song, each in its own beautiful key.

There is a time to lose oneself in a spouse's eyes, and a time to stand side by side, both looking outward together. Sacred love embraces both, the sweetness of deep emotional intimacy and the strength of a shared vision. In truth, even greater than the closeness of gazing into one another's eyes is the deeper unity of two souls gazing toward the same horizon, joined in an alignment of dreams, purpose, and a shared future.

TO COMMUNICATE AND DIALOGUE IS TO BE HUMAN & INTIMATE

ויאמר האדם / "Then Adam said, 'This one at last, is bone of my bones, and flesh of my flesh…,' And therefore…they become one flesh." This moment marks the first instance in the Torah where human speech is recorded. Up until now, only the Creator has spoken, but here, humanity finds a voice. This is the dawn of human expression, the beginning of the possibility of dialogue, and the first step toward authentic, reciprocal communication.

Prior to this, Adam (at this point, actually the fused being of

Adam-Chava) *Kara* / 'called' the animals by their names: "And Adam *called* names to all the cattle and to the birds of the sky and to all the wild beasts; but no fitting counterpart for a human being was found."* That is, Adam named the animals and defined them with language. Yet, this act of 'calling' was one-sided, a declaration without anyone necessarily listening. As distinct from Kara, אמר / *Amar* / 'saying', is an act of speech that implies the presence of a listener, however it is only saying something *to* them — a monologue. Another form of speech is דבור / *Dibbur* / 'speaking', implying dialogue. Amar is speaking *to* and Dibbur is speaking *with*. For example, אמר לו / *Amar Lo*, means 'He said *to* him,' while דבר עמו / *Dibber Imo*, means 'He spoke *with* him.'

After Adam names the animals, the Torah uses the word אמר / *Amar*, 'said', for the first time in reference to a human being: ויאמר האדם / "Then Adam said, 'This one at last, is bone of my bones...'" This is another stage of development of being human, a *Medaber* / 'communicating being'.

Kara, 'call', means to dictate information; one is able to call another person by some label, without their participation or consent. This is not yet 'communication'. Only *Dibbur*, 'speaking (with)' is full communication with another, as it recognizes them as an equal, and implies also listening to them.

This is why the Torah says, "And Adam *called* names...but no fitting counterpart for a human being was found." Adam was able to 'call' the animals and even define them according to their names,

---

* *Bereishis*, 2:20: ויקרא האדם שמות לכל־הבהמה ולעוף השמים ולכל חית השדה ולאדם לא־מצא עזר כנגדו.

but he was not able to have a genuine relationship with them. He did not regard them as an 'other', a partner capable of communication. As there was no capacity there for *Dibbur*, dialogue, or even *Amira*, monologue, there was no relational dynamic, and Adam remained lonely.

This is another essential and important ingredient in marriage: true communication. While speaking to each other, always keeping the channels open for genuine dialogue — listening and conversing.

Don't Label, Listen.

Don't Complain, Communicate.

Don't make Monologue, make Dialogue.

"THIS ONE AT LAST" BODY VS. IMAGINATION.

"Then Adam said; This one, at last, is bone of my bones, and flesh of my flesh." What does "This one, at last," mean? Does it imply that there was 'another one', another potential mate in the picture, before this? Rashi quotes the Gemara, "It teaches that Adam endeavored to find a companion among all cattle and beasts, but found no *satisfaction* except in Chava."* In other words, this time, in contrast to the past, he realized he could be intimate with the 'flesh of his flesh', the appropriate species, someone with a human body and essence corresponding to his.

---

* *Yevamos*, 63a.

It could also mean, "this time" and not in the future; in the future, husband and wives will no longer be from each other's actual flesh and bone, as Adam and Chava were.

One of the classic commentators on the Torah, the Even Ezra, mentions here a medrashic character called Li'lith, implying that the verse means, "*This one*, as opposed to Li'lith," whom Adam seemingly had 'dated'. What medrashic tradition is the Even Ezra speaking about?

Let's go a little deeper into this, by focusing more deeply on the *Pesukim* / verses that describe the creation of man. The *Pasuk* / verse says, "And Hashem cast a deep sleep upon Adam, and while Adam slept, [Hashem] took one of מצלעתיו / his sides."

This moment is rich with metaphor and mystery. The emergence of Chava, the 'other', the beloved, unfolds not in waking consciousness, but within the hidden, liminal realm of sleep, the place of dreams. When Adam awakens, he no longer beholds a figment of his imagination, a hypnopompic phantom of his longing. Now, standing before him is his soulmate, not a projection, but a presence, no longer 'within him' only; she stands before him, fully real. Only then does he proclaim, "This one at last, is bone of my bones, and flesh of my flesh." In other words, 'This one, whom I am looking at right now in my awake state, is bone of my bone and flesh of my flesh, but the previous one, just existed in my dreams.' Thus, our sages say, "The original creation of the woman was only in a dream.'"*

Adam first dreams Chava into existence, and since Adam origi-

---

שמתחלת בריתה אינה אלא בחלום *: *Medrash Rabbah*, Bereishis, 18:4.

nally included Chava, so too does Chava at first dream Adam into existence. Before actually seeing each other, Adam only existed for Chava in her imagination, and Chava only existed for Adam in his imagination. But then, "at last," they stood before each other in flesh and bone. Adam and Chava could finally behold one another not as mental images, but as fully embodied 'others', real people with whom they could have a real relationship.

On one level, this teaches us that in relationships people often encounter one another not as they truly are, but as projections of their own inner world, reflections shaped by personal fantasies, hopes, and desires. Rather than meeting the other in their full, independent humanity, with their own dreams, struggles, and complexities, they unconsciously reduce them to characters in their own internal narrative. Yet for a relationship to mature, these illusory images must be released. The fantasy must give way to reality. One must awaken, as Adam and Chava did, and see the other not as a projection, an extension of themselves, but as a real, distinct, living, whole person, standing before them.* Only a separate individual who is nonetheless of the same source and essence, "flesh and bone," has the independence and affinity necessary for authentic connection.

* A person is whole in themselves; no one can even rightfully claim, 'This is *my* husband,' or '...*my* wife," as no one can own someone else. Once, as the Alter Rebbe stepped out of his room, he overheard his wife remarking to several women, "Mine (my husband) says..." The Alter Rebbe commented: "With one Mitzvah I am 'yours'; with how many are we Hashem's!": *Hayom Yom*, 23rd Shevat. We ultimately do not even own ourselves—everything and everyone belongs to Hashem alone, the Infinite Wholeness. Even our children, though we call them 'ours,' come through us, not from us. They are made in the Divine image, not our image.

See and honor the other as genuinely other,

not merely as a reflection of your desires,

nor as an extension of your imagination,

but as a sacred mystery, a whole universe unto themselves,

deserving of wonder, reverence, and authentic recognition.

Rather than Suspect... be Surprised.

Rather than Analyze... Appreciate.

Sometimes people carry within them an ideal, an idealized, dreamlike image, of the one they hope to marry. It is a fantasy spun from the threads of imagination, untouched by life's realities. Then, when they get married and everyday life unfolds, they encounter their spouse in their true, complex humanity "flesh and bone," facing both their virtues and their flaws. If they remain emotionally attached to the fantasy image, they may feel disillusioned, or even frustrated and confused. For this reason, the Torah gently guides us toward clarity, saying, "this one, at last," urging us to step out of the shadow of our imagination, let go, and bravely embrace reality. We are asked to see, accept, and love the real person standing before us, in all their beautiful-yet-imperfect wholeness.

Perhaps you have dreamed of the one who would fulfill your heart's deepest longing, an image crafted within the sacred realm of your imagination, the one with whom you wished to share your journey through life. You should not remain stubbornly attached to this fantasy image alone, exclusively bound to the fleeting or fragile confines of your dreams.

The Torah's gentle whisper in fact invites us to hold both truths within our heart and soul simultaneously. Your spouse is both your perfect imagination *and* a real, separate person. For as the Torah reveals, "Hashem cast a deep sleep upon Adam, and while Adam slept, [Hashem] took one of מצלעתיו / his sides... bone... flesh." The word *m'Tzalosav* / מצלעתיו, besides meaning simply his sides, hints profoundly to *Tzel* / צל / shadow, image, reflection. This teaches us that Chava, and also Adam, emerge from the delicate fabric of idealistic dreams and loving imagination, shadowy yet luminous images brought lovingly into tangible reality.

As such, your beloved is indeed the fulfillment of your dreams, an embodiment of your deepest subconscious images. This is why soulmates sometimes recognize each other at first glance. Yet, at the very same time, your beloved exists fully in the realm of the real, in flesh and bone, a separate and wondrously unique individual. They are not a mere image, and will not always conform to your expectations.

We need to allow both truths to weave together:

The mystery and the mundane,

The concealed and the revealed,

The inner image and the outer flesh and bones,

The dream and the reality.

Only through embracing both of these truths does love thrive — balancing your enchantment with openness and respect, allowing your dreams to dance gracefully with the beauty of everyday reality.

THIS ONE IS BONE AND FLESH—
THE FIRST ONE WAS NOT

What was the Even Ezra hinting at by saying, "This one at last" refers to Chava, the woman of flesh and bone, whereas there was a 'first' version of Chava, or some other partner of Adam by the name of Li'lith? (In other contexts, her name is also spelled *Lil, Leil* / Night or *Lilin*).

Chazal, our sages, connect Lil with the worlds of demons and negative forces.[*] In fact, they also say that "It is prohibited to sleep alone in a house, for anyone who sleeps alone in a house will be seized by the evil spirit Lil."[**]

Chazal also speak about two versions of Adam's wife, and only in the second version is she is 'bone from bone, and flesh from flesh.'[***]

On a profound metaphysical level, *Lil* is in fact understood as the feminine embodiment of Kelipa, a negative, distorted force of the universe. She is even characterized as the spouse of the *Samach Mem* or 'the Satan', the personification of harsh spiritual opposition

---

[*] *Niddah*, 24b. *Zohar* 1, 19b. 28b. *Zohar* 3, 76b.

[**] *Shabbos*, 151b.

[***] ויאמר האדם זאת הפעם, רבי יהודה בר רבי אמר בתחלה בראה לו וראה אותה מליאה רירין ודם שתי יצירות הוו. 18:4 *Medrash Rabbah*, Bereishis, :והפליגה ממנו, וחזר ובראה לו פעם שנייה לו אחת נוצרה עמו מקודם וברחה ואח"כ ברא לו חוה מצלעו: Rashba, *Kesuvos*, 8a. Although, in Chazal, this 'first' version is not named. See also, Chidah, *Pnei Dovid*, on the Pasuk.

and concealment. Together, these two negative characters represent the 'shadow side' of union, coupling rooted not in true connection, but in illusion, ego, and estrangement from Source. But let us bring this concept down from the spiritual worlds into the realm of lived relationships. What does *Lil* mean, and what does she represent in our own lives?

As explained, when Adam and Chava were back-to-back extensions of each other, their spouse existed in their imagination alone. From the perspective of Adam, his wife existed as an extension of his fantasies.

Lil represents a demonic shadow realm of false imagination and self-centered, distorted fantasy. Lil whispers seductively to a person that intimacy can be experienced without genuine connection, and that pleasure can be extracted at the expense of another without consequence or accountability. Lil is the dangerous illusion of pleasure severed from the covenant of marriage, the tragic emptiness of intimacy stripped of sacredness and meaning.

Lil signifies the destructive consciousness behind the wasteful dissipation of life's potential, the 'wasting of seed', which is literally and figuratively a loss of new life. At its core, Lil embodies the perilous mindset that seeks gratification without commitment, intimacy without obligation, and desire without responsibility, a path that leads only to emptiness, loss, and spiritual devastation.

Lil is the world of pure fantasy, in which the other is present not as a real person, rather, as an object. Such a fantasy is a projected image rooted in one's own unresolved issues of shame, fear, or insatiability. This 'illusory spouse' is not one's real partner, but a reflection of one's own shadow, an echo of one's own unrectified sub-conscious imagination and buried trauma. The relationship, then, is not between two people, but between one person and their own darkness, their own repressed, subconscious states of hatred, deg-radation, and despair disguised as attraction, pleasure, and passion.

Lil represents the temptation to see the world and others as mere extensions of oneself. Such selfish fantasies lead to ignoring the consequences of actions and failing to acknowledge the real, in-dependent existence of others. In such a fantasy realm, everything is self-serving, as if other people exist merely to fulfill one's person-al needs or cravings. It also seems as if there are no repercussions or consequences for their actions because everything just exists within the world of imagination. These fantasies seem to promise limitless pleasure, but they eventually cut a person off from authentic plea-sure, wholeness, personal integrity, and real human relationship.

In this way, Lil is the 'first version' or previous image of the spouse of Adam, as the Even Ezra writes. In the first chapter of Bereishis, Adam and Chava were in a primitive, back-to-back state of consciousness, in which there was no other. They were both like a toddler in a self-centered fantasy world, perceiving no repercus-sions for their actions.

In the second story of Adam and Chava's creation, in the sec-ond chapter in Bereishis, there is a leap of consciousness and they meet face-to-face; they are flesh-and-bone physical beings. Unlike a self-generated fantasy image, a real person has needs and prefer-ences, and they give feedback. They do not tolerate selfishness or objectification from their partner. Also, as physical beings, when they become intimate, there is an actual physical result: getting pregnant, giving birth, and raising children, requiring challenging responsibilities and sacrifices. When attached to fantasies, a person does not want all of that challenge, effort, and feedback; they just want passion with no responsibility, certainly no children. This is why Lil becomes associated, in the writings of the *Mekubalim / Kabbalists*, with the idea of infant mortality.

Because of this mortal danger, when a woman gives birth, there is a time of vulnerability, whether it be related to postpartum depression, lack of sleep, or being in physical or emotional discomfort. In this vulnerable state, one might have a fleeting, illogical longing for there having been no consequences of the intimacy nine months ago. Almost against one's conscious will, one could have a thought of regret for the overwhelm of the consequences of intimacy, the birth of the child and ensuing commitments. For these reasons, there is a custom to hang *Kameios* / 'amulets' in the home and baby carriage, specifically traditional diagrams with Torah verses which help ward off the Kelipa of Lil. These also help one focus on the beauty of the soul of the child who was born, and the miracle of birth, and stimulate prayerful thoughts that the child should be protected from all spiritual or physical negativity and danger.

Now that Chava and Adam are physical beings, the Torah is saying, "this time," and from now on forward, know that the person you are intimate with, your spouse, is flesh of your flesh, not just there to feed your own imagination. Your spouse is not a phantom, but a real person, and as the Torah concludes, "Therefore a man shall leave his father and mother and cleave to his *wife*." Both partners need to fully leave their childish longings and fantasies, and join with their real spouse, uniting in sacred physical creativity and mature responsibility.

Now, in the second version of the creation of Adam and Chava, we are fully human with a Divine soul, as the Pasuk says, "And He blew into his nostrils and breath of life." We are no longer mere animals programmed to propagate through 'promiscuous' relationships. We are now conscious of our Divine self and that of our soulmate, capable of an exclusive, truly loving, face-to-face relationship.

In his 'second creation', Adam is created in the 'image of the Creator', and he too becomes a creator, conscious that he is a creator. When he wakes up and sees Chava eye-to-eye, he realizes that everything he does in this world creates an effect. Intimacy creates a living soul, whether it results in a physical baby or not. Something is sown and created in every act, and we will eventually reap its effects. Adam will need to learn that in his relationship, he is not the victim or automatically at the effect of Chava's actions, rather he has a choice of how to respond. All of this is our inheritance, too. We are called to wake up, become conscious that in all our actions we are a creator, to acknowledge that all our actions have effects, and to choose our actions and reactions.

Being created in the Divine image means not just passively 're-sembling' the Creator, but actively embodying that attribute of Divine creativity. Particularly in the context of relationship and intimacy, we are designed to participate in the Divine creation process itself. Intimacy is inherently sacred because it mirrors the Creator's own process. Through the act of intimacy, one can produce physical life but also infuse the relationship with life, with intention, love and covenantal commitment.

Someone who recognizes himself as a creator shifts from a more passive existence into a deeply active mode of participation in life.

He transcends the role of a 'victim' or a mere recipient of others' choices, and consciously becomes the author of his own actions and responses. He attains free will, an ability to make self-directed choices in relationships and all areas of life. By seeing oneself as a creator, a person can approach every interaction with people as an opportunity to contribute meaning and purpose to their life. This transforms even 'mundane' relationships into a 'genesis' of benefit.

Another crucial element in nurturing a healthy, flourishing marriage: ensure that you never objectify your spouse, never reduce your beloved to an impersonal object of desire, existing only to fulfill self-centered or superficial fantasies.

Moreover, stand firmly as a creator of your relationship, not a passive victim of circumstance, but an active participant, consciously shaping your shared reality and rooting it in responsibility, care, and mutual growth. In doing so, you reclaim your sacred role as co-creators, infusing your union with intentionality, purpose, and lasting beauty.

WAITING EXPANDS OUR VESSELS

After telling us, "This one at last, is bone of my bones, and flesh of my flesh." The Torah continues with a profound 'therefore': "And *therefore*, a man leaves his father and mother and clings to his wife, so that they become one flesh."

To transition from the type of relationships we have with our parents, which are shaped by shared genetics, history and familiarity, into the relationship of marriage — with someone who was, perhaps recently, a 'stranger' — we must *leave*. This does not mean just to leave physically, but also emotionally and psychologically. We must step away from our original home, from the comfort of the known, in order to encounter an unknown other in a face-to-face relationship.

For a deeper unity to be born, one that creates not only a shared life, but a shared essence, a "one flesh," we must pass through the threshold of separation. We must honor the space between us and our family of origin, release the old, and embrace any grief in leaving our past, in order to fully meet our present and future life. For some time, there may be a sense of being in between, neither here nor there.

Whenever we are about to receive a higher, deeper form of *Ohr* / light, there is a risk. Our *Keilim* / vessels are not yet large enough to contain the new experience, meaning we are not fully ready or open to receive the gifts destined for us. In such moments, Hashem places us in a state of 'waiting', in which the old has already faded and the new has not yet arrived.

In the context of marriage, this waiting period is especially significant. It is the time between leaving the home of one's parents, stepping out of the familiar past, and before fully entering into the covenant of marriage, the new future. In this gap, we are invited to expand our inner vessels, to refine ourselves, and to cultivate the readiness to truly meet and commit to another person. The waiting itself is part of the gift, shaping us so that when the new light comes, we can hold it with strength and grace.

This waiting refines and expands our *Keilim* / vessels, preparing us to receive correctly. Only then, when the Ohr, the light of love and marriage, descends, can it be properly absorbed, integrated, and assimilated. Waiting opens us, and prepares us to receive the higher Ohr, light of marriage, in a way that can be transformative and integrated.

Chazal tell us a very interesting principle in *Avodas Hashem* / serving Hashem, and by extension about the service of life itself, Reish Lakish said: "He who comes to defile himself is given an opening (פותחין לו), but he who comes to purify himself is given assistance" (מסייעין אותו). The school of Rebbe Yishmael taught: "This can be compared to a person who sells petroleum and balsam. When someone comes to measure and buy petroleum, the owner says to the potential buyer, "Go measure it yourself." But when someone comes to measure the balsam, the owner then says: *Hamtein Li* / המתן לי / 'Wait for me, so that I can measure it with you, so that I too can enjoy its fragrance'."*

A person seeking to defile himself, to step onto a negative path of behaviour, to deviate from the path of righteousness and justice, holiness and wholeness, can achieve his aim easily. He is immediately "given an opening," and "In the path that a person wishes to walk in, (Hashem) will lead him in that path."** Yet, one who seeks to purify himself must wait. Hashem says, "Wait for me," I want to lead you and accompany you on your path to greater purity and wholeness, but I want you to be still and wait a moment so that you can create the vessel to receive My guidance.

What is the significance of this waiting? Why is it necessary? Why does someone who seeks to acquire a cheap and foul smelling

* *Yuma*, 38b, 39a.
** *Makos*, 10b.

commodity like petroleum receive it immediately, while someone who seeks to acquire a valuable, fragrant commodity like balsam must wait? If you wish to receive great light, expansiveness, openness, and abundance, and in our context, a wonderful spouse with all the tremendous blessings that he or she brings, including joy, protection, wholeness, and Torah,* you need to expand your vessel, beyond what you think you are ready for.

Waiting cultivates longing, which fashions within us a vessel of appreciation that is deep and wide enough to allow us to truly receive, hold, and cherish the blessings that are coming to us.

Moreover, the act of waiting shapes and refines us from within, clarifying our heart, illuminating our desires, guiding us to discern what truly matters, and revealing to us what we most deeply yearn to embrace. When you have the power to wait for a blessing or pleasure, it builds you up and allows you to recognize what you truly want. If you do not have the ability to delay gratification, you increase your tendency to misperceive reality and stimulate your reactivity, and it is more likely that blessings will slip through your fingers. A good thing is worth waiting for.

THE COSMIC MARRIAGE

As explored earlier, in the "beginning" there was only the Infinite Light, where 'finitude' only existed within the Light of In-

---

* The Gemara, *Yevamos,* 62b-63a, says, "A man without a wife is a man without *Simcha* / joy, *Beracha* / blessing, and *Choma* / Protection; he is not a (fully-realized) Adam, he is not *Shaleim* / complete, and he is without *Torah* / spiritual wisdom." The Chidah notes that the acronym of these elements spell out the words שבח אשה / praise of the woman, for a meritorious woman is the one who can most powerfully bring the man joy, blessings, protection, wholeness, and Torah.

finity. Then arose a Divine desire. A longing, not from a place of lack, for there is no lack in Infinity, but a will to Self-express, to share, to give, to create space for an apparent 'other'. Although it is difficult for us to fathom the concept of desire emerging from unified wholeness, either way, this primordial yearning gave rise to the very possibility of Creation. And so, the first step was not Self-expression, rather, paradoxically, withdrawal. Before anything could be created, there needed to be a *Challal* / 'empty space' within the inseparable oneness in which a 'separate creation' could emerge, and this occurred through the *Tzimtzum* / Self-withdrawal or Self-constriction. There was a contraction, a withholding of the expression of the Infinite Light, allowing for finitude, for a vessel, an entity 'separate' from the Infinite Light, to emerge.

On a deep level the desire to create is itself the Tzimtzum, the freely chosen *'need'* for an other.

On a deeper level, the act of Tzimtzum, which outwardly appears as an expression of Gevurah, of restriction, withdrawal, inwardness and 'waiting', is, at its core, a profound act of love.

The foundation of the Tzimtzum, the Maggid of Mezritch, Rebbe DovBer teaches, is love. Tzimtzum is an act of tender restraint, much like a parent who lowers themselves to the floor to be with their small child, entering their world and playfully joining their game.

Divine Love creates the Tzimtzum, giving space for creation and otherness. Hence, Love is not merely an attribute, rather, the very foundation and thread woven through all of reality. We are created from Love, and the purpose of our creation is that we, as a separate being, will lovingly seek to reconnect with our Creator, in an awake face-to-face relationship.

In summary: in the pre-individuation stages, *Gevul* / finitude, the Power of Limitation, is merged within Infinity as if 'back-to-back'. Individuation is created by the Tzimtzum, which is rooted in love. Trans-individuation is created when we, who feel ourselves independent and separate, seek out and enter a love relationship and unity with HaKadosh Baruch Hu, the Holy One.

We, and all of Creation, move

From Singularity

To separation

And "at last" to Unity

PERFECT IMAGINATION

"Elokim created man in His own image, in the image of Elokim created him; male and female He created them." Which means that there is a male and female within Hashem's image—as it were, but what does this mean?

'Image' can also be understood as your 'perfect imagination'. An image is not merely a reflection; it can mean your deepest imagination, your most cherished vision of becoming. Think of that quiet Monday morning, as you sit at your desk, and your mind begins to wander. You imagine yourself on a distant island, time moving more slowly, life feeling fuller. Or perhaps you see yourself years from now, older and at peace, and feeling comfortable in simply being. That vision is your image, the inner whisper of what could be. And then, day by day, you work, strive, and build to close the gap between who you are and who you envision for yourself. This is the type of image the Torah is describing.

'Before' creation, there was only the Infinite. But within Infinity stirred a longing, a yearning to love and bestow love on something 'other', something distinct. Hashem, the Boundless One, desired a relationship (so to speak). To love and be able to express love with a finite other, to behold the beauty of contrast, of difference, of duality, and so, from this Divine yearning, worlds were born.

This is the Divine image we are created in, the sacred dance of opposites, and the ultimate embrace of the masculine and feminine, the male and female, the soul and body, the giver and the receiver. And so we wander, we yearn, we seek, we dream, we envision, not merely for companionship, but for love, for connection, for unity, and ultimately reunification. This is the great cosmic game of hide-and-seek. The Creator creates an 'other', and the 'other' feels the void, the emptiness, yearning for the apparently hidden Infinite One—and yet, the game is won, the Holy Other is found, and all Creation joyfully enters the wedding canopy of the One.

THE FULLNESS OF SELF & 'I' IN UNITY WITH THE ULTIMATE 'I'

As we joyfully return to Oneness, after experiencing separation and concealment, we are not united through an erasure of our individuality within the Infinity. We do not dissolve our selfhood into oblivion in order to become One; rather, we unite through the mystery of transparent individuality. In a sense, this is no less than an exaltation of our individuality, even while embraced within the context of Unity. The soul and the body are not eclipsed, rather, in their fullness, they come into alignment with the will of Hashem.

The great, humble sage Hillel would say, "If *Ani* / I am here, everything is here. And if I am not here, who is here?"*At first glance, this declaration seems oddly self-centered, hardly the words one would expect from a man renowned for his humility. In truth, it is a statement of profound spiritual awareness. The 'I' that Hillel speaks of is not the 'small i', the lower self, the fragmented ego, isolated and reactive, functioning from flight or fight instincts, rather, the *Ani* / I, he refers to is his 'big I', the I of the soul that is one with the Ultimate I (Ani) of the Creator. Thus, when the big I is present and revealed, then indeed, everything and everyone is here too, within It. But if the big I is not present, and just my small, egoic i is present, then who is really here, at all?

The goal of life, then, is not to diminish ourselves, but to live fully, to awaken every talent and activate every potential with which we are imbued. We are to write our story with great flair, but not from a place of ego or small i, rather from a place of *Bitul* / self-transparency to the true and Ultimate I of Being.

When we become transparent to the Ultimate I and our life is a clear channel for the Infinite to be expressed, then the fullness of

---

* *Sukkah*, 53a.

the Creator (so to speak) is reflected in the fullness of our beautiful self, our I. Our becoming, our story now becomes part of the ultimate story of Creation.

THE COSMIC PROCESS OF CREATION AS A MICROCOSMIC TEMPLATE FOR HEALTHY RELATIONSHIPS

Much like the process of Creation began with a Divine desire to create an 'other', followed by the cosmic Tzimtzum, the contraction of Infinite Light within itself, so too must the unfolding of all relationships begin.

Thinking that perhaps, we may want to get married and it sounds like a good *idea in theory*, means that it may never materialize , or the marriage that will materialize may not be a true meeting of souls. To be married in the way described above, a real desire to *be* married is first cultivated, and that desire comes from deep within. It is not borne of parental, peer, or social pressure. It is a feeling in the gut, a yearning for deep connection and a shared life. This inner spark of desire is what truly creates a marriage that is a merging of souls.

Desire is where it begins, but it is not enough. The Creator performed a Tzimtzum to make space for the world, and we, too, perform a conceptual 'Tzimtzum', a contraction within ourselves. A space within ourselves is carved out for another person to be able to enter our life. This is not merely making room in your home for another person and their belongings; this is making space for another on emotional, mental, psychological, and existential levels. It is opening the heart, softening the ego, and creating a place where the self is no longer your center of gravity. It is a deep welcoming of otherness into your being.

After one meets and marries their soulmate, their practice of Tzimtzum continues indefinitely. The cosmic Tzimtzum, too, is an ongoing event, making room for Creation to exist.

Practicing Tzimtzum means making room for the other, allowing them to be. It means listening, resisting the urge to fill every silence with your words. It is about creating a setting where our spouse can reveal themselves, gently, in their own time and on their own terms.

In fact, the most profound *Gevurah* / strength is often expressed not in speaking, but in the silence that holds the space, in the presence that does not crowd out, and the attentiveness that does not possess.

As explored earlier, Creation rests upon two primal forces: *Chesed* / loving-kindness, expansion, generous giving and Gevurah or *Din*, restraint, discipline, the art of holding back. A healthy relationship has both. The capacity to be impossibly kind to our spouse, overflowing with affection, support, and giving. And simultaneously refraining: listening without offering advice or correction, holding our emotions in when necessary. Withdrawing from constant expression and emoting, too, is love. For just as the cosmic Tzimtzum was an act of ultimate Chesed and giving disguised as withdrawal, so too in our relationships. Inward restraint, silence, patient waiting, and making space for differences, are acts of deep love. They are echoes of the Divine pattern of creation.

To truly love is not only to give, but to give space.

MARRIAGE NEEDS A "THIRD," TRANSCENDENT, PARTNER

When two people marry, they do not simply join together to share a home and a life, they actually form a new space, a new container that can hold and support them both. For such a union to last, something beyond the finite efforts of two people is required. Hashem is needed. More specifically, the Divine Name Yud-Hei-Vav-Hei, the Name that represents the Transcendence of time, space, ego, and duality itself is invited in. The Name 'Hashem' represents the Infinite beyond all form, structure, and boundary, the world of possibility beyond limitation.

In the creation story, the Name 'Hashem' does not appear in the first chapter of *Bereishis* / Genesis. This narrative refers only to the Name 'Elokim'. 'Elokim' is the Name associated with *Din* / judgment, order and structure. 'Elokim' is the Divine force that creates boundaries: light and darkness, day and night, water and land, this and that. 'Elokim' is the Name through which the finite world comes into being, where everything has its place, time and clear definition. The Name 'Hashem' introduces the ability to go beyond all form, beyond the strict order of things.

Because the world of the Name 'Elokim' is a closed system, Chazal, our sages tell us, that the grasses and plants were already formed beneath the surface of the earth, poised at the edge, waiting to emerge. But they could not break through, not until Adam was created and prayed for rain. Only then did the rain fall and the vegetation grow.*

Creation as a whole is originally rooted in this realm of 'Elokim'. Nothing in that realm can move beyond its assigned boundaries, and every element remains confined to its place; boundaries define existence. Nothing overflows and nothing crosses over. Thus, in the initial stage of creation, even the grasses and plants, though already formed beneath the surface, could not break through the earth. No vegetation could rise upward, and every living thing remained locked in its space, waiting. For something to transcend its limitations, to rise beyond itself, another force had to enter the scene: the force of 'Hashem', the Divine Name that represents transcendence and infinite possibility. When Adam came along, a being connected to 'Hashem', who prayed to Hashem, life was finally able to move beyond itself, beyond the boundaries of 'Elokim'.

In marriage, boundaries are essential. Each person must have their own space, their own identity. This is the realm of 'Elokim': respect, structure, and discipline. But a marriage cannot flourish on 'Elokim' alone. For two distinct individuals to truly unite, to step beyond themselves and feel the reality of the other, they need something more: they need to be connected to Hashem, to a sense of Transcendence, and the *Emunah* / faith that there is something much larger at play in their union.

---

* "This teaches us that the grasses emerged (on day three of Creation), stood at the entrance of the ground, (and waited) until Adam the First Human came and prayed for compassion upon them, and then rains descended and they sprouted": *Chulin*, 60b.

A connection to Hashem, the Infinite Transcendent, allows a couple to go beyond their own spaces, to become one with each other without dissolving, and to create a presence that is larger than the sum of its parts. Just as the earth needed Hashem to bring forth life beyond itself, so too every marriage needs Hashem to become more than just two individuals living side by side.

This is why it is taught that *Ish* / איש / man, and *Isha* / אשה / woman, both contain within their names the word *Aish* / אש / fire, passion and desire, and sometimes anger. Yet, they also each carry a letter from Hashem's Name, Yud-Hei-Vav-Hei. *Ish* has the י / Yud of Hashem's Name, and *Isha* has the ה / Hei of Hashem's Name. When these letters of the Name are present, the relationship is infused with a 'third partner', the Divine Presence. Then, the fires of passion are tempered, and the Divine Presence rests between them. But if the Yud and Hei are removed, if transcendence is absent, all that remains is Aish and Aish, two unchecked fires. When fire meets fire without higher guidance, one will consume the other.*

AFTER THE TZIMTZUM: SPEECH & COMMUNICATION

Following the Tzimtzum, there begins a process of creation, in which "Hashem said let there be light and there was light." Here,

---

* *Sotah*, 17a. The Name of Hashem is י-ה-ו-ה. *Ish* and *Isha* contain the letters י-ה. Every married couple has a כתובה / *Kesuvah* (marriage obligation contract). The word כתובה is כתב / writing and the letters ו-ה, hence together we have י-ה-ו-ה, the Name of Hashem.

Creation emerges into existence through the medium of Divine speech ("Let there be..."). On the microcosmic, human level, a parallel process unfolds. After the *Nesira* / severing of Adam and Chava from each other, the 'Tzimtzum' on a human level, there emerges a new creation of 'otherness': Adam and Chava existing as two distinct people. This relationship, too, was ushered in through speech. After awakening from surgery, "Then Adam *said*: This one, at last, is bone of my bones...." This is the first time Adam truly 'speaks', not merely 'calling' and naming the animals. This saying is the first stage of the development of language and eventually genuine communication between spouses.

Painfully, two people can be married for years and both still feel devastatingly lonely. True connection is not born out of physical proximity or fulfilling technical obligations. To genuinely connect with one's spouse requires face-to-face and heart-to-heart encounters, meaningful communications, and not just small talk and 'instructions' for chores and expectations. We speak with our spouse, not *at* them. Always a dialogue, never a monologue.

Without real communication, every need can be met, every chore completed, every responsibility upheld, and still a spouse can feel unseen, unheard, and unrecognized.

NAMING & CONTROL

In the Torah's account of creation, we find that Adam—at this stage still an androgynous being—names all the animals. After naming them all, a deep loneliness lingers within him, for although he had named the animals, he had not truly known them. In fact, naming them becomes an act of domination and control, not 'self-Tzimtzum' and togetherness. Naming anyone or anything is a subtle act of exerting control. When we label something, we define it, assuming mastery over it. This is why we often categorize people, putting them into boxes, such as 'smart', 'funny', 'open-minded,' or 'stuck'. By labeling them, we subconsciously assert control.

Children, in particular, are known to assign nicknames to their teachers as a subtle act of rebellion, a subtle way to gain control where they feel small and overpowered. Sadly, adults who may still be trapped in childish patterns, continue this habit, naming and labeling others, often as a defense mechanism against their own sense of vulnerability or perceived lack of control.

It is challenging to avoid labeling, as naming does give us an easier sense of understanding who a person is. But labeling limits our relationships and dulls the mystery of encounter. To refrain from labeling is to meet another without reducing them to a definition. This requires great inner maturity, asking us to access mental, emotional, and spiritual depth. It demands that we resist the urge to sum someone up, and instead remain open, curious, and willing to be surprised. The challenge lies in the discomfort of ambiguity. If we do not define the other, how do we relate to them? Who is this person if they are not easily categorized? To behold someone as fluid, unfolding, and essentially mysterious is to live with awe and curiosity, and also to be comfortable with some measure of uncertainty.

It is precisely in this openness and uncertainty, this refusal to confine the other to a concept, that the possibility of true relationship is born.

Our Sages tell us that when the Torah says, 'Adam named the animals,' this means that Adam sought to engage with each creature intimately, metaphorically speaking.* Adam tried to exert control over the animal kingdom, assert dominance over creation and nature, in doing so, he sought connection, perhaps even companionship. He called out to each creature, hoping that through this naming, through defining and relating, he might find unity, a bridge across the chasm of his loneliness. But the opposite occurred. The more he tried to assert mastery over nature, the more his isolation deepened. Instead of soothing his solitude, this exercise in control only magnified the absence of true companionship. And so the Torah says, "And Adam called names to all the animals. And Adam did not find an *Eizer* / helper to stand and be a *Kenegdo* / against or 'opposite' him." These sentiments of loneliness were only augmented by trying to fill the gap with calling to, speaking *at*, and dominating other forms of life.

ADAM RECOGNIZING THE NEED FOR AN OTHER

The turning point in the story comes when Adam's loneliness is no longer just Hashem's observation, but it has also become Adam's own perception. Before the episode of naming, it is Hashem who declares, "It is not good for the man to be alone." This is a declaration of the Divine plan, a 'decision' that aloneness is not ideal, and an intention to change the situation. Yet, the creation of a partner, an Eizer Kenegdo, does not occur immediately. Only after Adam

---

* *Maharsha*, Yevamos, 63b. *Tosefos Chochmei Anglia*, Avodah Zara, 22b.

has named the animals, after he has reached outward and found no reflection of himself, no one to truly stand opposite him, does the process of forming Chava begin.

Hashem did not wish to impose a solution before Adam himself could sense the lack. It was essential that Adam himself awaken to the longing for companionship and the presence of another who could truly meet him. Not merely as a decree from Above, but as a yearning from within. Hashem makes a 'Tzimtzum' and waits for Adam to develop the vessel to receive and appreciate Chava, and create with her a new reality.

From that moment forward, the experience of separation, duality and longing, becomes embedded in the fabric of human existence. The yearning for connection and reunion with our soulmate is woven into our very life. This yearning is nothing less than the echo of Eden, calling us toward wholeness through the other.

To bring about this new state of being, Hashem caused a sleep to descend upon Adam. Moreover, the fact that this transformation takes place in a state of sleep is deeply symbolic. Sleep alludes to the realm of *Dimyon* / imagination, of vision beyond the confines of waking consciousness. Adam's 'name' shares a root with *Adamah* / earth, but also shares a deeper linguistic connection with the words *Dimyon* / imagination and *D'mus* / resemblance, as in אדמה לעליון / "I will resemble the Transcendent One.* The meaning behind this is that humanity was created not only from the dust of the earth, but in the resemblance of the Divine image. Also, just as the Divine 'imagines' us into being, we too can create and shape our reality through the power of our own creative imagination.

* *Shaloh*, Toldos Adam, p. 3.

As the narrative of humanity begins, G-d proclaims, "Let us create Adam (/Chava) בצלמנו כדמותנו / in Our image and resemblance…Elokim created Adam (/Chava) בצלם אלקים / בצלמו בצלם אלקים / in His image, with a Tzelem of Elokim…." Later on, Adam/Chava is put to sleep, and Hashem removes a part *m'Tzalosav* / מצלעתיו / "from his sides." The root of this word for 'part' is Tzel / צל / shadow / image, the same root as the word Tzalmo / צלמו / the Divine image, and fashions the complete form of Chava from it. Adam and Chava, as individuals and as a married couple, are thus created through dreams, so to speak: in the *D'mus* or *Dimyon* / 'imagination' of the Creator ("Let us make an Adam/Chava"), and in the dreams of Adam (and Chava) themselves. The act of creation becomes layered and reciprocal: Adam / Chava was originally dreamed up in the Divine imagination, and now, within Adam's (and Chava's) sleep, Chava is dreamed and imagined into being.

Chava is brought into being while Adam sleeps, in a state of dreaming, of Dimyon, where imagination envisions and creates. Chava as the other, is formed within Adam himself, yet now, stands apart from him. Although she is no longer a mere image or echo of longing, but "bone of my bones," the dreamlike quality of her origins and emergence leaves a trace, a lingering longing. This longing, so central to the human experience of love, is born from the awareness that the person who stands before us is both 'other' and a part of us. Your spouse is not simply someone you meet out in the world, but an inner 'part' of you that has been lost and now returns. Finding one's soulmate is like finding a lost object that belongs to you.* There is recognition, but also yearning; reunion, but also mystery. Marriage, then, is not only the forging of a bond,

* *Kiddushin*, 2b.

rather, the rediscovery of an integral piece of yourself. This return to wholeness is shaped by love, imagination, and the eternal desire to be reunified.

TO MOVE AHEAD WE NEED TO LET GO OF THE OLD

"Therefore a man shall leave his father and mother, and cleave to his wife, and become like one flesh." This is a description of the journey towards individuation, towards becoming a self. Becoming yourself, and then eventually being able to marry, begins with 'leaving', not only in the literal sense of leaving one's childhood home, but more profoundly, emotionally, and intellectually.

To leave your 'parents' home' means to release the paradigms, stories, and unconscious patterns inherited from your past. It means stepping out of familiar, limiting narratives, in order to make space for something new, something whole, mutual and real.

A healthy marriage requires releasing the narratives from your upbringing and past relationships that no longer serve you. This is the only way forward. The present is the only place we truly live.

How do we release old stories and soften our grip on what has passed? Maybe the question is, how do you *not* let go? Because the only place where we actually live is in the now; everything else is either replayed memories or projected fantasies. The only objective reality is the one appearing at this moment. How, then, are we able to hold on to the past?

The past only exists in our thoughts, and we ultimately have a choice of how to respond to our thoughts. Say someone experienced a trauma or real negativity, G-d forbid, and it is now a year later. If they are repeating the same story in their mind and allowing the memory of that experience to take over their consciousness, their body will not fully differentiate between the story and an actual recurrence of the trauma. They are, at least subtly, re-traumatizing themselves.

The same is true with every experience. We have a choice at every moment to live without baggage in the clarity of the present, or to live weighed down by a past that does not truly exist outside of our mental story. That is why our Sages tell us that the word *V'ata /* "and now" means Teshuvah, transformation. To transform yourself requires living in the present. This is not just a nice idea; there is actually no other place to live.

OUR PAST CAN CLOUD OUR PRESENT

Consider a few examples of how past narratives, when left unexamined, can quietly follow a person into their present relationships and slowly erode them from within. Perhaps you grew up in a home where conflict was met with shouting, or where communication was avoided altogether. Now, as an adult, you find yourself reacting in the same way, either with explosive anger or silent withdrawal, without realizing it stems from a learned script. Or maybe you struggle with wounded self-worth. Perhaps you carry beliefs from childhood that you are not lovable or not good enough, and now as an adult, in a marriage, this negative narrative is making it extremely difficult for you to fully receive love and to trust that what your spouse is giving you is genuine.

Fear of vulnerability can be another issue you carry with yourself from your youth. Perhaps if showing strength was idolized in your upbringing, and tenderness was seen as weakness, you may go around hiding your true feelings and needs and instead walk around wearing strength as an armor, but sadly, feeling painfully alone and vulnerable beneath it.

Perfectionism can be another lingering burden. You may have absorbed the message in your upbringing that anything less than perfection is a failure; if you did not come home with a hundred percent mark on your test, there was a sense of disappointment. These impossible expectations may now be poisoning your marriage, creating unnecessary tension and emotional distance.

These are the kinds of patterns the Torah alludes to when it says, "A man shall leave his father and mother." Certainly, if you have been hurt in a previous relationship, you may unknowingly project those wounds onto your spouse, expecting them to behave as others did, and never give your marriage a real chance to survive and thrive. However, the option to "leave" our past is always open; it is not a one-time act, it is a continuous invitation to return to presence.

Now the context has been set to explore the five basic keys to a happy marriage: joy, love, kinship, peace, and friendship.

Part Two

THE FIVE KEYS
TO A HAPPY MARRIAGE

Our sages speak of the number five in relation to the wedding ceremony.* Indeed, in the blessing for marriage we say, אשר ברא ששון ושמחה... אהבה ואחוה ושלום וריעות / "...Who has created **joy** and gladness...**love** and **kinship**, and **peace** and **friendship**.**" These are the five ingredients for a healthy prosperous marriage.

Each of these five qualities is vital in its own right, and each will be explored in depth, uncovering its unique role in sustaining and deepening our most sacred bond. For now, consider that there are five dimensions or modes of self which correspond to the five keys. You are a multidimensional being, with physical, emotional,

---

* *Berachos*, 6b.
** *Kesuvos*, 8a.

mental, and spiritual dimensions, plus an all-inclusive self-essence. Each of these layers carries the potential for a deeper stage of connection and harmony with your spouse. This potential is activated when you are able to weave together your five dimensions with the five dimensions of your spouse. To build a bond that is whole and fulfilling, a couple connects and aligns with each other through all five, by means of the Five Keys.

THE FIVE KEYS AS OUR FIVE DIMENSIONS

Physicality is our tangible bodily presence. On this level of being, connection with one's spouse is activated both through caring touch and physical closeness, and through respecting physical boundaries and giving space. It usually includes sharing in material support and physical tasks, and maintaining one's health and physical appearance.

Emotionality is the language of the heart. It is the ability to love and be loved, to feel and be felt. The connection on this level is emotional.

The mental self is the meeting of minds. Here ideas intertwine; shared values, ideals, and goals take root. The connection of this level is at its peak, a mental and intellectual compatibility , and at the very least, a mutual interest in exploration.

Spirituality is the part of self that seeks meaning and soul connection. The union on this level transcends the immediate, leading to a commitment to living towards a shared higher purpose.

The fifth key beyond all these is the very essence of being. This speaks to the deepest truth of who people are. It is here that two souls go beyond connection and resonate as one. This is a level beyond all boundaries and distinctions, a resonance of harmony so deep it becomes eternal.

Through this section, we will explore in depth these five keys as they relate to our five dimensions of connectivity within a marriage.

Chapter 1

JOY | שמחה

*I*n the blessings recited over a wedding, we say, "You are the Source of All Blessings, Hashem... Who created joy and gladness...delight, exultation, happiness, jubilation — love and kinship, and peace and friendship."* The first six terms refer to various forms and expressions of joy, as there are in fact ten types of joy in the Torah.**

For example, there is the 'joy' of contentment, a joyful satisfaction with one's life or circumstances. There is joy experienced in growth and in doing what we love. There is a joy of anticipation, being excited about an event in the future, and there is a joy of

---

* *Kesuvos*, 8a.
***Avos d'Rebbe Nason*, 43:9.

receiving what you desire. Joy is experienced when something un-expected and wonderful happens to us, and there is joy when we experience an alleviation of stress, worry, or fear. There is a joy in the resolution of doubts, and a joy in finding or reclaiming some-thing you lost, or someone who was missing from your life. There is inner joy, and there is ecstatic joy. There is joy experienced in the mind, and joy that is felt in the heart or body.

TO BE JOYFUL

The highest aspiration is to be in a state of *Simcha* / joy at all times.* Having an ongoing joyful disposition contributes to our mental and physical health,** and profoundly impacts our home and marriage.

Joyfulness is a gift not only to ourselves but to everyone around us, particularly those who share our living space. Emotional states are indeed contagious. Individuals who present with gloom, annoy-ance, or despondency create a heavy and unpleasant atmosphere. And when joy is expressed outwardly, a happier environment is cultivated. This radiance uplifts everyone in the home, including our spouse and children.

One does not become joyful simply by relying on external cir-cumstances or objects that stimulate joy; it comes from a deliber-ate and mindful decision. We ultimately have free choice whether to be joyful and hopeful or morose and pessimistic. We choose

---

* *Tanya*, 26. Joy is a 'Mitzvah' in itself: *Keser Shem Tov*, Hosofos, 169.
** *Orchos Tzadikim*, Sha'ar haSimcha.

the lens through which we look at this world, and this determines the tone of all of our thinking and ultimately our behavior. For this reason, the Hebrew word b'Simcha / בשמחה / "with happiness" contains the same letters as Machshavah / מחשבה / thought.* At any given moment, we can decide to stop ruminating on, or complaining about, our circumstances. In any case, even if we do not *feel* joyful, we can choose to *act* joyfully, our mood will then follow our behaviour.

We may occasionally find our joy depleted, and our 'positivity lens' to be muddied to the extent that our mind loses control over our heart. In this case when we cannot 'think ourselves into' a more joyful state, then we can resolve to take a proactive approach to rejuvenating our joy. For example, sing or hum a cheerful song, or play uplifting music.** The power to change our mood is within our grasp. When we listen to joyful music, no matter how we are currently feeling, there is an urge to sing, to move the body. Notice how such physical acts can positively influence the mind and alter consciousness. Actions *affect* our mind and heart as much as they *reflect* our feelings. In this way one can create a continuous loop of inner joy and satisfaction. "The heart follows actions."*** Our inner emotions are influenced by our physical actions. Simply choosing to smile releases neurochemicals which trigger an internal welling up of joy.

---

*   *Tiferes Shelomo*, Sha'ar haTefilah, p 10.
** *Ma'amarei Admur haZaken*, Inyanim, p. 403.
*** *Sefer haChinuch*,16:2.

Not only is it within our capability to be joyful, but it is in fact a moral and spiritual responsibility—to ourselves and to our loved ones—to cultivate joy. Our moods affect not only our thoughts and our behavior, but they either uplift or pull down everyone around us.

JOY OF PURPOSE

Examining sadness can provide insight into the nature of joy. Often, sadness and depression are rooted in a sense of purposelessness and lack of direction. People who struggle with sadness may feel their life lacks cohesiveness and meaning, making them feel aimless or like victims of random events. In contrast, joy springs from a clear sense of purpose, mission, and direction.

People who wake up every morning infused with passion for their mission and purpose have a sense of inner drive, and experience more joy in their day-to-day life. The nature of the human being is to work, grow, move, and evolve: "Man is born for toil."* When we work hard, when we have something in life that we *want* to accomplish, that is often when we feel most human, most alive. and most joyful. In a marriage, the joy of being married is sensed more when spouses have similar overarching goals and ambitions for their marriage.

The Hebrew word שמח / *Samach* / happy is similar to the word צמח / *Tzamach* / plant,** meaning *to grow, to sprout, to blossom.* This linguistic kinship reveals a beautiful truth: to be truly happy is to grow. Happiness is not merely the result of attaining what we de-

---

* *Iyov*, 5:7. See *Sanhedrin*, 99b.
** As Shin and Tzadik are interchangeable, see *Tehilim*, 105:9.

sire, but is born from the very process of becoming, of unfolding, evolving, and reaching upward like a plant toward the light. The simple act of movement and inner expansion is, in itself, a source of joy. Of course, when our efforts bear fruit, when we see the results of our labor and our dreams take form, our joy deepens.

When we have exercised or cared for our body and feel stronger and healthier, or when we have set financial goals and achieved them, a natural joy arises. When we learn a new skill or cover ground in *Limud haTorah* / Torah learning, when we realize we have grown emotionally and become more mature or whole-some, or when we have grown spiritually and are living with more *D'veikus* / connection with the Infinite Creator, joy awakens ac-cordingly. Clearly, the joy of an exercise routine usually pales in comparison to the joy of deep emotional healing, and certainly to that of D'veikus, but each level of joy is integral in its own realm.

In marriage, finding joy in purposefulness involves setting and achieving shared goals, whether taking walks together, or working together toward financial stability or spiritual growth. Each level of accomplishment, no matter how small, contributes to the overall happiness in the marriage.

A sense that you are both growing together is fundamental to a joyful marriage. In the Shabbos *Piyut* / liturgy, we recite regarding the angels of Shabbat, "They experience Simcha when they go out and Sasson when they return" (שמחים בצאתם וששים בבואם). Simcha is, in this way, associated with outward movement and growth, while Sasson signifies contentment.*

---

* *Gra*, on Iyov, 3. There are in fact ten such terms of joy: *Avos d'Rebbe Nason*, 43:9.

In a marriage, as in life, growth brings Simcha. As both spouses evolve and support each other's growth, they experience deeper joy, for when there is *Tz'michah* / growth, there is Simcha.

Deeper forms of Simcha are revealed when we attain *Yishuv haDa'as* / settling of consciousness. In this settled mind state, we know our purpose, our mission, what we need to be doing in this world, and how we can go about doing it. Chasing the next high, the next momentary excitement or relief, does not bring us lasting Simcha. We need Yishuv haDa'as in order to rise out of that addictive cycle of the next great thing, to focus on what we need to accomplish in this world and how best to direct our energy and talents. The more we live with this settled, purposeful awareness, the more Simcha we experience in our lives.[*]

Attaining a settled consciousness, the centeredness and presence that is Yishuv haDa'as, helps us foster profound and lasting joy in our marriage, and by extension, in all our relationships.

SENSING THE PURPOSE & UPWARD TRAJECTORY OF CREATION BRINGS JOY

Just as we experience joy when we are aware of our own personal purpose and mission, deep inner joy also arises from the awareness that everything in life has purpose. There are no accidents or ran-

---

[*] Simcha is from something that is *constant*: *Malbim* on Tehilim, 96:11 and Mishlei, 23:24-25. The *Gra*, however, writes (on *Mishlei*, 23:24) that Simcha comes from something *new*. Regarding Sason and Simcha, see also the Rebbe, *Hisva'aduyos*, 5745, vol. 4, p. 2181. The Mitteler Rebbe, *Sha'arei Orah*, "V'Kibel HaYehudim".

domness in our lives, in Creation, and throughout history.[*]

Everything is constantly evolving toward the ultimate purpose of perfection and redemption. There are obvious setbacks and regressions, since history is not a straight line, but from a wider lens we will always see that the universe is marching forward and upward, with humanity at the forefront. The movement is gradual, (sometimes it feels too slow for our liking,) but everything will reach its ultimate purpose. Individual and cosmic redemption are actually unavoidable. Joy is experienced when we are able to sense this positive evolution of all beings and all things, together as one.

Likewise, joy in marriage comes from sensing that every moment we share together has a higher, deeper purpose. Despite any challenges, in a marriage that is evolving, everything is moving toward a better place. This is palpable when we consciously choose to live according to this perspective. Despite setbacks and lows, recognizing that the totality of the journey together is part of a greater upward trajectory, and that each person in the marriage is an agent towards this process of positive unfolding, we can choose to grow in our marriage and do our part, and as we grow so will our joy.

By embracing these aspects, finding joy in purpose, growth, and being, spouses can create a marriage filled with lasting happiness. Supporting each other's missions, celebrating growth, and cherishing each other's presence helps build a joyful and fulfilling relationship.

---

[*] *Reishis Chochmah,* Sha'ar HaAhava, 10.

It is wonderful to grow together and share a common purpose with your spouse, which brings much more joy into the marriage, but it is not the role of one spouse to enforce this growth upon the other. Our personal growth is our own responsibility, our business and not that of our spouse. A spouse may not have the same purpose or sense of direction that you do. Certainly, it is not our role to be our spouse's *Mashpia* / spiritual and moral guide, nor their 'Rabbi' or therapist.

What we can do is focus on living *our* life, *our* purpose, and do so with enthusiasm, optimism, and with a positive mindset and lightness. This inevitably creates an inspired environment in the home that encourages growth organically. One's genuine and passionate commitment to their own mission and the joy that comes with it, can and will be contagious, and hopefully will inspire their spouse towards that same upbeat enthusiasm and positivity.

THE LEVELS OF JOY MIRROR THE TEMPLATE OF COSMIC AND MICROCOSMIC CREATION

Within the joy of 'becoming' there are many grades corresponding to the levels of becoming, such as finding purpose, growing, achieving, and accomplishing. In marriage this is a joy of growing together and living with shared purpose. There is also a joy of 'being'; in marriage this is the simple joy of being in each other's company, of being in oneness with the aspect of your soul embodied in the other.

Earlier, the meta structure, the inner template of Creation, was discussed at length. This template evolves and is structured on three stages. Initially, there was and is only the Bli Gevul / Unlimited, the Ohr Ein Sof / Infinite Light. Then comes the Tzimtzum, the contraction of the Infinite Light and the revealing of the finite light. Finally, once there is already a finite reality of time, space and perspectival consciousness, the purpose arises for this finite reality to reconnect and unify with Infinite. Singularity to separation, to synthesis.

This structure of three—singularity, separation / individuality and finally unity—plays itself out as well in each of the five dimensions and keys of marriage and healthy relationships; joy, love, kinship, peace and friendship.

There is the joy of becoming, the exhilaration of growth, movement, and transformation. But there is also the deeper joy of being, the quiet contentment of resting fully in one's own place, one's own essence. Yet, the highest form of joy is when these two dimensions merge, when we are wholly present in our own being and place, yet harmoniously united with the other in theirs.

עז וחדוה במקומו / "Strength and joy are in His *Makom* / Place".* As a reflection of this, when we are in our place, that is—when we uncover our *Makom* / place in the world—we feel joy, alive, alert, conscious, and empowered. This is the joy of being.

Everything in nature is essentially in a perpetual state of joy, the joy of being. Only a human being who can be misaligned and estranged from their true place, their deeper self, can feel a dichotomy between joy and existential depression. Everything in its true place of *being* is in a constant state of joy. Marriage is a return to our

---

* *Divrei haYamim*, 1, 16:27. *Chagigah*, 5b.

Makom. We were once part of a greater whole, a greater soul, and then experienced a Tzimtzum, a *Nesira* / severing. After decades of being apart, now we are rejoining and becoming even more whole again. This is why marriage *is* joy, the joy of finding the one who was 'lost'; the joy of being back in the right Makom, place. And this is the reason the sages say that someone who lives without a wife (or husband) is a person that is without this particular joy.

Marriage is the third level in the template, the finite fullness of each spouse coming together in an even greater unity than the singularity before the division. The first level, the joy of being alone, is healthy and appropriate for the first stages of growth. Yet, "it is not good to be alone" too much or to stagnate in loneliness, and thus the second level, the Nesira, the separation, comes to free us from stagnation. In the separation of Nesira we feel a tremendous desire to reconnect with our soulmate. This is the joy of becoming, ie; dreaming and idealism, which drives us toward the ultimate joy, the joy of pure being, of reunification.

It should be noted that these three levels of singularity, separation and reunification and synthesis, are not only a linear progression. Even once a person is already married, one still needs to feel their own individuality and integrity while alone, and the tension, desire and ambition to connect, which comes from being separate. And of course the joy of being, expressed in simply being in each other's company, which is the joy of reunification.

BRINGING LAUGHTER INTO THE HOME AND RELATIONSHIP

However one defines the concept of *Simcha* / joy, it is vital that we bring joy, laughter, and lightness into our marriage, and in fact into all our relationships. Any form of *Avodas Hashem* / serving Hashem, should not feel heavy and burdensome. Marriage is one of the greatest forms of Avodas Hashem, and arguably the most important training ground for loving and respecting Hashem.

There is a principle in the Torah that the first mention in the Torah of a topic, a word, or even a letter, holds significant importance. This initial reference is considered the archetype or foundation of that concept.* Yitzchak and Rivka are the first couple in the Torah, not the first to be married, but the first couple where the Torah describes their meeting, getting married, and living together in love. When the Torah describes the deep intimacy between this 'first' couple, the paragon of marriage, the holy patriarch and matriarch, Yitzchak and Rivkah, the Torah says, "And behold, Yitzchak was frolicking (מצחק / laughing with) Rivkah, his wife."**

---

* *Toldos Yitzchak*, p. 39b. *Bnei Yissaschar*, Iyyar, Ma'amar 3.

** *Bereishis*, 26:8. Avimelech saw through divination, and not literally: *Zohar*, ad loc. It is important to keep in mind that we are talking about the Avos and Imahos HaKedoshim, our holy patriarchs and matriarchs, who were profoundly modest in every way. The idea of שׂחק / laughing is essential for harmonious relationships and intimacy. *Berachos*, 62a. *Chagiga*, 5b: סח וצחק ועשה צרכיו. Note *Avoda Zara*, 20a. Note also the ruling of the Rambam that intimacy should be ברצון שניהם ובשמחתם. *Hilchos De'os* 5: 4.

The term *MeTzacheik* / מצחק / frolicking, comes from *Tzchok* / צחק / laughter, which is essential for a thriving relationship. Incorporating healthy, productive, and positive humor into our marriage relationship and family life can transform the atmosphere and basic feeling of our home. While it is crucial to take our physical, emotional, mental, and spiritual well-being seriously in a growth-oriented relationship, this should not come at the expense of lightness and joy. We need to be mindful that the pursuit of greater accomplishment and thriving does not lead to heaviness and stress.

Heaviness often arises from a feeling and attitude of weakness or tiredness, which, unfortunately, is frequently a consequence of transgression. As *Dovid HaMelech* / King David, tells us, "My strength fails because of my sin."* Before Adam and Chava ate from the Tree of Knowledge, they were warned, "On the day you eat from it, you will die," meaning they would become mortal. Being connected to the Tree of Life, they were intended to be immortal. However, once they ate from the Tree of Knowledge and identified with the world of duality and separation, Hashem declared, "Dust you are, and to dust you will return."**

These two statements, death and dust, are interconnected. Adam and Chava's departure from the reality of oneness and unity, caused the element of earth—or dust—within them to become most dominant. Earth, unlike the lighter elements of fire, wind, and water, is heavy and pulls us into its gravity. Thus, with death, dust returns to dust.

---

* *Tehilim*, 31:11. *Gittin*, 70a.
***Bereishis*, 2:17. ibid, 3:19.

Acting against our true nature can create a profound sense of heaviness within us. And, if we then further burden ourselves with shame, blame, or self-criticism for those actions taken or not taken, this weight can become almost unbearable, compounding our pain and distress and making us feel heavier and yet heavier, worse and still worse.

It is for this reason, among many others, that our heart and home should be a sanctuary overflowing with genuine joy, purpose, values, holiness, and positive goals. A healthy dose of humor goes a long way in creating such positivity.

Part of having a nurturing home is having laughter and humor in the home. "One who whitens his teeth to his friend (by smiling at him) is better than one who gives him milk to drink."* Just as a child needs to be nurtured, and milk is symbolic of that nurturing, children are nurtured by the smile of their parents. The same is true between spouses: we bear a sacred responsibility to nurture one another with kindness, warmth, and love.

A well-balanced sense of humor can transform our environment into a haven of happiness. When life throws us curveballs, humor becomes our ally, soothing difficult situations and helping us bounce back with ease. If you happen to slip and fall, whether literally or figuratively, lying there and berating yourself won't help. Instead, try to find a bit of humor in it, laugh it off, choose to get back on your feet, and take swift measures to prevent similar mishaps in the future.

---

* *Kesuvos*, 111b. טוב המלבין שינים לחבירו יותר ממשקהו חלב.

HUMOR DEFUSES TENSION

With just a touch of humor, we can create a pleasant and joyful atmosphere in our relationships, and when things go unexpectedly wrong, humor can act as an antidote to dispel the tension that this causes. This approach helps us feel safer, more valued, and loved, especially during moments of conflict, and can clearly help spouses get out of conflict. For example, if one's spouse accidentally breaks a valuable object or responsibility, and this causes hurt or anger, introducing a bit of (appropriate) humor before addressing the issue, or making a joke to defuse a quarrel, can restore the balance and equilibrium of the relationship. This approach can increase the likelihood of the other person, or one's own self, accepting responsibility and sincerely apologizing.

In the same vein, if we want to suggest something beneficial to our spouse — like dedicating more time to a specific task — using humor can be incredibly effective. Instead of sounding preachy or condescending, a light-hearted approach can help us to convey our point. This way, the message comes across warmly and is more likely to be received positively, and without making anyone feel threatened or lectured.

This is even more essential when tensions are high. For example, if one spouse is already feeling frustrated and expressing disappointment, even if their frustration is justified, humor can still help soothe the situation. If a disagreement becomes too intense, a light-hearted joke or even a playful gesture can defuse the tension, allowing both spouses to reset and tackle the issue with renewed energy and a fresh perspective of the issue at hand. This works, of course, only as long as the humor is not demeaning or seen as a means to claim victory. Humor should only serve to lighten the mood and pave the way for more constructive communication.

Additionally, humor should never be used to ignore the situation or trivialize the real issue at hand. Humor which is cynical and used to belittle a person, group, or situation is counterproductive and worsens things. Humor is a powerful tool and one that we should employ wisely and wield with care. A careless or misplaced joke or jibe can cause real damage to a loved one's sense of security within the relationship.

A 'make-up joke' is when, after a verbal disagreement, one spouse tries to defuse the tension with humor or light-heartedness. As the recipient of the humor, it is important to receive the gesture with grace and not to play the victim card. Choosing to be an active participant and creator of your life means allowing ourselves to laugh, to be appeased by our spouse, and appreciate their effort to mend the situation. Just as we use humor to lighten a situation by being the one who maintains their sense of humor, we equally embrace and receive the lightness our spouse offers.

Rather than fixating on the quarrel or falling into sadness, embrace the gift of letting your spouse make you laugh. As the Pasuk says, "Yitzchak was delighting and making Rivkah laugh," but for him to make her laugh, she needed to allow him and open herself up to it. Without this mutual humor and delight, there is little hope for the relationship to survive or thrive. Perhaps, the humorless relationship can continue to go through the motions of what a relationship looks like from the outside, but a genuine, face-to-face, intimate, loving, alive relationship requires openness and vulnerability. This openness shows up in the ability to laugh at the other's sense of humor and not to take oneself too seriously.

LAUGHING TOGETHER

The practice of embracing laughter and lightness means that we are taking life very seriously but taking ourselves very lightly. This benefits our own life, allowing for genuine growth, and by extension it benefits all those around you. This posture of lightness is a profound way of serving Hashem, as it is beautifully exemplified by Dovid HaMelech, King David, who said, "I have laughed (or played) in front of Hashem."*

The book of Jewish law which details our daily practices begins and ends with two *Temidim* or constants. It opens with the verse from Tehilim, שויתי ה׳ לנגדי תמיד / "I have placed Hashem in front of me Tamid / תמיד / at all times"**: "A person's way of sitting, his movements and his dealings while he is alone in his house are not the same as his sitting, movements and dealings when he is before a great king; nor are his speech and free expression as much as he wants when he is with his household members and his relatives like his speech when in a royal audience. All the more so when one takes to heart that the Great King, the Holy One, Blessed Is He, Whose glory fills the earth, is standing over him and watching his actions."***

---

* Shemuel 2, 6:21.
** Tehilim, 16:8.
*** *Shulchan Aruch*, Orach Chayim, 1:1

The other teaching of Tamid / constant, which appears at the conclusion, states, "The good-hearted feast Tamid / תמיד / always."*

These two constants—both feeling ourselves to be always in the presence of the Divine, and being in a state of joyfulness always—which bookend the masterpiece of Jewish Law, are the truest expression of how we are empowered to live our daily life.

We strive to be like Dovid HaMelech and be playful in front of Hashem, as joy and laughter allows us to go beyond our *Gevul* / limitations in serving the Source of Life more and more deeply.

LAUGHTER AND THE
OHR EIN SOF | INFINITE LIGHT

In Hebrew, the word for laughter is שחוק / *S'chok*, which has a numerical value of 414, as do the words, אור אין סוף / *Ohr Ein Sof* / the Infinite Light.**

Laughter touches Infinity, allowing us to leave our finite, defined space and encounter another.

Everything in the natural world has its own distinct *Gevul*, its unique *Makom* / space, and the most any living creature can do from a place of Gevul is to cohabit with another and create new life. This utilitarian relationship is called *Achor-b'Achor* / back-to-back. It is not intimate or personal. Only human beings, created in

---

* Regarding Purim Katan. *Shulchan Aruch*, Orach Chayim, 697. Mishlei, 15:15.
**As the Tzemach Tzedek teaches, *Ohr HaTorah*, Ba'alosecha, p. 331a. Or twice the word אור / Ohr. Arizal, *Sha'ar haMitzvos*, Vayelech.

the Divine image, have the ability to encounter an other as *an other*, and be intimate. Humans are created with the potential to enter into a relationship with a spouse in a way that is *Eizer Kenegdo* / helper, opposite the other. A relationship in which the spouses are *Kenegdo* / opposite the other, is where each spouse is anchored in their own fullness of life and Makom. And precisely because of that groundedness, each spouse can also be a true *Eizer* / helper, someone that can enter the shared space, naturally and harmoniously stimulating growth and depth in the relationship, and producing holy angels and souls.

Humans are the only creatures that can experience true *Panim-El-Panim* / face-to-face encounters, and humans are also the only creatures that can truly laugh. Most of the other eleven 'senses' that the Sefer Yetzira speaks about are also found throughout the animal kingdom, but a developed sense of humor is uniquely human.* While certain primates appear to exhibit a sense of slapstick humor, if we observe them more closely we will see that it is still only humans who possess the ability to appreciate irony, intellectual incongruity, and more sophisticated forms of humor.

Parenthetically, it is for this reason that a sense of humor is also individual and idiosyncratic. People laugh at different things and in very different situations. To a certain extent, you can tell what type of person someone is, or what kind of subculture they are from, by the jokes they tell or laugh at. "A person's true character is ascertained by his behavior in three areas: his 'cup', meaning, his behavior when he drinks, his 'pocket', meaning, his conduct in his

---

* Gra, *Sefer Yetzirah*, 5:2. Yavetz, *Mitpachas Sefarim*, 8:8.

financial dealings with other people, and the charities he gives or does not give, and his anger. And some say, a person also reveals his real nature in his laughter."* You can tell a lot about a people, a nation, and even a person by his particular sense of humor.

Ultimately, when we approach life with a healthy, sacred, and positive sense of lightness and joy, and ensure that joy and laughter are the prevailing atmosphere in our home and marriage, we become more open and receptive to our own self and to others. This attitude allows us to release our narrow, ego-driven thinking and the confines of our own Gevul and live more expansively. In doing so, we create a nurturing space, an open Makom, an infinite, all embracing space, where both spouses, and all in the household can flourish. The *Shechina* / Divine Presence can then rest therein and embrace each person within Its sublime, joyful shine.

LAUGHTER CREATES SPACE

All relationships, and certainly marriages, are harmonious fusions of two distinct individuals, with their own unique perspectives, ways of thinking, feeling, and being in this world. While they share a soul connection, to be sure, they also bring their own defined barometers and prisms into the marriage. Every person has their own Gevul, their defined comfort zone and defined personal space. Marriage requires an opening of your own Gevul to welcome the Gevul of the other, to expand the contours of your way of life to respect and cherish those of the other. This opening of

---

* *Eiruvin,* 65b.

borders is often challenging, especially for those who are deeply protective of their space.

Laughter helps alleviate and soften our borders, allowing us to let in a little more movement and light, and welcoming in the spark of Infinite Light in the other. Laughter is a magical key that opens our heart and makes us more transparent and light. This is why laughter is often a telling sign of whether two people will come together, and also whether their union will flourish and endure, G-d willing.

שחוק / *S'chok* / laughter also shares a numerical value with the word ואהבת / "You shall love." Love, just like laughter, allows us to leave our space, hold space for the other, and be there fully for them. Love also allows us to open our finite *Gevul* / boundary, so that our spouse can enter our space. In this way, love has an element of *Ein Sof* / Infinity, transcending boundaries.

It benefits a marriage to learn to laugh together, to always make each other laugh, and also to be open to allow your spouse to make you laugh. Letting your spouse make you laugh is a willingness to let down your guard, and allow your spaces to blend.

Practical Takeaways

CHOOSE JOY DELIBERATELY:

Joy is a conscious and mindful choice, not simply a reaction to favorable circumstances. Joy emerges from the deliberate decision to see the world through a lens of optimism and hope. While practices like contemplation and inner reflection can nurture joy from within, the company you keep plays a powerful role as well. Surround yourself with positive, optimistic, uplifting people whose energy amplifies joy. As a spouse, be intentional about the people you welcome into your home, as they will directly affect the atmosphere within it. Similarly, be mindful about the circles you spend time with, as you will inevitably carry their energy back into your home. Always seek out friends and company who embody joy and optimism.

BRING JOY INTO YOUR HOME:

Be mindful of the energy you carry. When we walk through the door with a heaviness or dour expression, when our face is tight with tension or resentment, that energy does not stay with us; it spills into the room, and everyone feels it. As the adults in the home, we can either drain the life out of our space, or breathe vitality into it. We have a sacred responsibility to make our home a space of warmth and joy.

NEVER THINK ABOUT "THE MARRIAGE" WHEN TIRED:

Avoid evaluating your life or your marriage when you are physically or emotionally exhausted, or going through a particularly difficult season in life. Similarly, refrain from evaluating yourself or your life at the end of a long and exhausting day, when fatigue clouds clarity. Indeed, fatigue distorts your perspective and casts a shadow over everything. What may feel like deep dissatisfaction with your life, or your marriage, may, in truth, be nothing more than simple exhaustion. Sometimes, all you really need is a good night's sleep, not a radical life change.

ENGAGE IN JOYFUL ACTIVITIES:

When you are feeling down, take proactive steps to rekindle your joy. Singing, playing uplifting music, dancing, or other physical expressions of joy, even as simple as smiling, can powerfully uplift your mood and shift your mindset. To cultivate a joyful atmosphere at home, make it a habit to fill your home with joyful music. Having music in the home creates an environment that naturally invites lightness, warmth and joy. *

---

* "A chassidic melody…brings joyfulness, and places the home and family in a state of light" *Hayom Yom*, Tamuz 22.

ENGAGE IN INDIVIDUAL AND COLLECTIVE GROWTH:

Encourage and support each other's personal growth. Recognize that growth brings joy and a sense of fulfillment in your relationship. As such, it is important for each spouse to discover their unique *Makom* / space in the world and in the relationship, who they are and what is their unique contribution, but simultaneously, also find joy in shared goals, whether they are personal, financial, or spiritual.

PRIORITIZE SHARED JOY:

Make it a habit to create and share moments of joy together. Whether it is through shared hobbies or activities, or simply spending quality time together, prioritize these experiences to strengthen your bond.

DEFUSE TENSION WITH LAUGHTER:

Use humor to ease tension and soften conflict within your marriage and home. A light-hearted joke or playful gesture can help reset the emotional tone and open the door to a fresh perspective. The goal is not to avoid an issue, but to approach it with gentleness. Humor, when used with humble sensitivity, can be a powerful tool, so long as everyone feels safe, seen, and valued.

BE OPEN TO LAUGHTER:

Welcome your spouse's attempts to lighten the mood, and allow yourself to be delighted by their humor. Laugh at their jokes even if you do not find them all that funny. Even a small effort to bring joy deserves appreciation. Besides, shared laughter not only defuses tension, it strengthens the bond between you and deepens your emotional connection.

Chapter 2

LOVE | אהבה

*T*he second element in the blessing over marriage is Ahavah / love. To feel, give, and receive love, is essential to a marriage. Marriage thrives on love, expressed as kindness and empathy.

On a basic level, empathy means understanding your spouse's
struggles, joys, and needs, and responding with attention and compassion. Empathy and compassion in a relationship means far more
than simply demonstrating care. Compassion is the courageous
willingness to truly inhabit the emotional landscape of your spouse,
to deeply experience them in their uniqueness, and to encounter
their otherness without diminishing it. It means seeing the world
through their eyes, feeling their joys and sorrows, comprehending
life as it appears to them, molded by their individual experiences,
upbringing, and innermost thoughts and feelings.

When genuine empathy and compassion permeates the relationship, one's spouse experiences something far more profound than mere support. They feel genuinely seen and profoundly understood. They no longer bear their burdens alone, for they sense that we do not merely stand beside them as a sympathetic observer, but walk intimately alongside them as a true partner. In this depth of connection, their feelings are no longer foreign or distant; rather, their happiness and pain become ours as naturally as our own.

Compassion is an expression of love. In *Lashon Kodesh* / the Sacred Language of Hebrew, the word for love is *Ahavah*, a term that reflects deep connection, giving, and oneness. But when this word is translated into Judaic Aramaic — the language of the sages of the Talmud and Zohar which reveals the 'back' or external layer of Lashon Kodesh — the word for love becomes רחימו / *Rechimu* / literally 'compassion'. This is no accident; it reveals to us that the true expression of love is not just desire or affection, but the ability to feel with the other, to care from a place that transcends self.

But what is love, on the deepest inner level, beyond desire or affection or attraction?

To love someone is not about shaping the other in your image; it is to carry their pain as your own, to rejoice in their joy as if it were yours, and to see not only their appearance, but also their inner lived experience. Even deeper, loving someone means creating and holding a conceptual space in which they can safely grow, evolve, and unfold into their fullest self; a safe place where they are free to *be*, and to gently and beautifully *become*.

Parents, by nature, love their children, and from this love, they instinctively make space for their children to grow, to become, to unfold into who they are meant to be. In many ways, marriage can be like a 'second birth', especially for those who may not have received enough nurturing love in childhood. Marriage can offer a profound Tikun, a deep opportunity for healing for anyone, but especially for those who grew up feeling unseen, inadequate, or as if others were disappointed in them.

When we love our spouse with presence and patience, and carve out an emotional space for them to be, evolve, and feel safe, we help them heal and repair what may have been broken in their early story. In doing so, we do not just build a stronger marriage, we are participating in a profound act of restoration, rewriting the inner script that once said, "You are not enough," with a new truth: "You are loved, and you are free to become."

In the language that has been employed earlier, love is an act of *Tzimtzum* / contraction and withholding of self that creates space for the other person. Just as Hashem's love, the attribute of *Chesed* / giving that led to the Tzimtzum of the *Ohr Ein Sof* / Infinite Light prompted the emergence of a world other than Himself, so too, in marriage. We emulate Hashem's act of creation. Though Tzimtzum is an act of *Gevurah* / restraint and self-limitation, it is in fact the very expression of love that allows the other to exist, flourish, and unfold within the space we make for them. In this way, marriage mirrors the Divine love that gives the other space and nurtures their becoming.

THE MICROCOSM IS A MIRROR
OF THE MACROCOSM

Previously, the template of the macro-creation and the micro-creation was explored, and how the creation of humanity mirrors the creation of the world, and how the process unfolds in the three stages of singularity, separation, and synthesis.

The Divine act of love, which is Tzimtzum, means leaving the first stage, the 'immature' state of singularity, and allowing for the second stage, the emergence of multiplicity and the creation of time and space, and finally the third stage of reunifying Creation with the Infinite Light. Within the context of marriage and human relationships, love means making a Tzimtzum, making room for the other, and holding space for them to be and become. Love is to hold the other person, to hold the 'otherness' of the other, so that you can be a synthesis; two and one at the same time.

Adam was first a singularity, as one 'male and female', similar to the undifferentiated Ein Sof, and therefore, they needed to be put to sleep, sleep itself being a form of contraction, Tzimtzum. In Adam's sleep state, there was a Nesira, a severing, and when Adam awoke, Chava emerged as a separate being.

These same three stages are reflected in every relationship and marriage. We begin our adolescence as a single person, learning to express ourselves and our individuality, as an unconscious, self-centered 'singularity'. Sometimes people even get married with an adolescent mindset, seeing only themselves, and there is an unchecked expansion and expression of ego, leaving little room for their spouse. Such a relationship is sadly back-to-back and trans-actional. The connection is as yet unrefined, unconscious, and lacking mutuality; it is not a true soul merger. Maturity demands the practice of Tzimtzum, the movement from self-centeredness to an awareness of the other, and from there, entering the state of soul synthesis.

In simple day-to-day life, the practice of Tzimtzum of self means not always saying what we want to say right now, and making room for the other to speak. Love is not just giving an object to someone, rather it is giving a part of one's self, making room within oneself for the full existence of the other.

In this way, love is Tzimtzum, both the openness to the other and the bridge that allows us to connect and come together as two people with "one flesh," one essence.

STAGES OF RELATIONSHIP DEVELOPMENT

For there to be a stage three reality, there must first be a developed stage two of Tzimtzum, and that is an outgrowth of a refined and matured stage one, which is the sense of self. Throughout one's marriage, we are required to hold the tension between individuality and unity.

We start with a sense of self, as there first needs to be two selves to enter into a relationship. When there is a 'me' and 'you' there is the potential of an 'us'. But when a person is full of himself or herself, with no capacity for Tzimtzum, then their opinions, perspectives and needs will dominate, and the partnership will not be a face-to-face encounter. As one matures, there is a realization of the necessity of lovingly limiting oneself for the sake of the other, so that they can be themselves authentically and without being overshadowed. Only through this self-limitation can both spouses draw close in love in a way that sustains and deepens the bond.

CREATING SPACE WITHIN SELF IS LOVE AND IT ALLOWS FOR LOVE

The second stage, opening up space for your spouse to emerge, starts well before you enter the relationship. Even before an individual can contemplate being in a relationship, they need to empty out a place within their heart and psyche for another person. We need to make room for a relationship, before it can begin to manifest.

The Zohar, in the beginning of the portion *Tazria*, asks a question. The Torah tells us, "A woman gives seed and gives birth to a son" (Vayikra, 12:2), but is this true? It seems to mean that the moment of insemination is the same moment the woman gives birth. Perhaps the Torah could have said, "A woman becomes pregnant and then gives birth to a child," for prior to birth there has to be pregnancy. And Rebbe Yosi answers: "A woman, from the moment she becomes pregnant until the day of the birth, continuously speaks about the idea of having a son" (אתתא, מן יומא דאתעברת עד יומא דיולדת לית לה בפומא, אלא ילידו דילה אי להוי דכר).

In other words, while the actual birth of the child occurs after nine months of pregnancy, from the moment of conception there is already a 'birth' of a child in the psyche or in the soul of the mother. In the mother's mind, heart and then in her speech, there is a space carved out for the son to be born, and therefore, the Torah says, "A woman gives seed and gives birth to a son," because from the moment of conception, this child already exists in her mind, and only after the entirety of a pregnancy, is the actual baby born.

Beyond the simple meaning, the Zohar is alluding to the creative process itself. In the creation of any meaningful reality, such as a marriage relationship, there is a pattern of progression. Before anything is born into the world, it must first be conceived in imagination. It then takes form through speech. The act of speaking is the articulation of the dream and is essential. Speech is what transforms dreams into direction, and intention into form. Before a child is born, there is already a kind of inner birth within the mother. She opens a space within herself, mentally, emotionally, and of course, viscerally, in which the actual child can be born.*

To marry and begin living with another person is like a birth. Not only is a relationship and a new home born, but the other person is born into our own life, into our being. For this to happen, there first needs to be within us a space that is created, making way for them to arrive. We think, speak and dream within ourselves the space for a new person in our life. Just as one might prepare a house or apartment where they will live together, we prepare with-

---

* The Gemara says, אשה מזרעת תחילה יולדת זכר איש מזריע תחילה יולדת נקבה / "If the woman emits seed first, she gives birth to a male, and if the man emits seed first, she gives birth to a female": *Niddah*, 31a. If the female opens a space within herself first, the gender opposite to hers is created, a son. If the man opens within himself a space first, the gender opposite to his is created, a daughter.

in ourselves a dwelling place for their soul, body, character, opinions, preferences, viewpoints, talents, lifestyle, spirituality, and way of being.

MAKING THE SPACE TO ENTER RELATIONSHIPS & CONTINUALLY MAKING THAT SPACE

Often, there are those who have been searching for their life partner for a long time and wonder why they have still not found their *Bashert* / 'destined one' or soulmate. It is possible that they have not yet made the conceptual, mental, and emotional space within themselves for another. They may be standing just two feet away from their Bashert, but because the space for them in their life and identity has not yet been carved out, their personal 'space' is fully occupied. Sometimes there is no room for anyone at all, much less someone who will naturally challenge them to grow as only a spouse can. Even more challenging, they might be unconsciously pushing away their soulmate and blocking their entry.

We do this inward practice of opening up space within ourselves before we entertain the possibility of entering into a relationship. And this practice is continuous throughout the marriage. For a marriage to flourish, we constantly make space and hold space for our spouse. This is not meant just for the beginning of the relationship or to initially attract our soulmate, but every single day thereafter.

Marriage, like the creation of *Gevul* / finitude from the Infinite Light, is a *Chidush* / novelty. This means that it is something that will not happen on its own; it must be deliberately and consciously created. Much like any Chidush, and especially the ultimate Chidush which is the creation of the world, it needs to be continuously created for it to be sustained. Every moment the world is being created and recreated from nothingness, from the Ein Sof. Consider a ball that sits on the ground. To keep it airborne, contrary to its natural state of groundedness, it requires a continuously renewed force. It is not the nature of a ball to fly; a flying ball is a 'Chidush', and therefore it needs the continued momentum of the toss to keep it airborne.

This is a metaphor for the entire Creation, and also for marriage. In many ways, it is a Chidush, a complete novelty, for two individuals with their different genetics, upbringings, experiences, and perhaps even cultural backgrounds (even while sharing the same soul-root), to come together and create a unified entity. Marriage thus demands continuous work. The union of marriage requires continuous reunification, and this means renewing our effort, tenderness, clear communication and mindfulness, and holding space for our spouse again and again. In the beginning of the relationship this effort may be relatively superficial, as there is a natural momentum in the newness of the relationship, but it needs to deepen and increase over time to maintain the momentum.

LOVE IS BEING FULLY PRESENT. SHOWING UP AND BEING THERE.

After the space for the other has been created and our Bashert has appeared in our life, the next step is to be totally present for them.

The Torah says, "You shall love your fellow as yourself,"* and the very next *Pasuk* / verse, says, "You shall observe My laws. You shall not let your cattle mate with a different kind; you shall not sow your field with two kinds of seed; you shall not put on a garment of (*Shatnez*) a mixture of linen and wool." These are the laws of *Kilayim,* prohibited mixtures of species.

As these two verses are juxtaposed, they suggest a connection between 'love' and 'prohibited mixtures'. The Baal HaTurim writes that the message is that a person must not, G-d forbid, be intimate with his spouse while thinking of another person.**

Love cannot exist with 'mixed, or unfocused' attention. Love means being fully present with the other. In fact, the first verse regarding loving another as ourselves applies not only to marriage, but to loving any person. Whenever we speak or listen to another person, it should not be in the manner of 'Kilayim' or 'Shatnez'. We focus on our spouse as if they are the only person in the universe; showing them with our undivided attention that there is nowhere else we would rather be, nothing else we would rather be doing, and no one else who is more important. We are completely open to them, and never mix even a subtle hint of competition into our marriage.

Not only does love avoid thinking about a third person while you are focusing on your spouse, child, parent, student, or any other recipient of your attention, but also avoiding comparing them with

---

*ואהבת לרעך כמוך. *Vayikra,* 19:18. The great principle of the Torah. *Medrash, Bere-ishis Rabbah,* 24:7.

**In the words of the Baal HaTurim, האוהב אשתו לא ישמש עמה ועיניו באשה אחרת.

others. When we say to our spouse, or even think, 'Why can't my spouse be like my friend's spouse (or like my sibling's spouse, etc)?' We are practicing Kilayim. In a second marriage, one would never think or say things like, 'My first husband would bring me such and such a gift,' or 'My previous wife used to say it this way…' One should never reference other love relationships, whether verbally or mentally. To truly love someone, we need to let go of past perceptions and dynamics, whether positive or negative, and commit fully to the relationship with the person we are with right now. Creating even a hint of jealousy through comparison undermines building a genuine connection based on openness, love and without any trace of 'relational Kilayim'. The Divine Presence rests upon spouses who are doing the 'Mitzvah' of being completely present with each other.

NO ONE COMPARES TO YOUR SPOUSE, EVERYONE ELSE IS LIKE ANOTHER SPECIES

As explored earlier, after their 'surgical separation', the primordial human being, Adam, beheld his wife, and declared, "This one at last, is bone of my bones, and flesh of my flesh; this one shall be called woman…." Says the Zohar, "'This one is called woman' — as there was no one like her. She was the precious one, and all other women of the world were like apes (in his eyes)."* Adam says, 'My wife Chava is so precious and beautiful to me that all other women have nothing to do with me at all; they are of a different species, they do not belong to my world, and thus there is zero attraction or tension.'

---

* In the language of the Zohar, לזאת יקרא אשה דא היא דלא ישתכח כוותה. דא היא יקרא דביתא כלהון נשין גבה כקופא בפני בני נשא. *Zohar*, 1, 49b.

When you marry, you are accepting the challenge to honor your spouse with unshakable devotion. Perhaps it is not possible for a person to close their eyes to the world or shun all human interactions, yet, a person should absolutely practice *Shemiras Einayim / safeguarding the eyes*, by looking only where it is appropriate. At the forefront of your heart must always be the awareness that no one, no matter how captivating, brilliant, or beautiful, can compare to the one you have chosen as your spouse. Any necessary encounters with others should feel as emotionally irrelevant as observing a creature of another species, no more significant than noticing a fascinating animal in passing.

Married life means fully committing to one person, exclusively and wholeheartedly, for in love and true intimacy, there is space only for one. This means cherishing our spouse as our 'home',* our entire world, valuing their presence above all else. When this truth is deeply etched into one's being, the eyes will not wander, and the heart will not waver. This devotion not only honors one's spouse, it becomes a powerful example for their children and family. Within one's self, this unwavering loyalty brings a sense of stability, confidence, and strength. You feel more grounded, more powerful, and ultimately, better about who you are. Everybody wins.

---

* Regarding the woman. *Yuma*, 2a. *Shabbos*, 118b. *Yevamos*, 44a. *Sotah*, 2a. Regarding the man. *Yevamos*, 2a (Rashi). *Chulin*, 31a (Rashi). *Nidda*, 5a.

BEING PRESENT MEANS LETTING GO OF OLD PERCEPTIONS AND BEING OPEN TO WHAT IS NOW

When the Torah says, "Therefore a man shall leave his father and mother and cleave to his wife, and become like one flesh," it speaks to a literal and profound truth. To have a successful marriage, we must leave our parents' home and build a new life with our spouse, becoming one unit and creating our own unique family. For years, one is defined as so-and-so's child. As an adult, they are defined more by who *they* are. Once married, they are still defined by who they are, but also as someone's spouse. This is a completely new identity; we now belong to a different family — our family.

It is vital to forge a bond that belongs solely to the two of us, free from the voices and images of our parents. When one catches themselves thinking, "My mother would never behave that way," or "My father always handled things differently," they are neglecting the call to "Leave father and mother." Such comparisons only sow seeds of discontent and invite marital strife. Even seemingly innocent and harmless comments, such as "My mother bakes the best bread," when one's own wife bakes bread, or praising one's father's patience whenever their husband shows impatience with the children, erodes trust and sows seeds of discord. Ultimately, comments such as these, adding up over the years, can be disastrous for a relationship.

By gently closing the door on parental comparisons altogether, we open the door to genuine intimacy, giving our marriage the freedom to flourish on its own terms, rooted in mutual respect, trust, and deep, unfiltered devotion.

One also needs to resist the urge to bring their parents' advice or opinions into their marriage. Of course, we must still honor and respect our parents, but, must also nurture a marriage shared only between us and our spouse. Even if both agree, at times, to seek their parents' counsel, one's spouse's perspective should always come first and be the most important. Relying too heavily on parental input can be detrimental: one spouse may feel judged or undermined, and parents may feel entitled to weigh in on private matters that belong solely to the marital unit.

On a deeper level, the 'leaving' of the past, of 'father and mother', symbolizes letting go of old paradigms, ways of thinking and behaving that may have served well during childhood or while growing up, but no longer suit the new relationship. To fully embrace and nurture a marriage, one must leave behind these outdated patterns and create new paradigms for the new experience called marriage.

To enter into the dynamic of marriage, where 'me and you' become 'us', we are called upon to embrace a fresh start, avoiding 'mixing' (Kilayim) past perceptions and ideas with the present. This process involves leaving behind old negative, pessimistic, and destructive beliefs and ways of thinking, acting, and reacting based on your perception of your childhood home. Even if one is carrying old beliefs that are not negative per se, it is still vital to open our mind to our new life and to the soul of one's spouse, to the best of our ability.

Part of leaving our parents' home is consciously leaving behind the dynamics imprinted upon us from our upbringing. One might have grown up observing their parents' interactions with each other and come to believe that their behaviour defines how a husband and wife should interact or what their respective responsibilities should be. We might find ourselves thinking, or even worse, saying, to our spouse, 'Why are you acting this way? When I was growing up, my father did this, and my mother took care of that.' It is essential to let go of these expectations. Our spouse and our marriage are unique. If we try to make our spouse conform to the image of our parents, or to always be the opposite of our image of our parents, we are not ever leaving the parents' house. Besides not being fair to our spouse, expecting our spouse to be different than they are prevents you from truly appreciating who they are, and sadly, it does not allow us to truly be present with them and for them.

Any difficulties, struggles, or arguments in one's marriage should not be discussed or even shared with parents on either side; parents naturally will want to side with their child, sometimes even if it means criticizing or withdrawing from the other spouse, or looking down upon them. This can erode trust and cause an avalanche of insecurity and defensiveness, and a problem that could have been resolved can become intractable. If there is a need to speak to someone about a severe challenge, it is best to rely on an unrelated, professional third party who will remain neutral whenever possible, and help to implement a balanced change.

One cannot be fully present in the moment if they are relying upon their parents as they once did. 'Leaving' one's parents' home, letting go of our dependency on it, or our reaction to it, is essential for cultivating a healthy, vibrant, and presence-imbued marriage relationship. Letting go of perceptions of marriage based on one's childhood home allows for new experiences and the emergence of

something unique and wonderful within the relationship, fostering true "cleaving and becoming one flesh." It means being open
to experiencing life and situations differently than one did growing
up. This openness allows for something new and unique to tran-
spire, enabling both spouses to create their own distinctive bond
with each other.

Let the uniqueness of our spouse and the uniqueness of the
marriage emerge and allow for the "cleaving… and becoming like
one flesh," for something new and wonderful to sprout.

LETTING GO OF NEGATIVE THOUGHTS ABOUT YOURSELF

To the best of our ability, one should try not to bring into their
marriage any negative beliefs about themselves as well. We release
lingering thoughts collected from childhood experiences that seem
to tell us that we are not good enough; disorganized, inattentive,
or undeserving of love. It may be necessary to heal parts of one's
self that have been 'exiled' and pushed down internally, due to not
feeling loved, safe, or secure in childhood or adolescence. Holding
on to beliefs and traumas can hinder the marriage by preventing us
from being present with vulnerability, openness, and love.

Letting go of self-doubts is crucial for being present with our
spouse and not being guarded or unavailable. Thinking we are undeserving of love will block us from accepting love from our spouse.

To truly embrace and nurture our marriage, we work on self-acceptance and understand that we deserve love and respect. This shift allows us to receive and appreciate our spouse's affection.

BEING OPEN TO RECEIVE LOVE

To be open to giving and receiving love is essential not only in marriage but in life in general.* Many people find it easier to give than to receive. There can be a measure of false pride that prevents them from being open to receiving, as it makes them feel vulnerable, unprotected, and fragile, and there is always the fear of being hurt. However, these qualities—vulnerability, openness, and the ability to receive from another—are precisely what are needed in a healthy marriage.

It is important to learn how to be open to receiving love, even though it may feel risky. Being open to receiving not only strengthens the bond between spouses but also nurtures a deeper connection built on trust and mutual respect.

---

* Healthy living depends upon balance, both physically, as in breathing, and spiritually, as in *Ratzo* V'*Shov* / 'running' or ascending and 'returning' or descending (*Yechezkel*, 1:14). V'*Ahavta* / "You shall love…," calls for movement in both directions: Ratzo and Shov, drawing closer and moving back, rising upward and returning. The Hebrew letters that comprise the word V'*Ahavta*, *Vav*/6, *Aleph*/1, *Hei*/5, *Beis*/2, *Tav*/400, have the numeric value of 414 twice the value of the word *Ohr* / light: *Aleph*/1, *Vav*/6, *Reish*/200 = 207. Genuine love, on all levels of reality, has direct light, as in giving, contracting and reaching out (Ratzo), and reflective light, as in receiving, expanding and opening up (Shov).

GIVING TO THE OTHER CREATES CONNECTION AND LOVE

If at times we feel that love does not flow naturally or organically, and we are not 'feeling it', remember that a simple act of giving to our spouse can generate love. Giving creates the bond and thereby the love.

Giving is not only an expression of love, it is also a path to cultivating love. While we often imagine that we give because we love, the deeper truth is that love often flows from giving. The more we give to someone—our time, attention, effort, resources—the more we become invested in them, and the more naturally love takes root and grows in our heart. If you are struggling to feel love for someone, especially your spouse, try giving to them. Not only material gifts, but also your presence: your attention, your patience, your time, your encouragement. Offer a listening ear, a kind word, a moment of understanding. Even when our heart feels distant, the simple act of giving softens the space between us, and will bring us to love. The act of giving fosters love, and the more sincerely we give, the more our love will blossom. "The heart follows actions": focus on active giving, and your heart will open.

Conversely, if we ever feel a lack of love from our spouse, we can gently invite them to give to us, and allow ourselves to receive with openness and vulnerability. Often, we block love not by withholding, but by resisting what others wish to offer. When we receive their gift—be it time, help, affection, or attention—with grace and gratitude, we create a connection. The more one's spouse gives to them and sees their gift welcomed, the more love they will feel.

Receiving well is itself a form of giving, and it draws forth the love that may be lying dormant in the heart of the giver.

Speaking of giving and receiving, and the subtle art of receiving, which in itself is a form of giving, here are a few words regarding how to correctly receive a gift.

HOW TO TRULY RECEIVE A GIFT: THREE LEVELS

If you are the spouse being given a gift, be open to receive it, not just materially, but emotionally and relationally. Generally speaking, there are three distinct ways we can receive a gift, and each reveals something deeper about the nature of love, presence, and relationship.

Let's use the analogy of a husband returning from a trip with a gift for his wife. (Of course, the roles can be reversed, but we will use this version for simplicity.)

Scenario 1: Receiving the Gift, Forgetting the Giver: The husband comes home, and with warmth and excitement says to his wife: "While I was away, I thought about you deeply. I wanted to bring you something special. I chose this for you with love and care." He hands her a beautifully wrapped gift. She opens it, and her eyes light up. It is an exquisite bracelet, elegant, thoughtful and exactly her style. She gushes: "This is perfect! I have wanted something like this for so long! It's gorgeous, the design, the color—everything. I love it!"

She goes on praising the gift, but she never once thanks him directly, never acknowledges his thoughtfulness or emotional investment. Her focus is entirely on what she received, not who gave it or why.

This is level one. The gift is received, but the giver is forgotten. The relationship behind the gesture is overlooked. Gratitude remains shallow because it ends with the object.

Scenario 2: Honoring the Giver, Ignoring the Gift: Now imagine a similar scene: the same husband, the same heartfelt gesture. He says excitedly to his wife: "While I was away, I kept thinking about you. I wanted to bring something meaningful back." He hands her the gift, still wrapped. But this time, before even opening it, she bursts into gratitude: "I can't believe you thought of me! You were so busy, and yet you still made the time to get me something. That means so much. Thank you, thank you!"

Her appreciation is overflowing, but it is all directed toward him. She never opens the gift. Or if she does, she barely looks at it. She focuses entirely on the emotional gesture, not the physical item. The love is felt, yes. The relationship is honored. But the actual gift, which her husband thoughtfully chose, with care and attention to what she would like, is barely acknowledged.

This too leaves something missing. The giver might feel appreciated as a person, but the effort he put into finding the right gift is overlooked.

Scenario 3: Receiving Both the Gift and the Giver: The deepest and most beautiful form of receiving is when the two are held together. The wife receives the gift, opens it, and genuinely admires it: "Wow, this bracelet is stunning! It is exactly my style. I love the design. I will wear it all the time!" And then she turns to her husband and says: "Thank you for thinking of me. I can tell how much care you put into choosing this. It means the world to me that you know me so well, and that you wanted to bring me something that would make me feel special."

In this response, both the gift and the giver are acknowledged and cherished. She fully receives what was given, and she also feels and reflects back the love that motivated the giving. This is the essence of deep connection: to hold both realities simultaneously, the tangible gift, and the invisible thread of relationship it carries.

This is the deepest way to receive a gift, not only from your spouse, but from anyone, and ultimately, from the One who bestows all of life's blessings. To receive with full presence, with heartfelt gratitude for both the gift and the giver. This itself is the greatest gift we can offer in return, the gift of receiving with an open heart.

UNCONDITIONAL LOVE

As explored, there is a form of love which is conditional, also known as transactional, but the deepest expression of love is unconditional and not dependent on any particular response from the beloved.

An employer may appreciate and even celebrate an employee for their contributions to the company. However, the moment the employee ceases to produce, the employer's acceptance may wane.

Similarly, when someone expresses love after receiving a favor, it is often the act of kindness they appreciate rather than the person who did the favor. If this can be called love at all, it is, at best, 'conditional love'.

Mature and meaningful love is a connection. There is a level of love that is based on mutual interests, understanding, and feelings, and often a shared history, such as being married for a long time. This form of love is still contingent love. It may still be bolstered by physical or intellectual attraction, or emotional attachment. The highest level of love is a love that is completely unconditional. Those who are in this highest paradigm of love never ask themselves, 'What has my spouse done for me lately,' as their love transcends issues of what they are receiving. While this love may have originated in the mind or in the heart, and the original connection may have been founded on *Meshichas HaLev* / 'drawing of the heart' through attraction, with time and experience, the love has become deeply ingrained and absolute. In the context of marriage, the husband and wife have truly understood and sensed that they share a soul connection, a profound spiritual bond, and a shared purpose and Tikun.

I DO NOT 'NEED' YOU, I 'WANT' YOU

A defining distinction between conditional and unconditional love lies in their source. Conditional love arises from a place of need and lack, and therefore, it gives in order to receive, always seeking something in return for its efforts. It is transactional by nature, tethered to expectations and outcomes. Unconditional love, by contrast, flows from fullness. It is self-sufficient, generous without calculation, and does not hinge on reciprocity. It gives not to get, but, just because.

When spouses 'need' each other, their love tends to be conditional, for need arises from a sense of lack, from an inner absence of wholeness. In such a dynamic, love becomes a means to fill a void, and the relationship often hinges on what each spouse can provide. In contrast, when both spouses feel whole and self-sufficient within themselves, their desire for one another emerges not from deficiency, but from fullness. From this place of inner wholeness, love can become truly unconditional, freely given, not out of necessity, but as a sincere expression of abundance and choice.

In other words, in immature love, *need* precedes love, expressed in the sentiment, "I need you, therefore I love you." Love, in this case, is born out of dependency. In mature love, however, love comes first. It is not driven by lack, but by genuine connection and choice. Mature love says, "I love you, therefore I need you."

Unconditional love can be seen as innate, as in a child's love toward their parent, and a parent's toward their child. With a spouse, however, unconditional love is on a higher level since it is a conscious choice. Spouses might recognize their soul-connection from the beginning and immediately attain unconditional love, or, in most cases, they might grow and evolve from conditional to unconditional love.

Chosen unconditional love is based in wholeness, not need and lack. Due to this, it is contagious and attractive. The more unconditional love we give, the more it draws those we love towards us. Neediness (from a place of lack) is unattractive and repels. People turn away from those who 'need' them, and towards those who 'want' them.

From a place of wholeness, we can know another as whole. In this way we can embark on a journey of life as two 'wholenesses,' unfolding the greater Wholeness known as marriage.

LOVE & VULNERABILITY

There are those who argue that pure, unconditional love in marriage is unrealistic. They suggest that at the beginning of a relationship, one may be immersed in a dreamlike haze, seeing the beloved not as a full human being, but as an idealized image, ethereal and flawless. Others say that even when the spouse is seen with their imperfections, the overwhelming intensity of new love renders judgment impossible. But as time unfolds, and the emotional high of newness begins to settle, reality reasserts itself. The illusions begin to fade, and the very real, human flaws of one's spouse gradually come into view.

Perhaps, true unconditional love is something far deeper than these two options. It does not deny imperfection, it embraces it. It does not require blindness to faults, but rather, the vision to see through them. It can recognize the so-called 'negative' traits as part of the beloved's complex beauty, or at the very least, hold space for their full humanity without any judgment.

When we truly love someone, judgment has no place, not because you choose to ignore their faults or do not see them, but because your heart and mind are occupied with something higher and more important: giving to them, listening deeply, and being fully present for them. And when one's spouse feels that they are not being judged, they open up. They can speak freely, and do so without fear or shame.

In this way, unconditional love becomes not just a bond, but a safe space. A place of healing. Unconditional love allows one's spouse to unburden their heart, to reveal their pain, their doubts, their darkness, and in doing so, something profound occurs, a mutual Tikkun, correction and healing takes place. When a person feels safe enough to reveal their vulnerability and is met with presence instead of judgment, both husband and wife participate in a sacred act of healing.

Much of the emotional pain people carry stems from a fear of being truly seen, and thus rejected. But when one feels deeply seen and still fully embraced, the healing and Tikkun begins. This is the power of unconditional love in marriage.

UNCONDITIONAL LOVE FOR SELF AS THE FOUNDATION OF UNCONDITIONAL LOVE FOR OTHERS

To truly love someone else unconditionally, we must first love ourselves in the same way. This does not mean 'being in love with ourself', rather to love ourself. This 'self-love' is the opposite of narcissism and arrogance, which are not love at all, but signs of a selfish, weak, and fragile ego. Unconditional self-love is to fully cherish and appreciate the value of yourself and being actively committed to your higher purpose in this world. You carry yourself with joy, and your love for others lifts them into this joy. If, instead of true self-love, we carry self-loathing, our 'love' for others can infect them with the same type of negativity.

Unconditional love is to give love without expectation or entitlement, and also to be aware of the ways in which the other is open to receive your love. Everyone has their unique ways of expressing and receiving love. Loving someone involves understanding the other person's needs and wants, and honoring their way of receiving love.

It is important not to selfishly impose our own definitions, conditions, or ways of experiencing love onto our spouse; this would be akin to Kilayim, a spiritually detrimental mixture of elements. Unconditional love means being attuned to them and offering them what they need according to their terms.

THE SYMBOL OF LOVE IS TWO FACING EACH OTHER

The universal symbol of love is a 'heart' shape, and this is because intellect is viewed as residing in the brain while emotions in the heart. Of course, all expressions and experiences are in the brain, yet, the heart is considered to house emotions.*

---

* In the words of the Alter Rebbe, מקום משכן נפש הבהמית ...הוא בלב. כל התאוות.. הן בלב, ומהלב... עולה למוח: *Tanya*, 9.

Today, in fact, we know that the physical heart contains neurotransmitters and hormones, such as oxytocin, which are connected with the experience of love.

Rebbe Avraham Abulafia teaches that the word לב / Lev / Heart) itself reveals the nature of love. The Torah begins with the letter Beis / ב and ends with the letter Lamed / ל, forming the word לב. The Beis has the numerical value of two, suggesting relationship, reciprocity, and the presence of another. And when we take two Lameds and place them facing one another, their shapes form the image of a heart. Thus, the very word לב / Lev / Heart hints that love is born when two distinct beings turn toward each other, face to face, heart to heart.

Love is when two people see each other face-to-face, support each other, carve out the space for each other, and hold that space, unconditionally and wholeheartedly.

DOING WHAT IS RIGHT WITH PRESENCE

Love means to be in a face-to-face relationship. A loving relationship is not just about doing all the right things. It is not enough to simply check off a list of responsibilities, no matter how complete that list may be, as a robot can do chores as well. A machine can be programmed to provide, to clean, to manage logistics. But a real relationship requires something that can be provided only by one's person and that is: presence. What we truly long for is a face-to-face connection. Not simply "I am doing all the right things" but "I see you."

There is a world of difference between living 'back-to-back', simply *doing* for the other, and living 'face-to-face', being *there* for and *with* the other. The actions may look identical from the outside, but the inner reality, how it is received, is entirely different.

We might think, "I am a good spouse, I provide, I help with the kids, I do everything I am supposed to do." And perhaps that is all true. But if we haven't paused for even five minutes to look into our loved one's eyes, to hold their space, to see them and let them know they matter deeply to us, then something essential is missing. Without that presence, our spouse may feel profoundly alone, unseen, and even unloved. Two people can live under the same roof, raise children together, and share a life, and yet may still feel emotionally starved if they don't feel truly *seen*. To enter a real relationship, we must not merely *do*, *solve*, or *fix*. Rather, we must learn to stop, to look into another's eyes, and truly *be* with them with our full presence.

A strong relationship begins not with *what we do*, but with *how we are*. One can do all the right things in a marriage, provide, help, participate, but without a face-to-face connection, as described above, the relationship risks becoming mechanical and lifeless. Actions, no matter how noble, must grow out of the fertile soil of love, presence, and mutual attentiveness to manifest a living bond.

TENSION CAN BRING GROWTH

In any real relationship, there will be disagreement. And in fact, it can be said that there must be disagreement. A healthy marriage includes tension, a dynamic of opposites that challenges and re-fines. This is the meaning of "a helpmate who also stands opposite you," not to negate you, but to offer another voice, a differing per-spective. That tension should not be seen as a threat to the relation-ship; it is its very engine for growth. True connection doesn't mean always agreeing; it means staying connected and loving even when you disagree. It means that even in conflict, we remain face-to-face, never turning our backs on each other. When there is presence, even disagreement becomes a form and expression of love.

At its core, relationships are built not merely on *doing*, but on *being*. This is the essence of true love: a face-to-face relationship where each one is reflected and cherished in the eyes of the other.

Practical Takeaways

CREATE INTERNAL SPACE:

Before entering into a relationship, take time to cultivate mental and emotional spaciousness within yourself. Ask honestly: is my inner world already too full, crowded with my own needs, thoughts, and preoccupations? To welcome another into our life, we must first make room. Creating this inner space is an act of generosity; it is clearing a place within your heart where love, presence, and connection can take root and grow.

CREATE SPACE FOR YOUR SPOUSE:

Just as the Creator created the world through a Tzimtzum—a self-withdrawal making space for another—practice love by creating a space for your spouse to be, to flourish, and become their best self. This involves actively making room for our spouse's individuality to be expressed, and for their needs and desires to be acknowledged. We can continuously be mindful of holding the space for our spouse throughout the marriage, ensuring that this practice is ongoing and not just present at the beginning of the relationship.

CREATE LOVE THROUGH ACTS OF GIVING:

When the feelings of love have faded or are difficult to access, we remember that love follows action. When I give, I create the conditions for love to reawaken. Loving acts, even small ones, have the power to stir deep affection. If we want to feel love for our spouse, we begin by giving to them. In the giving, love is born anew.

PRACTICE PATIENCE IN COMMUNICATION:

In our day-to-day life we can practice Tzimtzum by not always immediately saying what we want to say, thereby giving our spouse the space to express their point of view and to feel heard. This patience fosters a respectful and supportive environment. We should certainly try to avoid dominating conversations or situations, in this way allowing our spouse to feel heard and valued.

PRIORITIZE YOUR SPOUSE:

By unwaveringly supporting our spouse and choosing to stand by their side in every circumstance, we make our spouse feel like they are our main priority and they always come first. We can show them through our steadfast support that their needs and desires matter above all else and that their happiness is our greatest concern. One simple way that this can be done is by trying to always answer their calls, so they know that if they need you, they can reach you.

Another example of how this can be done practically, is to make an effort to get up and greet them when they walk through the door, after being away for the day or for a while. And if we are the ones walking into the house, making sure the first thing we do is ask our spouse about their day or how they are doing.

It is through these small yet meaningful gestures, that we show that our spouse's needs and well-being are foremost in our heart.

HONOR THEIR UNIQUENESS:

Instead of projecting our needs, desires, or assumptions onto our spouse, we can strive to truly see them as they are. A simple example of this would be that if one's spouse enjoys hobbies we don't share, we can honor their passions by supporting them and showing interest.

HIGHLIGHT THEIR POSITIVE QUALITIES:

If one person in the marriage struggles with low self-esteem or a diminished sense of self-worth, it may be difficult for them to fully give or receive unconditional love. In such moments, one of the most healing things we can do is to gently and consistently reflect back their goodness. We can make a habit of acknowledging their strengths, both the obvious and the more subtle ones. Saying things like, 'You're good at problem solving,' or, 'I admire the way you think things through,' are affirmations, that when offered sincerely, can slowly help them see themselves through our loving eyes and, eventually, through their own.

VERBALIZE GRATITUDE TOWARDS EACH OTHER:

One of the most essential ingredients in a healthy relationship is gratitude.

Over time, we have a tendency to take the people closest to us for granted. When someone consistently shows up for us, we begin to expect it, and in doing so, we risk losing sight of how meaningful their efforts really are.

Make it a habit to express gratitude to each other daily. Be specific in your appreciation, rather than just offering general thanks. For example, we can say, 'Thank you for hosting so graciously,' or 'I am so grateful that you cleaned up,' or 'I appreciate that you took the children to school.'

And gratitude is more than just words spoken, it is a posture of the heart, a way of moving through the world and a way of being in this world. Ultimately, we aspire to be a genuinely grateful person. When we live in a state of gratitude, our spouse will feel it. It shapes the atmosphere of the relationship and the home, and creates a space where both spouses feel seen, valued, and loved.

SURPRISE EACH OTHER:

Keep the excitement alive by surprising each other with small gestures. It could be a thoughtful note, a favorite snack, or planning a spontaneous outing. These surprises show that you care and are thinking of each other.

AVOID ALL COMPARISONS:

In our marriage, we want to refrain from comparing our spouse to others, including and most importantly past relationships or our other family members or parents. These comparisons can erode trust and intimacy, sowing seeds of unreasonable expectations and preventing us from truly cherishing our spouse's unique gifts. When we focus on the unique qualities of our spouse and the relationship we are building together, we can truly appreciate and be present with each other. It's a great practice in life in general, that when we are with someone, we try to see them for who they are, without making comparisons. Comparisons steal our ability to be fully present and engaged with another.

An easy reminder, *Don't Compare, Compliment.*

LET GO OF OLD PARADIGMS:

Embrace new ways of thinking and being in the relationship. Leaving behind old patterns and dynamics learned from our upbringing or previous relationships that no longer serve us creates an openness that allows for new experiences and deeper connections to emerge.

EMBRACE SELF-SUFFICIENCY:

Focus on feeling whole and self-sufficient on your own. By cultivating personal wholeness, our love for our spouse can come from a place of genuine desire rather than neediness. This fosters a healthier and even more unconditional love.

Chapter 3

KINSHIP | אחוה

*T*he very foundation of all good, lasting relationships, particularly in marriage, is deep and unwavering commitment. This commitment implies a profound awareness that you and your spouse are dedicated to each other for life.

Commitment means being there for each other through the highs and lows, the joys and challenges. Commitment is about building a life together with the understanding that both spouses are fully invested in nurturing and growing the relationship. This sense of commitment fosters trust, security, and a deep bond that can withstand the test of time.

A committed relationship means prioritizing one's spouse, making sacrifices, and working through difficulties together. Commitment is about being steadfast in our dedication to one another, knowing that we are both in it for the long haul. This unwavering commitment provides a solid foundation upon which love, respect, and companionship can flourish.

Commitment in marriage is not merely a commitment *while* the relationship lasts; it is a commitment *to* the relationship itself. This commitment is rooted in the awareness that beneath all the changing seasons of life, beneath every difference or difficulty, there lies something unshakable, *Achvah*, a deep, essential kinship. Achvah speaks of a bond not built on convenience or passing emotion, but on an unbreakable foundation. It means being married to someone who is not just close to you, but *part of you*. Like a brother or a sister, a sibling of the soul. This kind of commitment is not up for negotiation. It is not fragile. It does not depend on how I feel today or what you said yesterday. It rests on knowing that 'We belong to each other. We are bound by something deeper than circumstances, we are bound by essence.'

We live in a disposable generation. In a world where everything is replaceable, if a piece of furniture breaks, there is no need to fix it; we just buy a new one. If our phone slows down, we upgrade. Even the basic hardware in our homes is built to be temporary, to be discarded and replaced every few years. And, unfortunately, without realizing it, this consciousness may seep into our relationships and our marriage. When the thinking is that everything in life is temporary, why would marriage be any different? If everything else loses its value over time, becomes outdated, worn, boring, it would stand to reason that marriage does too. The very idea of permanence has lost its glow. Eternity no longer means *forever*, it means 'until I lose interest,' or 'until I am no longer entertained,' 'until it is easier to dispose of this configuration and acquire a new one.' But true marriage is built on something deeper, Achvah, a bond of inherent connection, of essential oneness. This is not disposable, temporary, or fragile.

Achvah is a union that says, 'You are not a guest in my life; you are a part of me, and what is part of me cannot be thrown away.'

Eternity in marriage means staying the course, being in it long term, even when it is challenging. It means standing within a sacred space that is not up for negotiation, not subject to the passing winds of mood or convenience. It is the quiet, unwavering knowing that this relationship is not something to discard when it becomes complex, nor to trade in when it loses its initial sparkle. Marriage is not a contract of convenience, but rather a covenant of presence. It is a promise that says, 'I am here — not just when it's easy, not just when it feels good, but always.'

The commitment to marriage is the courage to weather the storms, the patience to wait out the winters, and the faith to believe that even in the silent stretches, something holy is growing beneath the surface. Real love is not proven in moments of passion, rather in moments of perseverance.

Our sages teach us that a man can betroth a woman in three ways: with *Kesef* / money, *Sh'tar* / contract, or through *Bi'ah* / intimate relations. Says the Baal Shem Tov, every marriage progresses through these three stages.[*]

---

[*] *Kiddushin*, 2a. *Keser Shem Tov*, 10. See Yerushalmi, *Kiddushin*, 1:1. האשה ניקנית

The first stage, Kesef / money; is related to the word *Kisufim* / longing. This speaks to the initial spark of love, the burning passion, the fervent yearning that defines the early days of a relationship. It is a time of excitement, of hearts that race with anticipation and a dance of discovery. But as time passes, this initial fire may decrease (although G-d willing, it can always return), and then one enters the second stage: commitment.

Commitment is symbolized by the Sh'tar, the contract. A contract is not just a formal agreement; it is a commitment, and because one has committed themselves to it, it is a deep covenant and promise between souls. It speaks of resolve, dedication, and the steadfast decision to remain committed, despite the challenges and the changes that are wrought by time. Through unwavering resolve and commitment, the marriage will eventually arrive at a deep, authentic, and lasting intimacy. Through this dedication, the relationship is not merely sustained; it is nurtured and guided into progressively deeper intimacy. This is not the fleeting intimacy of the heart's first longing, but a true, everlasting closeness. It is a bond that is not subject to personal whims, the wear of time, or the ever-shifting nature of circumstances; it is rooted in resolve, faith, and love.

Absolute commitment is born from the awareness that we and our spouse are united on a soul level, Divinely destined to walk this journey of life together, with a shared purpose. Though each of us is a unique soul, complete in our individuality, there is a truth that runs deeper: we are two 'halves' of a whole, even while whole in our own right, and together, we are both fulfilling a greater calling.

בשלש דרכים כול׳. כיני מתניתא. או בכסף או בשטר או בביאה.

A marriage is not simply the merging of two lives, but the re-union of a part of one's self that was once lost. Marriage is a journey of discovery, of reclaiming the sacred pieces of our soul that were meant to be found in the presence of our spouse. As we walk this path together, we are not only sharing our lives, but rediscovering the essence of who we are, as two souls intertwined, unfolding a greater purpose with every step. In this shared destiny, we come to realize that our marriage is not just about the present, but about the eternal, a soul's journey back to wholeness, a dance of becoming who we were always meant to be, together.

IN MARRIAGE WE ARE RECONNECTING TO OUR SOUL

The root of this essential unity called Achvah is the awareness that we are deeply connected on a soul level. Although the relationship becomes *revealed* through our free choice, the marriage is formed from a bond that is deeper than choice. There is an indelible connection much like that between siblings. This idea is rooted, as explored earlier, in the template of the creation of Adam and Chava.

To review again, the Torah describes their creation as originally described: "Male and female He created them." Adam/Chava emerged into life as one unit, as a singularity, albeit in a 'back-to-back' relationship and paradigm. This back-to-back state symbolizes an unconscious relationship, lacking mutual recognition. Then came the process of Tzimtzum, the contraction, the "falling asleep" of Adam, and the Nesira, the gentle severing apart, through which another distinct human being came into being. And then, once there were two, the Torah continues, "Therefore, man should leave his father and mother's home and cleave to his wife." Now they can have a genuine face-to-face relationship, and become like one flesh.

In this way, marriage is a reclaiming of an ancient connection, one that existed in perfect unity before separation. It is not the joining of two halves, nor the search for a missing piece, but the reunion of two complete beings who once shared a single essence. Each was whole in themselves, yet together they reflect the original oneness from which they both emerged.

This singularity reflects a primordial oneness, a bond that transcends the physical and emotional. The unity of marriage, therefore, runs deeper than choice, though choice is essential to bring it into being. It is an eternal connection, rooted in the soul's essence, long before it took form in this world.

Marriage is not just the creation of a new bond but the reclaiming of a pre-existing one. A conscious reuniting of two souls that were initially one, separated to journey through the world as individuals until reuniting in love and purpose.

THE TREMENDOUS JOY OF MARRIAGE

This is the deeper reason why marriage evokes such profound joy. It is the joy of reunion, the coming together of two souls that were once inseparable, long before their descent into this world and the experience of division. Once separated, these souls were born into different families, shaped by distinct lineages, upbringings, and environments. Across years, and sometimes across continents and cultures, they journey through life, until they find one another once more. The ecstasy felt in marriage, whether by the couple, their families, or all who witness it, springs from this miracle of reconnection, two souls, once one, rediscovering their eternal unity.

The profound joy experienced at a wedding is greater than the joy of two people finding companionship; it is a celebration of a spiritual awakening, a soul recognition, and duality miraculously becoming unity, before our very eyes. It is a revelation of the essential oneness that existed before creation.

During the wedding, it is worth pausing to truly absorb the moments of pure elation, to take a mental snapshot of the joy and unity that fill the air. In the days and years that follow, especially amid life's inevitable challenges, return to that inner album and let those memories rekindle the sense of wonder and transcendent joy that first bound you together.

TWO HALF BUT COMPLETE SOULS BECOMING ONE

Here are the words of the Holy Zohar regarding souls reuniting: "The unity between male and female is called 'one'...for a male without a female is called a half of body, and a half is not one. But when these two halves come together, they become like one body, and then they are called 'one'."*

---

* In the language of the Zohar זיווגא דדכר ונוקבא איקרי אחד... בגין דדכר בלא נוקבא פלג פלג נוקבא בלא דדכר בגין ...אחד איקרי ונוקבא דדכר

גופא איקרי, ופלג לאו הוא חז, וכד מתחברן כחדא תרי פלגי איתעבידו חד גופא, וכדין איקרי אחד:

While the language used seems to imply that before marriage, a person is merely half a soul and half a body, this does not mean that a person is not whole before marriage; it is just a different register and kind of wholeness.

Recall that before the cosmic Tzimtzum, there existed only Divine Singularity, and before the Nesira, the separation of Adam and Chava, they too were one being, a unified male–female essence called Adam. As discussed earlier, the individual reflects the cosmic order: the microcosm mirrors the macrocosm. Just as there was absolute Wholeness and Unity before the Tzimtzum — recognizing, of course, that the Tzimtzum is neither literal nor confined to the past but an ongoing process — so too there remains absolute Wholeness and Unity even now. In the same way, Adam was whole before the Nesira, and he remained whole afterward, even when he beheld his counterpart, Chava, face to face.

Similarly, each human being is whole and perfect just the way they are, a total singularity, and can come to marriage from a place of wholeness and healthy desire rather than neediness and lack. The sense of being incomplete before meeting one's soulmate is

---

Zohar 3, 7b. Note the language of the Ra'avad, Hakdamah, *Ba'alei HaNefesh*, ועל כן ראוי האדם לאהוב את אשתו כנפשו ... ולשמרה כאשר ישמור אחד מאבריו. In a similar vein, the Ra'avad writes that the wife of a Menudeh, remains permitted to be intimate with him, for אשתו כגופו / a spouse is like part of one's own body. This ruling is recorded and explained by the Ran, *Nedarim*, 7b. (ומייהו הראב"ד ז"ל כתב דאשתו אינה חייבת לנהוג בו נדוי, וטעמא דמילתא משום דאשתו כגופו). Yet, at the same time, the spouse remains a fully independent individual. Thus, even if others may not engage in business with her husband due to his Menudah status, she may still do so with them, as his status is not her status. This reflects the dual nature of marriage: on one hand, they are one body and one soul, "male and female He created them"; yet, as the second account of Adam and Chavah's creation teaches, they are also distinct beings, 'full souls' as explained in great length earlier.

real, but it is only due to the fact that the soulmates have not yet consciously and physically actualized their latent status of oneness. They have not yet experienced the unity that is greater than their original singularity.

The great Egyptian sage and one of the last and most famous of the Geonim, Rebbe Saadia Gaon, writes, "They (the heretics) also inferred and posited that it is the action of the Creator, blessed be He, that created the souls of human beings as round spheres and divided them into two, placing each part in one person. Therefore, when each part finds its counterpart, it attaches to it... However, (regarding) the matter of the division of the spheres that they referred to...we have explained that the soul of every human being is created with its whole form, hence, their hypothesis (that each individual is only half a soul) is nullified."[*]

Rebbe Saadia Gaon teaches that every soul is born whole, for each of us is created in the Divine image, the image of ultimate wholeness. An unmarried person is not half a being or half a soul. You are already complete before meeting your Bashert, and it is from this inner Sheleimus, this sense of fullness, contentment, and peace, that you should live even while single. Entering marriage from a place of wholeness allows love to flow freely and authentically. To believe that you *need* your soulmate is to come to life from a place of lack, and that quality of neediness is often felt and subconsciously repels the very connection you seek. But when you

---

[*] In the original Hebrew, גם עלו מזה עד שאמרו שהוא פעל הבורא יתברך, וטענו שהוא ברא רוחות הנבראים כדוריאם עגולים, וחלק אותם לשנים, ומשים כל חלק באדם אחד, ובעבור זה כשימצא כל חלק את חלקו הוא נתלה בו... אבל ענין חלק הכדורים אשר נתלו בו....ובארנו כי נפש כל אדם היא נבראת עם השלמת צורתו, בטל השער הזה ושבור :*Emunos V'Deos*, Ma'amar 10:7.

know yourself as whole, and your desire arises not from emptiness but from the quiet knowing of the soul, from deep intuition that this person is truly your destined one, that energy becomes magnetic. Wholeness recognizes wholeness, and two complete souls are drawn together by that resonance.

Soul-based desire is a microcosmic reflection of the Ta'avah, the Divine yearning, so to speak, that moved the Creator to create, to enter into relationship with what appears as "other." Before the Tzimtzum, when all was seamless Divine Singularity, there was — in human terms — a yearning for relationship, for the revelation of the Infinite within the finite.

PART OF YOUR SOUL

A person is whole just as they are, and every individual person is born with a perfect and whole soul. This perfection and wholeness is our birthright and inherent condition. Yet, there is an even higher and more profound level of wholeness that is attained through marriage. It is in comparison to this deeper paradigm of wholeness in marriage, that single life can be viewed as deficient.*

The wholeness experienced through marriage elevates us to an entirely different plane. It is a wholeness that transcends the boundaries of the individual self, where each spouse expands beyond the confines of "I" and enters the sacred space of "we." In that union, a shared identity emerges, and the wholeness it brings is greater than the sum of its parts.

---

* *Zohar*, Vayikra, 5b: דאיהו פגים, ואקרי בעל מום.

Yet, even more profoundly, this wholeness is uniquely tailored to each soul. Every individual is distinct, and so too is every marriage. The completeness that arises within a relationship mirrors the singular essence of each person, a reflection of the soul's own design and destiny.

Moreover, the one you marry, your true soulmate, is, from the beginning, a part of your own soul. They are divinely tailored to mirror and evoke exactly what you need in order to grow toward higher and deeper levels of Sheleimus. Your soulmate is not merely compatible with you; they are intricately fashioned to awaken your fullest potential and meet the deepest needs of your being.

Speaking of the marriage of Moshe, and how Yisro, the father of Tziporah, gave his daughter's hand to Moshe in marriage, the *Pasuk* / verse says, ויתן את־צפרה בתו למשה / "And he gave Tziporah, his daughter, to Moshe.".* Amazingly, the name Tziporah, צפרה, is numerically 375, which is the same numerical value as the word למשה / "to Moshe."**

This indicates that Tziporah is perfectly matched to Moshe; they are uniquely crafted for each other. When any individual marries someone else, the other is exactly matched for them. When Esther, for example, marries Mendel, she is L'Mendel / 'to Mendel', and Mendel is 'L'Esther'.

---

* *Shemos*, 2:21.
** *Paneach Raza*, ibid.

Practical Takeaways

DON'T SECOND-GUESS YOURSELF:

"The wicked are full of regrets."* When we live in a constant state of "I should have" or "I could have," we lose alignment with the flow of life and with Hashem's presence in it. Everything that has already happened was meant to unfold as it did, for our free choice exists only in the present moment.

If we find ourselves in a marriage that, though imperfect, still holds moments of connection and possibility, we can choose not to dwell on whether we made the right decision. Continual second-guessing only weakens our resolve and drains the vitality from our relationship. Instead, we can lean in, invest with faith and openness, and trust that this very path, with all its flaws and challenges, may be the one through which growth, healing, and even deep joy are waiting to emerge.

MENTAL SNAPSHOTS:

When we experience a moment of true joy in our marriage, whether in its early days or within a particularly beautiful season of life, we can pause and take a mental/emotional snapshot. We stop for a moment to fully absorb the feelings, the sights, the sounds, and the atmosphere of that moment. Anchor it in memory with

---

* *Tanya*, ch. 11. *Sheivet Musar*, ch. 25.

vivid detail: what I was wearing, what was said, how the light fell, how my heart felt. Then, when we find ourselves moving through rougher seasons, we can open that inner album, revisit those moments, and remind ourselves of the beauty and possibility that still lives within our shared story.

FILL YOURSELF UP WITH GOOD FEELINGS IN YOUR TIMES OF PLENTY:

A wise person recognizes that marriage, like life itself, moves in cycles. There are seasons of joy and seasons of challenge, and the key is to prepare the heart for both. When we find ourselves in a time of happiness, let us consciously take it in, to truly feel the elation and fullness of love, allowing it to nourish us deeply. By doing so, we store light for the moments that feel dimmer.

This practice is called LeHazhir Gedolim Al HaKetanim / "to caution Gedolim / adults regarding the Ketanim / children." This statement can also be understood as LeHazhir, "to illuminate": to let the radiance of our times of greatness, our Gedolim, shine into our moments of our Ketanim, our seasons of smallness and constriction.

PERSONALIZED RITUALS:

Consciously cultivate personalized rituals that celebrate your unique bond. These could be special routines or traditions that are meaningful to both of you, be it walking a favorite trail together or celebrating an inside joke.

GRATITUDE PRACTICE:

Develop a mindful gratitude practice where you regularly express appreciation for each other's unique qualities and contributions to the relationship. This can be through verbal affirmations, notes, or shared moments of reflection.

Expect Nothing, Appreciate Everything.

Chapter 4

PEACE | שלום

*S*halom, loosely translated as peace and harmony, is one of the most important words in our lexicon. It is one of the Names of Hashem, and hence it needs to be treated with reverence.* Yet, despite its sanctity, Shalom is also a common word and a beloved name. The word Shalom is the way we greet people, and it is the word we use when we depart from people. This beautiful word serves as our greeting and our farewell. It encapsulates an ideal that we fervently seek and continually pray for in our daily prayers.

Before we delve deeper into *Shalom Bayis* / peace within the home, it is essential to understand that peace does not mean uniformity or sameness, nor does it require the elimination of individuality for the sake of unity. True peace is the harmonious union of two dimensions or individuals, with all their differences.

* *Shabbos*, 10b. *Shulchan Aruch*, Orach Chayim, 84.

Peace is about embracing and uniting opposites. Peace is not about erasing diversity but rather creating a unity that celebrates and honors individuality. Shalom is the integration of these differences into a greater, more harmonious whole, in which each person's uniqueness is valued and contributes to the overall peace.

Shalom is the radiant harmony that arises when opposing forces find balance, when Chesed, the energy of kindness, expansion, and outward flow, joins with Gevurah, the strength of discipline, restraint, and inward focus. True peace is not the absence of tension but the blending of contrasts into a living, dynamic unity. In this balance, each quality retains its distinct light, yet together they illuminate something greater than either could alone.

This truth of Shalom is relevant cosmically and within a marriage. In *Shalom Bayis* / marital peace, each spouse can celebrate the uniqueness of both themselves and their spouse and the beautiful harmony and synthesis that their relationship creates and cultivates. Each spouse comes to the marriage with their distinct qualities and together combine to create a symmetrical, balanced unity.

A marriage is not a 'back-to-back' relationship where one spouse leads and the other simply follows. Instead, we aspire to view our spouse as an *Eizer Kenegdo* / a dynamic helper standing against us in the unity of opposites. This creates a space where both individuals can each bring their full self into the relationship, merging their unique qualities to create an even greater whole. This mutual respect allows for a vibrant union, in which individuality is honored and celebrated within a context of Sheleimus.

THE MEZUZAH AS A SIGN OF SHALOM

The front door of our home represents the liminal space that holds the tension between the inside and outside. It is the transitional space that allows for what is on the inside to come out, and what is on the outside to come in.* This is the space where we affix a Mezuzah, as well as upon all the other doors of the home.

Affixing a Mezuzah to the doorpost is a sacred Mitzvah, and that, in itself, is reason enough to fulfill it. Yet this Mitzvah also carries profound spiritual and metaphysical significance. The Mezuzah serves as a source of protection, standing as a guardian at the threshold of the home. It wards off negative influences from entering, while at the same time allowing the positivity and holiness within to radiate outward. In this way, the Mezuzah becomes a conduit, channeling the sanctity of the home to illuminate the world beyond its walls.

The prevalent Ashkenazi custom is to affix the Mezuzah on a slant. This practice arises from an ancient discussion among the early commentators whether the Mezuzah should be placed vertically, "standing," or horizontally, "lying down." By positioning it on a diagonal, we honor both opinions, symbolically bringing them into harmony. In doing so, the Mezuzah itself becomes an emblem of Shalom, peace born from the union of differing views.**

---

* Hence, a home is not a 'home' without a door: *Tzafnas Paneach*, Rambam, *Hilchos Avodah Zarah*, 2:8. And hence, according to the Rambam exempt from a Mezuzah: *Hilchos Mezuzah*, 6:1. See also, *Baba Basra*, 53b. *Shulchan Aruch*, Choshen Mishpat, 275:21. ואין צורת אותו הבנין מועלת עד שיעמיד עד דלתות

***Menachos,* 33a, Rashi and Tosefos, ad loc. Rama, *Yoreh De'ah*, 289:6: והמדקדקים יוצאים ידי שניהם ומניחים אותה בשפוע ובאלכסון וכן ראוי לנהוג וכן נוהגין במדינות אלו. The Mechaber rules that the Mezuzah should be placed upright.

By placing the Mezuzah on a slant, we are symbolically showing the outside world that in this home, there is compromise. We are showing the world that this home is not a place for 'my way' or even 'your way', but a place that fosters 'our way'. But even deeper than compromise, which merely implies concession, meaning, 'I agree with you and I concede my viewpoint', we are demonstrating that this home is a sanctuary of Shalom, a place where individuality is fully expressed and celebrated. This is the idea of Shalom, true peace: two opposite perspectives come together to form a third perspective which includes both.

Through the Mezuzah on the liminal space of the door, the harmony inside our home radiates and ultimately transforms the outside world. The more Shalom Bayis we have in the home, the more Shalom there is in the Creator's Bayis, the entire world. The more we cultivate Shalom within our homes, marriages, and family dynamics, the more peace and tranquility will resonate throughout the universe.

THE COSMIC PARADIGM OF SHALOM

All of Creation is essentially about the turning of opposites into unity, all the while maintaining the richness of their distinctions. The unity beyond singularity is not about compromising to the point of losing one's identity, but about discovering a transcendent harmony that could not exist without the tension of opposites.

EACH SPOUSE HAS THEIR OWN CONTRIBUTION

As explained earlier, the entire creation process of singularity to separation, and separation to unity, mirrors itself in the creation of Adam and Chava and is reflected in every marriage and relationship.

When two individuals enter a marriage, it is crucial for each of them to contribute their uniqueness to the marriage and to play the role that only they can. Everyone excels at something, but no one person excels at everything. Knowing this well is an important ingredient to creating a healthy and holy marriage. We need to know what our unique strengths and talents are, and how we can offer them in marriage, and then learn to stick to our lane and area of expertise. Some people excel with numbers and finances, and some are better organizers and designers of living space. Some are better nurturers and caretakers, while others are better providers. Knowing ourselves, our strengths and 'superpowers', allows our spouse to bring their own talents and ways of doing things to the marriage as well.

The more we know ourselves and who we are, the easier it will be for us to stay in our lane and bring our particular genius and talent into the marriage. This will bring us to greater appreciation and reliance on our spouse's contributions as well.

The more confident you are in who you are, the more confident you will be in your role in the marriage and in the role your spouse plays in the marriage.

Part of knowing one's self is recognizing, as explored earlier, that we are 'whole' in who we are, in our singularity, and that we are entering and residing in the marriage from a place of wholeness and abundance.

Overstepping boundaries and trying to fill the role our spouse usually plays in the marriage can lead to friction and overall is not very helpful. Of course, there are times when we need to step up and take over certain responsibilities, but overall, Shalom means knowing our uniqueness, staying strong in our place, and coming together from a place of strength, clear definition, and mutual respect.

In a healthy marriage, each spouse both has and needs their own space — physically, emotionally, and conceptually. Honoring this space is essential, as it allows each of us to bring our unique strengths to the relationship without feeling overshadowed or diminished. On a literal level, this means respecting one another's privacy and personal boundaries. On a deeper level, it means recognizing and honoring each other's individual roles and contributions within the marriage.

For example, if one spouse typically manages the finances and does so competently, it is wise to trust their judgment and allow them to lead in that area. Of course, we can offer help or input when invited, but it's important not to overstep or take control where trust has already been placed. When we interfere unnecessarily, it can unintentionally convey a lack of confidence in our spouse's abilities, which can feel disempowering and erode the foundation of mutual trust.*

---

* Chazal teach us that most quarrels in a marriage are regarding finances — שאין מריבה מצויה בתוך ביתו של אדם אלא על עסקי תבואה: *Baba Metziya,* 59a.

Respecting each other's space, therefore, is not about distance; it is about creating room for both spouses to flourish and for the marriage itself to grow stronger.

By honoring each other's roles and responsibilities, we create a supportive collective environment where both spouses can thrive and feel valued. This mutual respect and trust are the bedrock of a strong, harmonious marriage.

Healthy boundaries within a loving relationship prevents the paradigm of codependency, ensuring that neither spouse becomes overly reliant on the other. Codependency is a behavioral condition characterized by one spouse having an excessive emotional or psychological dependence on the other, often to the detriment and sacrifice of their own needs and well-being. This can result in one spouse becoming the primary caregiver or enabler, while the other becomes overly dependent, struggling to be alone, avoiding all conflict, seeking constant approval and validation, and feeling responsible for their spouse's happiness and actions.

Healthy boundaries ensure that both spouses maintain their individuality and can pursue their own personal growth. Boundaries preserve a sense of mystery and respect for each other, keeping the relationship dynamic and vibrant. By valuing each other's space and autonomy, spouses can continue to discover new aspects of one another, fostering a balanced, fulfilling, and non-codependent relationship.

BORDERS & OPENNESS: BALANCING MYSTERY & INTIMACY

Shalom is where each spouse has their unique space within the marriage, and from within those respective spaces they come together. In this way, the Shalom Bayis is dependent on this delicate balance between honoring the distinct space of the other and simultaneously coming together.

In other words, a healthy marriage is one that is able to gently hold this tension of opposites; not singularity, not sameness, but rather unity, where two become one, but still remain, on some level, two.

Shalom in the home is nurtured within the sacred balance, the space that holds both openness and privacy, vulnerability and mystery, intimacy and respect. True harmony lives in this tension: where love and closeness do not diminish reverence, and familiarity never infringes upon one another's sacred inner space.

This dynamic is beautifully expressed beneath the Chupah, the very foundation of marriage. The custom of the Kalah, the bride, veiling her face recalls our foremother Rivkah, who covered herself upon first seeing Yitzchak.

Marriage is the union of body and soul, of two destinies interwoven. Attraction draws people together, yet the essence of marriage transcends the physical. It is a merging of souls, of shared hopes, dreams, and a higher purpose. External beauty may spark connection, but true love rests upon an awareness of the inner, eternal beauty that never fades.

When the bride veils herself, she and the groom affirm that their bond reaches beyond appearances. The covering itself becomes a declaration: *I love and honor not only what I see, but all that you are, both revealed and hidden. I am committing to your whole being, even the parts not yet known to me.*

The Kalah's veiling beneath the Chupah, and her later unveiling, reflects the delicate rhythm of married life, the dance of revealing and concealing, of openness and protection, of intimacy and sacred mystery. At the very root of marriage lies this quiet vow: *I am choosing you, even the parts of you that will remain forever beyond my sight.*

This is Shalom, the delicate balance between the revealed and concealed, between total openness and the recognition of the deepest hiddenness; the concealed that can never be revealed. Translated, this means, living with love, passion, and vulnerability, but not at the expense of respect and the honoring of the otherness in other, and ensuring that there is always also a deep sense of reverence in all loving relationships.

Sometimes people begin to lose respect for the person they love the most. The intensity of the love can overshadow the reverence and respect you once held for them. Sadly, the receiver of this overwhelming love can begin to feel unseen. If one's closeness leads them to take liberties with their spouse's space, privacy, and sacredness, it should be seen as a wake-up call. One might think, 'My spouse is so intimate with me, we are like the same person. If I can disregard my own boundaries and body, I can disregard theirs too." In this case, it helps to think of our spouse as a king or queen, deserving of being placed on a pedestal, so that we respect, give weight, honor and even revere them. This mindset helps preserve the sacredness of the relationship and ensures that love and respect coexist harmoniously.

WHEN INTIMACY TURNS INTO THE INVASION OF BOUNDARIES

The Torah speaks of a very peculiar form of idol worship called Ba'al Peor. For some bizarre reason, the way to worship this idol was through defecation and the release of bodily fluids. How exactly this practice arose is debated, but on a deeper level, in the context of this conversation, this most unusual behaviour makes sense. Love and passionate worship with no boundaries leads to a total breakdown of all reverence and respect.

The worshiper of Ba'al Peor would tell himself, 'Since I am so in love with my idol, so open, so comfortable, why maintain reverence? Reverence, after all, is reserved for relationships of separation, distance and unfamiliarity. I am so intimate with my deity, and it is so familiar to me, reverence is inappropriate!' This unbounded intimacy leads to an extreme demonstration of comfort, relaxation, and letting go of control: releasing their bodily waste upon the deity.

Marriage is a sacred bond, an intimate space where spouses find openness, vulnerability, and deep familiarity. Yet, these sentiments, beautiful as they are, should always coexist with a sense of mystery, reverence, and respect.

That which is meant to be done in private needs to always remain private. This is true on a literal and metaphorical level. Even in the most intimate relationships, some activities should remain private from the other. For instance, one should never come to a point of such 'familiarity' that one uses the restroom without closing the door.

On a deeper, inner level, no matter how intimate and familiar a person feels with their spouse, they need to cultivate a sense of awe for them, respectfully giving them their space and privacy as one would for royalty. One should guard an enduring sense of mystery in the other. Sometimes they should seem close, like a beloved sibling, and other times they should seem hidden and beyond you, like a great sage or leader. This fluctuation between familiarity and unfamiliarity keeps the relationship new, attractive, alive, and vibrant.

When the angels asked Avraham where his wife was, Avraham answered, "Behold, in the tent." Our sages comment: "The ministering angels knew where our mother Sarah was, but they asked this question in order to endear her all the more to her husband."* On a simple level, this accentuated and highlighted the mystery of Sarah in Avraham's eyes.

OPENNESS WITH REVERENCE MEANS NOT SHARING EVERYTHING

For every level of ourselves that we reveal, there are countless layers that remain hidden. While some might argue that complete transparency and total openness are vital for a healthy relationship, this is not always the best approach. There are times when what

---

* *Baba Metziyah*, 87a. Rashi, *Bereishis*, 18:9. ‏כדי לחבבה על בעלה‎.

causes us pain is better left unsaid. If we can resolve our own issues without causing our spouse unnecessary hurt, then why involve them and hurt them in the process of our own growth?

Consider a situation in which one has acted in a way that is unbecoming toward a spouse and now feels regret, seeking Teshuvah, a return to respect, integrity, and healing. It is natural to feel the urge to confess everything in the name of honesty, to believe that full disclosure will bring relief or purification. Yet, what purpose does such a confession truly serve?

If the act of sharing is merely to ease one's own guilt, it can become an act of self-centeredness rather than love, transferring the weight of one's pain onto another's heart. Though such openness may appear virtuous, it can, in truth, burden and wound the very person one wishes to protect.

If the sense of remorse feels too heavy to bear alone, it may be wise to confide in a trusted, unrelated third party for guidance. Ultimately, however, the true work lies in taking responsibility: to cleanse the heart, amend the behavior, and quietly repair what has been harmed. There are times when carrying the burden in silence is itself an act of atonement and love, owning what was created, rather than placing it upon another.

Teshuvah involves courageous self-reflection, taking responsibility, and working towards improvement, not necessarily sharing what we have done with anyone, especially not with one's spouse. One can always speak about any wrongdoing, mistake, burden, and one's resolutions to do better from now on to the Compassionate Creator; in that sense, one is never alone in carrying their burden.

HOME AS A SACRED SPACE

On a more day-to-day level, a key aspect of fostering Shalom Bayis in your marriage and family is establishing clear boundaries regarding what and whom is welcome in the home. For Shalom Bayis to flourish, spouses and family members must protect the sacredness and privacy of their shared sanctuary.

A crucial part of maintaining healthy boundaries is ensuring that your home remains primarily for your spouse and family, free from unwelcome or intrusive guests or even friends visiting at the wrong time. Of course, there is a Mitzvah to welcome guests into your home, but it is essential to strike a balance. Guests who overstay their welcome, or knowingly infringe upon private space, should be encouraged to leave, and perhaps no longer be invited.

The presence of guests should never come at the expense of the well-being and comfort of one's spouse or children without their explicit consent or permission. By remaining vigilant and sensitive to this delicate matter, we ensure that our home remains a place of refuge and respect for those we hold dearest, even if it is mutually agreed upon to have an 'open door' policy, or if all enjoy filling the home with guests and community.

OUR HOME AS A MINIATURE BEIS HAMIKDASH / TEMPLE

A home should feel, to oneself, one's spouse, and family, like a Beis HaMikdash: a sacred and safe haven imbued with holiness. Our sages teach that the family table is like the Mizbeach, the altar,* a place where everyday life becomes an offering of love and kindness.

Just as the Kohen Gadol, the High Priest, entered the Beis Ha-Mikdash with the soft sound of the bells on his garments announcing his approach, so too should one enter their home with mindfulness and respect, not abruptly or with haste, but gently, perhaps with a light knock or a warm greeting.** In this way, the atmosphere of the home becomes one of reverence, presence, and peace.

Entering one's home with intention and announcing one's arrival, is an expression of reverence and demonstrates respect for one's spouse and children, and for the sacredness of their privacy and boundaries.

Living our life as if our home is a miniature Temple, a Beis Ha-Mikdash, can profoundly transform our demeanor and behaviour for the better. Imagine if we treated our home with the same reverence and respect as the Beis HaMikdash. Would we ever raise our voice or lose our temper in such a place? Would we use disrespectful language or act carelessly in the Beis HaMikdash? Would we allow ourselves to be slovenly, unkind, or to act impulsively or greedily?

When we truly believe that the home is a sacred dwelling, even

---

* *Berachos* 55a.
** *Pesachim*, 112a. This is one of the seven things Rebbe Akiva told his son Yehoshua: "My son...do not enter your house suddenly, and how much more so, your friend's house." "Rabbi Shimon Bar Yochai says, 'Four matters the Holy One, Blessed be He, hates, and I do not love them, and they are: one who enters his house suddenly...'": *Niddah*, 16b. See also, *Medrash Rabbah*, Vayikra, 21:8. *Derech Eretz Zutah*, 5:2-3.

an extension of the future Beis HaMikdash,* our awareness and behavior naturally rise to meet that holiness. This consciousness encourages composure, mindfulness, and gentleness; it cultivates compassion and joy. From this inner awareness, our actions within the home begin to radiate outward, uplifting not only our household but every space we enter throughout the day. By embracing this profound perspective, the home, and all who dwell within it, are naturally elevated.

THE BENEFIT OF LONELINESS
IN PURSUIT OF SHALOM

Earlier, the three-part meta-structure of the universe was explored in detail: singularity to severing to synthesis. In this structure, the process of severance, reflected in the meta-narrative in the separating of Adam and Chava into two separate beings, is mirrored in the loneliness one feels as a single person in this life, prior to meeting their soulmate.**

* The Rebbe, *Torahs Menachem*, 5734, Chof Av, Sicha 4. See also *Chasam Sofer*, *Derashos* 2, p. 236, regarding the Night of the Seder.
** The story of Bereshis (Genesis) can be understood on multiple levels. One fascinating approach is to see it as both a description of the creation of the macrocosm — the universe — and a reflection of the development of the microcosm, the human being. Here's a brief exploration:

Day One: Creation of Light. In the story of creation, light emerges from darkness. Similarly, human life begins with birth. The fetus transitions from the dark womb through the birth canal into the light of the world. This first glimpse of light mirrors the experience of seeing the world for the very first time.

Day Two: Division. The second day speaks of separation—the division between waters. For the young child, this corresponds to an early developmental milestone: the recognition of self as distinct from the mother. The infant begins to

At a certain stage in life, the experience of being alone can be-

understand boundaries, like realizing that their tiny fingers mark the edges of their body. This is an early stage of awareness, symbolizing the concept of Havdalah (separation).

Day Three: Vegetative Growth. Day three brings forth vegetation, a metaphor for the child's early life. At this stage, the child resembles plants, growing and developing physically but still immobile. This represents the Nefesh Tzemecha / the vegetative soul, where life energy is primarily focused on expansion and growth.

Day Four: The Rhythm of Time. On the fourth day, the celestial bodies are created, introducing the rhythm of time. Similarly, a child begins to comprehend time's flow, recognizing the concepts of past, present, and future. A simple game like 'peek-a-boo' illustrates this newfound awareness, the understanding that a parent exists even when out of sight. This grasp of time sets the stage for spatial awareness.

Day Five: The Emergence of Movement. The fifth day introduces animal life, symbolizing motion and mobility. At this stage, the child moves beyond vegetative growth, gaining the ability to crawl and explore. On a deeper level, this ability to move through space is connected to their recognition of the movement of time (Day Four). The awareness of the rhythm of time allows them to move within space from one location to the next.

Day Six: Human Life. Then, on Day Six, the child becomes more conscious and developed to the point that they start to gain awareness and understanding of this world. This progresses until they start speaking, which is the definition of what it means to be a human being, speech (Nefesh Chaya means 'a creature of speech', as the Targum writes). They start talking, and then finally reach a level of understanding of a full human being with *De'ah* and *Dibbur* / understanding and speech. This continues until the age of maturity, when they have full Da'as, i.e., when they become Bar or Bas Mitzvah, and they are obligated in Mitzvos. Then they are able to sanctify Shabbos, which is Day Seven:

Day Seven: Shabbos. Now that they have Da'as their actions can sanctify time and space, such as in keeping the Mitzvah of Shabbos.

The subsequent story in the Torah represents teenage years, when a person starts realizing that it is not good for one to be alone and desires a higher level of gin to shift into a feeling of loneliness. A sense of separation may emerge—from others, and at times even from oneself—leading to moments of withdrawal or isolation. This kind of loneliness can be deeply painful, affecting one's mental, emotional, and even physical well-being. Research has shown that chronic loneliness can be as damaging to the body as smoking a pack of cigarettes a day. Those who live alone and remain lonely—even those who feel lonely within a marriage—face a higher risk of ailments such as dementia, strokes, and heart disease.

Yet within that very loneliness lies a hidden seed of longing, a profound yearning to connect, to be seen, to be united. It is often in that emptiness that the desire to bond with another soul begins to take root and bloom. This yearning reaches deeper than emotion; it is the soul's quiet pull toward its other half, the echo of a singular oneness that existed before division. In that space of longing, the heart begins to awaken to the possibility of reunion, with others, and ultimately with one's destined partner, one's Bashert.

The stage of loneliness is necessary in order that one's individuality will become fully articulated, and one will develop the will to create a conscious, face-to-face connection with the one who shares their soul root.

The loneliness stirs the soul with a quiet hope that another might fill the empty space within. It awakens in us the impulse to seek, to reach across the silent void, to touch a hand, to hear a voice, to soothe the hollow ache of being alone. Yet if marriage becomes merely an escape from that loneliness, it subtly turns into an act of quiet exploitation. The other is no longer encountered as a true completion and to be with a spouse.

other, but as a solution; not as a spouse, but as a remedy. In such a bond, one's spouse is reduced to an object meant to fill a lack, a distraction from one's own emptiness, a vessel to carry the weight of the self alone.

A true relationship is born from a place far deeper than need. It arises not merely from loneliness that seeks to be filled, but from a longing to *be*, to express one's truest self as a creator, as an embodiment of the Divine image. This yearning finds fulfillment not in receiving, but in giving, sharing, and building something greater than oneself. Our Divine nature compels us to offer our lives to another, not to fill an emptiness, but to pour forth the abundance that already flows within.

Love begins to mature when it evolves beyond the need to receive, and instead becomes a joyful impulse to give without expectation. It takes form when two souls nourish one another, not from deficiency, but from gratitude, generosity, and presence.

Even if loneliness is what first awakens the heart to seek love, it is the spirit of giving, gratefulness, and self-transcendence that allows love to take root and endure.

When the desire for connection arises from inner, pre-existing wholeness rather than from a place of lack and neediness, it opens the way to find and discover your soulmate and ultimately join them in marriage. And when two complete souls come together, two wholes forming a greater wholeness, there emerges harmony, depth, and Shalom: the peace that comes from unity in its highest form.

When there arises even a subtle sense of incompleteness, a feeling that one is not enough, or that another person is needed in order to feel whole, it can be helpful to pause and turn to gratitude. Take a moment to thank the Creator for all that has been given. In this gratitude, include not only the outer blessings of life, but also inner gifts: personal strengths, talents, accomplishments, and the unique qualities of mind and heart that shape who we are. Offer thanks for whatever measure of independence, courage, and resilience has been granted. Give thanks as well for emotions, challenges, and desires, all of which contribute to growth. As gratitude deepens, awareness begins to shift; the sense of lack starts to soften.

From that space, it may be possible to look at life with quiet objectivity. Are there hidden, subconscious beliefs, formed long ago, perhaps in childhood, that whisper of deficiency or unworthiness? If so, it helps to remember that such ideas were learned from the outside, they are impressions, not inherent truths. With warmth and gentleness, we can begin to question them: *Is it truly so that we are not enough? Is it truly so that we "need" another to be and feel whole?* In stillness, an inner knowing may arise: that these beliefs that were once perhaps protective no longer serve who we have become. We are not broken. We are not lacking.

When the grasping for wholeness is released, a quiet realization dawns: we were whole all along. When the feeling of *needing* a spouse is let go, the heart opens to meet the one destined to share life's journey. And when the need for another to complete us dissolves, we begin to sense the deeper unity—the super-wholeness—that already exists within and between us.

LONGING AND DEEPER LEVELS OF WHOLENESS

Yearning and longing, when combined with a sense of whole-ness, form the meta-structure of the universe, propelling it towards increasingly profound states of unity. This dynamic also serves as the foundation for a healthy marriage.

Duality—the experience of two-ness, separation, and other-ness—is the very condition that allows for reunion and the reve-lation of the super-wholeness found in marriage. There is indeed a form of wholeness within aloneness, for each soul is both com-plete in itself and simultaneously one half of a greater whole. Yet the deepest wholeness is revealed only through the sacred practice of marriage, in the art of living one's own fullness while, at the same time, surrendering to shared life with another. It is within this dance of individuality and union that true completeness is ex-perienced.

To attain this super-wholeness, one first experiences a Tzimt-zum, a 'slumber', a feeling of isolation and loneliness, which en-genders the necessary yearning for one's *Eizer Kenegdo* / 'helper opposite one's self' in a face-to-face relationship.

The yearning to connect with another arises from the recogni-tion of *otherness*, an inner sense that the presence of another will somehow bring completion. Yet, our soul itself, being that it is fash-ioned in the Divine image, is rooted in Oneness. Through self-re-finement and contemplative awareness, we can reconnect with this innate wholeness, the reflection of the Divine unity within. From this place of inner completeness, marriage is approached not as a remedy for lack, but as an expansion of what is already whole.

Within marriage, a new dimension of wholeness unfolds, one that transcends the completeness of the individual. The idea that a person is "half a soul" before marriage is true only in a relative sense; it points to the *super-wholeness* that becomes possible when two souls, each complete in themselves, unite in sacred partnership.

Paradoxically, it is the differences distinguishing each individual that combine to form the deeper level of wholeness. This is why super-wholeness cannot be attained alone, only with our soulmate. Marriage enables the two "half souls" to achieve the state of super-natural wholeness thanks to their unique qualities, their "opposite" natures. The *Kenegdo* / "opposite" personality of our spouse is actually our greatest *Eizer* / "help."

Of course, our differences can also give rise to challenges, such as one spouse wanting to arrange their shared life in a particular way, and the other spouse in a different way. Over time, what was originally charming and alluring, and the source of a profound revelation of deeper wholeness, can unfortunately devolve into a source of annoyance and even contention.

How can this be avoided?

OUR SPOUSE'S "FAULTS" ARE ALSO THEIR CHARM & GREATNESS

By thinking more deeply about the challenges or dilemmas that arise from differences, we may realize that the so-called 'faults' we find in our spouse, or what we may have grown to dislike, are directly tied to their unique greatness. In fact, they are closely related to what initially drew us to each other, and perhaps still, what we truly appreciate about them. Those same qualities are actually central to the attraction, the *Hamshachas HaLev* / drawing of our heart toward them, from the very beginning. Even now, they are most likely the qualities we appreciate in them, only this fact may currently be concealed from us.

It can be illuminating to reflect on the traits within a spouse that feel challenging or frustrating. Our spouse, for example, may seem disorganized or impulsive, acting swiftly, without much planning or structure. Yet, when we pause and consider what drew and draws us to them, we may discover that these very same traits are deeply intertwined. The spontaneity that sometimes appears as impulsiveness is also the source of their creativity, vitality, and initiative. What we call disorganization may simply be the shadow side of a free-spirited soul. When we look more closely, we begin to notice that the qualities we cherish and the qualities we struggle with often arise from the same root. Being impulsive and being spontaneous, being disorganized and being imaginative, they are not separate; they come as a single, living package. While habits can evolve and improve, understanding this connection allows us to nurture and support the fuller, healthier expression of our spouse's gifts rather than resisting them.

A spouse may also think, "My husband / wife overthinks everything, is slow to act, and can be quite rigid, which frustrates me." Yet, it is possible that the flip side of this same description is often the very traits we love about them. Their 'overthinking' may be the thorough and careful analysis of decisions that brings stability and focus to our lives. Our spouse's deliberate nature may show a deep commitment, and 'rigidity' may be a steadfastness that ensures their shared life is not haphazard or chaotic, all ultimately helping the relationships and their family stay grounded and focused. As the sages teach, a spouse is a "helper opposite," one who complements and refines through contrast, making deeper wholeness possible.

Often, what appears to be another's Cheser, their limitation or 'fault' so to speak, is intimately bound to their greatness. This principle applies across all relationships: between friends, colleagues, and family members alike. The qualities that challenge us in others are often the very ones that mirror what we most appreciate, the sparks through which we grow, balance, and discover greater wholeness together.

MARRIAGE CAN BE A *TIKUN* FOR A TROUBLED UPBRINGING

It's quite common for someone to marry a person who unknowingly mirrors the kind of parenting they experienced as a child. For example, a man who had a mother who was not particularly emotionally warm might find himself attracted to a woman who mirrors that same lack of warmth; a woman who grew up with a dominating father might seek out a similarly dominating husband. Such patterns are often subconscious attempts to recreate familiar situations in the hope of healing those deep or subtle wounds from childhood.

Tragically, adults who were abused as children, physically, emo-tionally or verbally, may end up being drawn towards people who resemble their abusive parents. In this scenario, the subconscious mind is in search of healing and Tikun for their soul and life story. By replaying the old scenario, the wound can be renegotiated and healed. This, however, is a difficult and risky path, since the patterns are often unconscious and the spouse with the abusive tendencies will have to overcome their own story to rewrite the script. If, G-d forbid, one's spouse does become abusive, even slightly, it will re-traumatize instead of heal, and the burdens will be compounded.

On some level, every person needs healing, but it is important to understand that choosing a spouse who is like a parent who failed us, specifically in order to heal our past trauma, isn't something we consciously should do. If our choice of spouse is truly conscious, it would be wiser to select a person who embodies the reverse of the harm we experienced. For example, one who grew up with an angry father, might consciously select as their spouse a person who is preternaturally calm and steady.

Although this is ideal, often the magnetic attraction to another person, which is integral to choosing our mate, is the underlying desire to be with someone who is familiar, and with that may come familiar negative patterns and challenges as well.

Speaking to what is often the case, we may find ourselves with a spouse who exhibits traits which remind us of our childhood wounds, and we might be—with our own traits and behaviours—mirroring their own childhood pain.

For example, imagine a man who grew up with a mother who

rarely listened to him. She was often anxious, distracted, and preoccupied with herself. Years later, he marries a woman who, without consciously realizing it, shares a similar pattern. After a few years of marriage, she too becomes distant and self-absorbed in the same way his mother once was.

Unconsciously, this resemblance may have been part of what drew him to her, the familiar echo of his childhood. If the wife can recognize that she is, in some sense, reliving his early experience, at least in the eyes of his wounded inner child, she can begin her own Tikun, as well as his. By consciously stepping out of her old patterns and learning to listen to him with genuine attention and care, she can help heal not only her husband's old pain but also correct something important within herself.

One of the mysterious, deeper purposes of her marriage to this specific person is to transform herself into a calm listener, developing a capacity for understanding and support. This will also empower her husband to provide her with the care and attention she herself may have missed during her upbringing which led her to these negative patterns of behaviour.

Our Tikun is not to come into marriage to fix our own hurts, but as we give our spouse the love and understanding they need, we often discover that we're being healed along the way.

Our spouse is one of the greatest keys to our Tikun, our life's mission and soul correction. To fulfill the purpose we were sent here for, we are invited to embark on a journey of awareness, learning to recognize our own patterns and tendencies. When we notice ourselves tuning out or becoming distracted at the very moments when our spouse most needs our attention, we can begin to study what triggers that impulse—both within and around us—and choose, in that moment, to be present.

As we do this, our relationships deepen and our truest selves begin to emerge. Marriage becomes the greatest laboratory for growth, correction, healing, and the awakening of genuine free choice.

SHALOM IN THE HOME CREATES SHALOM IN ALL WORLDS

We all have an ability to reenact the cosmic creative process. The Divine, as Creator, is metaphorically associated with the 'masculine' quality of outward expression and giving. The Divine contained within the universe is metaphorically associated with the 'feminine' quality of receiving. A healthy, balanced, respectful, loving, faithful union between a male and a female is reflected in the unity between the 'masculine' Creator and the 'feminine' Creation. Any distortion of a sacred human marriage has a ripple effect throughout the cosmos; a 'microcosmic' disruption of unity within the marriage creates a disruption of the unity within Creation, the unity between the Creator and Creation. In a sense, marital disturbances disturb the revealed Unity of the Creator. In the same way, peace in the home creates peace throughout all worlds.

Shalom is one of the Names of Hashem, as mentioned. Out of respect and devotion to certain Divine Names, we avoid erasing their written forms. However, the sages teach that Hashem allows His Name to be erased if doing so will bring peace between spouses.* This is because peace, wholeness, and unity in the home preserves the wholeness and unity of the Divine Name itself, in the inner worlds Above and within Hashem's Name itself.**

Cultivating wholeness within oneself, by directing our love and desires towards our spouse while avoiding inappropriate or detrimental thought, speech, and action, brings peace and sanctity to the home. A ripple effect then extends beyond our home and immediate surroundings, until it influences the entire cosmos. By fostering harmony in the universe, we invite the Divine Presence, 'the Name of Hashem', into the world, and ensure that it is never 'erased'.

THE FOUNDATION OF A HEALTHY SOCIETY ARE HEALTHY FAMILY UNITS

On a sociological level, Shalom in individual homes is the root

---

Shabbos, 116a.

**Although, the Name is erased, but since the erasing is a Mitzvah, and כל התורה נתנה לעשות שלום / "The entire Torah is given to bring Shalom" (Rambam, *Hilchos Chanukah*, 4:14), hence, the erasing itself brings Shalom and unity. "If [a person has the opportunity to fulfill only one of two Mitzvos,] lighting a Shabbos Candle or lighting a Chanukah Candle...the candle for Shabbos in the home receives priority, since it generates Shalom within the home...and the entire Torah is given to bring Shalom" (*ibid*). In other words, when a person kindles a Shabbos candle that brings Shalom, they are also fulfilling the Mitzvah of lighting Chanukah candles, since the purpose of Chanukah candles is also to bring Shalom: See *Likkutei Sichos*, 15 p. 372. On an even deeper level, since one of the Names of Hashem is Shalom, and since there is only One Divinity, erasing the Name 'Hashem' creates the Name Shalom.

of all moral, ethical and civil human communities. Before the sons of Yaakov became a nation of twelve tribes—as depicted in the Book of Shemos (Exodus)—they first had to forge themselves into a cohesive and harmonious family. The Book of Bereishis (Genesis) concludes with Yoseph forgiving his brothers for selling him into slavery. This led them to reunite on a higher level of unity and be transformed into a powerfully functional family and only then a holy nation.

This narrative underscores the importance of the family as the cornerstone of society. Healthy family dynamics create the bedrock for thriving societies. Just as a building needs a solid foundation to remain standing, society relies on stable families to maintain order, compassion, and continuity. Families are where values are first taught, identities are formed, and individuals learn how to relate to others. When the integrity of the family begins to erode, the very fabric of society begins to unravel. Across all cultures and times, societies that prioritize and protect the family unit tend to flourish, while those that neglect it often face moral and social decline. The world is built upon the strength and unity of harmonious families.

Our home is the sacred space where our children discover the values of commitment, mutual respect, sharing, loyalty, friendship, and healthy boundaries. We strive to ensure that our home becomes a nurturing environment for both giving and receiving, where love and a sense of belonging can flourish. Within this haven, children grow and thrive as individuals, while also learning how to navigate and contribute to the dynamics of family and community life. Shalom within the family is a direct reflection of the Shalom within the marriage. The unity that flourishes internally between spouses manifests outwardly, shaping the future resiliency and wise choices of the children. This is one way that the bedrock of a loving, cohesive family environment fosters a healthier community and society and contributes to a holier, more loving world.

PEACE DEMANDS KNOWING WHO YOU ARE

As explored, true and genuine Shalom requires both spouses to be fully present as their complete selves within the context of their union. Peace does not come from sameness or self-erasure, but rather from each spouse being whole and coming together to create an even greater sense of wholeness. To do this, self-knowledge is essential. Without it, we cannot hope to be present. Knowing who we are and what we contribute to the relationship, as well as understanding the roles of husband or wife more generally, are crucial for fostering a healthy marriage.

Every relationship is composed of two dynamics; giving and receiving. The giver dynamic, often expressed as 'masculinity', is characterized by outward-facing, proactive movement. It manifests as assertiveness, extroversion, ambition, and a focus on *process*. On the other hand, the receiver dynamic, termed 'femininity', is expressed through the inward movement of receptivity, introspection, hiddenness, and *presence*.

While masculinity in this sense is generally predominant in males and femininity in this sense, in females, every person has a combination of these qualities. Some of these different capacities are hardwired into the nature of our biologies, while some may have more to do with nurture and socialization; however, these two basic behavioural patterns are enacted by people in numerous ways. Familiarizing ourselves with their inner dynamics provides us with fresh insight into various character types, including our own, allowing our relationships to flourish and be more conscious.

GOAL ORIENTED VS. RELATIONSHIP ORIENTED

Femininity is also called *Malchus* (or *Malchut*) / royalty, human nobility, meaning the majesty of things as they are, within. Malchus seeks to share this nobility by creating trustworthy friendships. A person with Malchus thinks in terms of caretaking and nurturing, cultivating community and holding presence for others.

Masculinity, also referred to as *Yesod*, is characterized by an outward focus, constantly striving to overcome challenges and achieve goals. It embodies a process-driven and goal-oriented approach. Individuals who possess this quality tend to think in terms of accomplishments and progress.

While Yesod focuses on a destination, Malchus appreciates the beauty and presence of the journey itself. To truly grasp this concept, try a simple experiment: as you are walking to work or an appointment, focus on your inner intent. Are you mostly focused on reaching your destination, moving from point A to point Z, or do you also find value in the walk itself? Is walking merely a means to an end, including 'getting' exercise, or does the walking have an intrinsic value in itself? When you become present with the act of walking—mindful of what you see and feel, and the miraculous life-force that enables you to put one foot in front of the other— how does the nature of the journey change?

Our orientations toward 'Yesod / process' and 'Malchus / presence, influence many aspects of life, including our communication styles. When confronted with a challenge, someone embodying the feminine quality of Malchus may focus on describing the problem to a compassionate listener. In this manner, being 'present with the journey' can be even more significant than seeking solutions. Just knowing that you are being heard can often resolve the sense of difficulty or any anguish or anxiety in the challenge that you are facing.

Someone inhabiting the masculine quality of Yesod may be inclined to seek help to find a *practical* solution to a problem. If a male is deeply entrenched in this perspective, it will be difficult for him to listen to a female who just wants to be heard as she describes a challenge. He may attempt to offer unsolicited solutions, and then feel surprised when she doesn't accept them and instead continues to elaborate on her challenges. She is focusing on the journey while he is fixated on the destination. This can frustrate both parties. Another way of saying this is that men are more connected to Chochmah / 'masculine' intelligence, and women to Binah / 'feminine' understanding. *Chochmah* is the *Koach* / potential of *Mah* / 'what'. The 'fifty gates of Binah' are connected to *Mi* / 'who' (*Mi* in Hebrew is numerically 50). Men often speak to find out 'what' is going on and to find 'what' the solution is. Women, of course, can do that as well, but are also often interested in 'who' is the one talking.

PROGRESS VS. UNITY, ELEVATION VS. INTEGRATION, VERTICAL VS. HORIZONTAL, LINE VS. CIRCLE

Although generalizations are never completely accurate, men seek progress while women seek unity; men seek elevation while women seek out integration; men move vertically, women expand horizontally. Men are connected more to the inner world of *Kav* / lines and women to the inner world of *Igul* / circles.

In a circle, everyone has an equal place; there is no one ahead or behind, and there is no need in the psychology of the circle world to surpass others.

Connection is part of a circle-reality, as each point on a circle is connected with the other; each person standing in a circle 'sees' everyone else. This seeing of others creates an interconnectedness in the group, and the potential for communication and dialogue with each other as equals.

In line-reality, there is a beginning and an end, and the objective is to move forward, aiming to be at the front. No points within the line are looking at each other; rather, each one is above the next, and striving, so to speak, to get ahead.

A line implies hierarchy and exclusivity; there are leaders and followers with different privileges and a strong sense of one-way communication. This is a complete contrast to a circle, where everyone has a place; no one is a head or a tail, and everyone is seen and valued as having something unique to contribute.

LANGUAGE TO COMMUNICATE
INFORMATION OR TO FOSTER UNITY

Women and men generally have very different communication styles, which are rooted in their respective spiritual roots. It is important for both spouses to recognize and understand this dynamic. For example, women often find comfort in speaking to others, while men may find comfort in achievements and victories.

Men use language and words to communicate information, or to achieve specific objectives, such as solving problems or making decisions. Women use language as a form of intimacy and connection, organically building relationships. When both spouses deeply comprehend these natural propensities and preferences, it can significantly reduce misunderstandings and prevent unproductive arguments.

We all have both feminine and masculine qualities within us, and we need to exercise both in a balanced way. A masculine trait of goal-orientation, when not checked by the corresponding feminine trait of connection, can lead to insensitivity, impatience, and an inability to learn from mistakes. A feminine trait of sympathy, when not checked by the corresponding masculine trait of competition, can lead a person to become oversensitive and indecisive.

We all need to cultivate skills of nurturing, listening, and sharing presence, as well as skills of decisiveness and striving resolutely to attain a goal.

COSMIC CIRCLES & LINES

Through the Tzimtzum of the Ohr Ein Sof, as explored earlier, the emergence of duality, time and space began to come into focus.

The Tzimtzum caused the displaced Light to encircle the *Chalal* / Vacated Space in the 'shape' of *Igulim* / circles or spheres. In the world of Igulim, there are circles within circles. The most expansive circle is *Chochmah* / wisdom, and within it is *Binah* / understanding, and within that is the circle of Da'as, knowing, and so on, until the centermost space within all the circles, Malchus. In this way, Chochmah has within it Binah, Da'as, and all the other seven lower Sefiros (*Chesed* / kindness, *Gevurah* / restriction, *Tiferes* / compasion, *Netzach* / endurance, *Hod* / humility, Yesod, and Malchus).

Circularity is a metaphor for a space of perfect equality; any point on the circumference of a circle is equidistant from the center, and there is no inherent hierarchy between one point and another. Neither is there a beginning or ending on the circumference, as distinct from a line. On the surface of an Igul, all energies and potentialities are equal, free from distinctions, individuation, or reification, beginnings and endings. The world of Igulim is thus a reality of undefined potentialities.

An Igul can be likened to a seed which holds within it the potential to grow into a fully blossomed, multifaceted tree. Just as the entire tree exists in an undifferentiated state within the seed, so too does all of Creation exist within the Igul as a singular, unmanifest, pure potentiality.

Once the Infinite Light is set aside in the Tzimtzum, finite creation can begin to manifest. The first manifest stage of creativity is the possibility for everything, synonymous with the Igul. Following this, a thin line or ray of direct Light, known as Kav, enters the Chalal, the vacuum. This Kav, still connected to the pre-Tzimtzum Infinite Light, begins to illuminate the perimeter of the Chalal, forming concentric circles of light as it progresses inward.

The world of circles holds all potentials. The actual process of revealing potentials occurs in the world of Kav, line, and follows the paradigm of *Yashar* / straightness.

Principally speaking, male souls reflect the inner world of Kav, the cosmic line, whereas feminine souls reflect the world of Igul, the cosmic circle.* The Igul contains all of the actuality of the line, and it manifests 'first', before the emergence of Kav. These dimensions of lines and circles are reflected in the physical anatomy and biology. For example, according to current scientific understanding, all humans begin as female. For the first five to six weeks after conception, only the X gene expresses itself, helping the estrogen development. Later, after these five to six weeks, the Y gene (as males are X and Y, and females X and X) begins to express itself, releasing androgens like testosterone. By the ninth week, the internal gonads start to differentiate, moving either upward to become ovaries or downward to develop into the male reproductive organ.

---

* Kav is connected with the *Ohr* of *Chesed* / the light of giving, the masculine and the *Reshimu* / imprint of that light is connected to the *Ohr* of *Gevurah*, the vessels of receiving, the feminine.

MEN = LINES, WOMEN = CIRCLES

To better understand the distinctions between 'line' and 'circle' paradigms as manifest within human traits and behaviours, some more sweeping generalizations about men and women will be explored.

Spiritual sensitivity, faith, faithfulness, and a desire for commitment, can often be found more in women than in men. Insofar as men are programmed and built for physical conquest, they tend to be more aggressive, and also more inclined to promiscuity.

Men can see others in the context of their own 'linear' goals, and once the goal has been accomplished, the relationship can be deprioritized. Women tend to see others in terms of wholeness, completeness, and a 'circle' of eternal commitment.

A businessman sometimes sees the CEO of another company in one dimension: he is a competitor. He may even be seen abstractly, as 'competition'. Whereas a woman, by contrast, may see that same CEO as a real person with a spouse, a person with parents, with children, with feelings and needs. The woman can, more often, see the full 360-degree panorama (circle) of a person, while the man is focusing on a certain trajectory or outcome (line).

Insofar as women want affirmation and acknowledgment, when a husband remembers a milestone in the relationship, this can stand out for her more than an expensive gift given without sentimentality. For a man, a valuable gift may stand out more than a sentimental gesture.

Men seek 'progress' while women seek 'unity'. In spiritual pursuits, men often seek elevation and gain, while women seek integration and ways of giving. In terms of social standing, males climb vertically, while females expand horizontally in circles of inclusion or withdraw into circles of protection.

DIFFERENT FORMS OF RELATIONSHIPS:
BENEFITS & THE PITFALLS OF THE DIFFERENT RELATIONSHIP STYLES

These dual dynamics of line, masculinity, and circle, femininity, play out in the understanding of the basic 'purpose' of interpersonal relationships and marriage.

In the masculine mode, relationships often serve external objectives or processes. They can frequently resemble alliances for mutual gain or contracts in which one party benefits or serves the other. For example, a man might form a friendship if he believes it will help him acquire information, wisdom, notoriety, honor, or financial advantages. To some degree, his interest lies in linear mobility within the world. However, a pitfall can arise in this mode of relationship if profit becomes the sole motivation, overshadowing any personal warmth, connection, or even ethics.

In the feminine mode, the purpose of a relationship can be in the relationship itself. One can be present with people just for the sake of being present with them. Relationships are about sharing thoughts and feelings and being there for others. No person is regarded as a means to an end. Yet, a pitfall can form in this mode of relationship if one spouse becomes overly dependent on the other's empathy and all 'linear' individuality is erased.

As mentioned above, an exclusively masculine posture can lead to impatience and an inability to learn from mistakes, whereas an exclusive feminine posture without competition can lead a person to become oversensitive and indecisive.

These different qualities are meant to bring husbands and wives toward a more profound state of wholeness, surpassing the wholeness they may have had as single people. This profound sense of wholeness unites the best qualities of masculinity and the best qualities of femininity into a harmonious alchemy, counterbalancing and greatly enriching both partners.

RELATIONSHIPS BASED ON WANT, NOT NEED

We all need and crave deeply genuine relationships with others, not just profitable alliances or comfortable friendships with like-minded people. Yet, it is also a benefit to not 'need' to be relating to others at all times, and certainly not to base our self-esteem on the teamwork, camaraderie, or warmth of others.

Genuine love is unconditional and comes from a place of wholeness. Conditional love, by contrast, always wants something from the other, whether it be utilitarian gain (masculine Kav) or empathy (feminine Igul). Conditional love is never satisfied, because attempting to enforce reciprocity or grasping for loyalty incites an ever-deepening sense of *Cheser* / lack and self-deficiency.

Unconditional love fosters a sense of self-sufficiency, not only in the recipient but also in the giver. When we offer love without expecting anything in return, we empower the recipient to grow, develop self-confidence, self-sovereignty, and to realize their own potential. At the same time, acts of unconditional love enrich the giver, instilling a profound sense of fulfillment, purpose, and abundance.

A spouse who gives because he or she needs something in return is not self-sufficient as an individual, and their lack of independence can become suffocating to their spouse. Conversely, spouses who have a high drive to share life with each other feel whole in themselves individually, and also feel supported by the relationship.

Mature love says, 'I can stand on my own, and yet I am choosing to love you.' The desire for the relationship comes from a place of fullness and 'want', not from a place of emptiness and 'need'. When people feel 'wanted', they feel honored and tend to reciprocate the honor. Only a distortion in masculine or feminine qualities makes love conditional and self-oriented. When we refine and elevate the masculine and feminine traits we have been given, and value and show appreciation for the traits given to our spouse, then we can love unconditionally.

With the unifying force of a *Bris* / covenant, an indelible commitment between souls, masculine and feminine qualities and "two parts of the same soul," are able to reconcile while remaining distinct, and the relationship can become a *Binyan Adei Ad* / an eternal bond.

EIZER KENEGDO / HELPER AGAINST HIM

Adam and Chava are the prototype and the paragon of the first marriage in the Torah, albeit a marriage where Hashem was their Creator and 'matchmaker'.*

The Torah tells us that Chava was created as an *Eizer Kenegdo* / "helper against him," this means that a spouse can either "help" their spouse or work "against" them. This dual possibility may be especially pertinent to 'Chava,' the wife in the marriage, but it applies to whoever plays the role of 'nurturer' in the marriage at the moment. A husband, even while perhaps trying to help his wife manifest her gifts and accomplish her life's mission, could unwittingly work "against" her or stand in her way.

There are 'serene' relationships, in which both spouses share a multitude of common interests, activities, and life perspectives. In this type of marriage, rather than balancing each other through the dynamics of tension and resolution, husband and wife often find themselves reflecting and reinforcing each other's traits and habits, essentially mirroring one another. The type of relationship may be characterized by the spouses peacefully supporting one another, the idea of *Eizer* / 'helping' without the tension of being *Kenegdo* / 'against' the other. This category of relationship may be less challenging or more peaceful, it may also be less dynamic and vibrant.

The Torah describes the prototype spouse as one who is Eizer Kenegdo / "a helper against him," where there is a Kenegdo / an opposing force at play.

---

* Bereishis, 2:22. מכאן שתקנה הקב״ה לחוה וקשטה ככלה והביאה אצל אדם: *Avos d'Rebbe Na-son*, 4:3. Note, *Berachos*, 61a. Hence, the first marriage in the Torah orchestrated by human action recorded in the Torah is the marriage of Yitzchak and Rivkah, as mentioned.

Sometimes, it may feel like one's spouse is showing up as a Kenegdo, an oppositional force, more than an Eizer, a 'facilitator.' However, when the *Kenegdo stems* from a place of love and care, and it challenges us to be our best self, pushing us to think bigger, act kinder, study more Torah and to give more Tzedakah, this is actually helping us immensely. And it is precisely through this tension and pushback, through this other voice, that both people in the partnership can truly grow and become the people they are meant to be.

There is a structural principle called tensegrity, which can help us understand this idea. The word 'tensegrity' is a combination of the words 'tension' (against) and 'integrity' (helper), a condition of structural integrity that comes from a combination of surrounding or 'circular' interconnections and opposing linear tensions. In this type of relationship, two or more objects can be connected in an 'embrace', while remaining independent. Each object paradoxically helps the other stabilize by pulling against it.

Eizer and *Kenegdo*, 'an oppositional helper' is the dual dynamic of tension and integration. A spouse becomes a 'helper' precisely by being 'opposite' to their partner, a counterbalancing force. By challenging and even lovingly opposing each other, spouses 'help' each other. The tension forces each spouse to respond from their higher selves. This stimulates and reinforces profound mutual growth, higher order, and unification.

By providing each other with a counter force to wrestle with and then eventually align with, spouses can illuminate and draw out each other's unique, though perhaps latent talents and qualities. This process may reveal *Kochos* / physical, mental, emotional, and spiritual potentials that even the challenged individual was not aware of.

In this tensegrity, each spouse also illuminates the darker areas in which the other spouse needs encouragement and Tikun in order to become the best person they can be. In this way, a spouse can both mirror and challenge one another simultaneously. While each spouse sees their own beauty and perfection (feminine quality) reflected in the other, they are also shown where they can grow and reach greater heights (masculine quality).

Balancing help and opposition, and keeping the equilibrium in perfect balance requires tremendous sensitivity and mindfulness. An imbalanced pull in either direction is unhelpful and can even be detrimental.

Another truth to remember is that the very trait we believe our spouse needs to "fix" as part of their Tikun is often the exact quality meant to awaken growth within us, namely, our own Tikun. Each of us is called to focus on the work within ourselves, not on what our spouse must change. When both spouses turn inward, attending to their own areas of growth with sincerity, the relationship itself becomes a vessel for mutual healing and transformation.

Ultimately, marriage is the quintessential balancing act: giving while retaining self, seeing while remaining seen, and healing while being healed. By weaving these principles together, a couple creates a marriage that is not only enduring but also deeply fulfilling and holy.

Practical Takeaways

RESPECT YOUR SPOUSE'S SPACE AND TIME:

Dedicate specific times or activities where each spouse has their own personal space, both physically and metaphorically. This might involve having separate workstations at home, personal hobbies, or alone time to recharge.

DO THINGS TOGETHER AND ALONE:

It is vital to maintain healthy boundaries in marriage, as each person retains their individuality within the greater context of the relationship. Make time for personal growth or hobbies that are yours alone, and be encouraging of your spouse to do likewise.

GIVE EACH OTHER PRIVATE SPACE:

Your spouse wants alone time to read or learn, but you feel left out. If you can respect their space and use the time to focus on your interests, then later, you can reconnect more profoundly by having novel experiences to share with one another. Through showing interest in their experiences during their alone time, greater intimacy is fostered.

STICK TO YOUR LANE:

In a marriage and the cultivation of a home, it is not necessary—or for that matter, advantageous—for both spouses to be in charge of everything together all the time. Instead, each person can claim their responsibilities and focus on what they do best, sticking to what is 'their business' and not getting involved in their 'spouse's business,' (unless of course, one is specifically asked to get involved).

REMEMBER, MARRIAGE IS A PLACE OF TIKUN:

Tikun is about the possibility of doing things differently this time around. If one grew up in a family where showing emotion was discouraged, but one's spouse values emotional vulnerability, we make a conscious effort to express our feelings, with perhaps the caveat of saying, "I'm still learning to share my emotions." If one's spouse has a habit that triggers old insecurities—rather than reacting defensively, we can remind ourselves, "This isn't my past; now is an opportunity to create a new response," and act consciously versus reactively.

EMOTIONAL SAFETY:

Honor the trust our spouse places in us by keeping their intimate and vulnerable disclosures private. Never divulge to others something your spouse shared with you in confidence, and of course, we never use that information against them. That is the surest way to destroy trust.

CONSIDERATE COMMUNICATION:

Share with your spouse only when it will genuinely benefit them or your relationship, not to simply unburden yourself. Always consider the impact of your words, ensuring they offer support or insight rather than serving solely to make you feel better by being unburdened.

TREAT YOUR HOME AS THE
BEIS HAMIKDASH, A TEMPLE:

Just as the Beis HaMikdash was a place of tranquility and holiness, strive to make your home a haven of peace and serenity. Foster an environment of love and respect by avoiding conflicts, avoiding raising our voice or losing our composure. Attempt to always speak gently, listen kindly, and aspire to sensitivity and attentiveness. This will make our home a true sanctuary of love, patience, holiness, and acceptance. We can create a place where our spouse and children love being, and returning to.

FOCUS ON YOUR OWN TIKUN:

Always focus your attention and intention on your own Tikun, and what you need to fix or improve in yourself, and not what your spouse needs to do. You have your Tikun, your spouse has theirs. It is certainly never our place to be our spouse's *Mashpia* / spiritual guide or 'Rabbi'.

NEVER KEEP SCORE:

We need to stop keeping score. A statement or sentiment such as, "I watched the baby for eight hours, and you only did so for six, so now I'm owed two hours," may feel justified in a moment of frustration, but slowly erodes the spirit of the relationship. When there is a running tally of who did more, it is no longer a relationship, rather a competition, and where there is competition, there is no peace. Shalom Bayis asks us to understand that giving is not always measured in hours or tasks. What may feel like six hours to one person could be the emotional equivalent of eight to another. We each have different capacities, energies, and ways we contribute. What matters most is that both spouses are doing their best, giving what they can, with love, and without resentment.

Chapter 5

FRIENDSHIP | ריעות

*I*n the book of Malachi, the prophet beautifully captures the essence of marriage: והיא חברתך ואשת בריתך / "...For she is your friend and the wife of your covenant."* This poignant passage emphasizes that one's spouse should be the person with whom one has entered into the sacred covenant of marriage and simultaneously, someone who is and over time becomes even more, one's close and cherished friend.

Sometimes people 'love' each other but unfortunately do not 'like' each other. A healthy marriage shines with both *Ahavah* / love and *Rei'us* / friendship. This is why, under the Chupah, we bless

---

* Malachi, 2:14.

the bride and groom to have both Ahavah and Re'ius. And like everything that truly matters, friendship requires attention, time, and effort. We are called upon to cultivate the friendship within our marriage, as it is not assumed. Through conscious and continuous engagement, one's spouse can become not only someone they actively love, but also someone who is their dear friend.

And always we bear in mind that our friend in marriage is also our spouse, "of our covenant," the individual to whom we are eternally tied, a soul with whom we have rejoined as one, someone who is part of us. Unlike a 'normal' friend who may come and go based on moods or circumstances, the friendship with one's spouse is grounded in the absoluteness of the Bris, the covenant between them. Therefore, this friendship, more so than any other, requires conscientious effort and dedication because we are building an eternal relationship. With dedication and awareness of Hashem's participation, this bond will be a friendship for life.

ENJOYING EACH OTHER IN FRIENDSHIP: SHA'ASHUIM

Earlier, the macrocosmic and microcosmic processes of creation were explored, illustrating how the Infinite Singularity, the Ein Sof, contracted its Infinite Light to create finitude and otherness. This overarching process mirrors the microcosm, where Adam and Chava began as a singular entity, "...Male and female, He created them." Following a stage of sleep and separation, Chava is formed as an independent being from Adam. The purpose of the Eizer Kenegdo / 'helper against him' is for them to reunite and become "one flesh." This represents a journey from singularity to unity, where two distinct individuals come together as one, while remaining opposites.

In a deep teaching revealed by the Emek HaMelech, and later elaborated in the teachings of Chassidus, the foundation of Creation and its purpose, along with the inner reason for the contraction of the Infinite Light, is the arising of Sha'ashuim, the Divine desire to frolic to enjoy, to delight in the creation of otherness.

As previously explained in the teachings of the Magid of Mezritch, the example of a *Tzipor HaMideberes* / צפור המדברת / "a bird that speaks," illustrates this concept, as the speech of a parrot is the fun of novelty, excitement, pleasure, and frolic. This novelty, the creation of otherness that seeks to reunify and become one with the Infinite Light, is the inner reason behind the Tzimtzum, the contraction of the Infinite Light in the first place.*

The Infinite Light of Hashem is *Yachid* / One and is a Singularity. For the creation of an apparently finite reality to occur there must first be a Tzimtzum of the Infinite Light. But what ignited Hashem's initial cosmic desire for 'limitation' in order to create an 'other'? And even more perplexing, how can a movement of desire—implying the existence of something outside and 'other'— arise from within the stillness and 'sameness' of the Only One?

* In the words of the Magid כמשל הציפור המדברת לפני המלך, אף על פי שמדבר דברי שטות, יש למלך יותר תענוג מכל הדברים שמדברים דברי שכל / "This is like the parable of 'the bird that speaks' (a parrot) before the king, even though it speaks nonsense, the king finds more pleasure in all who speaks words of wisdom": *Ohr Torah*, p. 82. 86, 4. *Keser Shem Tov*, 407. *Likutei Torah*, Bamidbar, 20a. See, *Sichos Kodesh*, Yud Shevat, 5714.

In another highly original metaphor, the Emek HaMelech* illustrates the phenomenon of cosmic desire, revealing its cause and
how it manifests within boundless Infinity. He compares it to a
person who, when overcome with joy, begins to chuckle to himself.
Before the chuckle, the body is still. One's posture may be erect,
and the body placid and 'smooth' like the surface of a restful pond,
but when he chuckles, a ripple moves across his belly and through
the whole body. These ripples of laughter create crevices, indents
or 'spaces' throughout the body as the muscles tighten and release
with the vibration of laughter. This physical phenomenon that we
experience in our own bodies is a reflection of the One Above.
There was a Divine 'chuckle' within the placid Infinite Unity of
Hashem, which created a ripple-effect, manifesting the 'space' in
which the desire to create was able to appear.

This is a stunning image, Hashem 'laughing the world into
being'. But to take this further, what made Hashem burst into a
chuckle? What prompted the laughter in the first place? The Emek
HaMelech explains it as this: the Creator envisioned the wonderful
spiritual work that would eventually be done in the world by the
souls of the righteous. This image inspired laughter.

In our own lives, when we are startled by an awesome, new or
paradoxical creative insight, we may suddenly laugh out loud. This
is because we, the microcosm below, mirror the Macrocosm Above.
All of our creativity, birth and movement, begins with the opening of an inner space, a relaxing of rigidity and predictability. This
is rooted in the power of *S'chok* / laughter and lightness of being.
Thus, *S'chok* has the same numerical value (414) as מקור חיים / *Mekor
Chayim* / Source of Life.

---

* *Sha'ashu'ai haMelech*, Sha'ar 1. Chapter 2.

In the unfolding process of creation there is a level that is called "the Sha'ashuim of the King within Himself" (שעשועי המלך בעצמותו), which is, so to speak, the way Creation exists on a conceptual level, existing within the mind of the Creator, in the mind, as it were, of the Infinite Light. But then it is only the Singularity, and the purpose of the Creation was that there should be a deeper level of enjoyment, a deeper level of Sha'ashuim within the sense of otherness. And that is the ultimate enjoyment, frolic and fun, so to speak, of the Creator.[*]

This concept is true not only on the meta level, in the relationship between Creator and Creation, but on a micro level—in every relationship—as all relationships below mirror the ultimate relationship between the Creator and Creation, Groom and bride. Each relationship of husband and wife mirrors this ultimate relationship, the macrocosm reflected in the microcosm, and all of life below a reflection of the Source of Life above.

The foundation of our relationships is similar to the creation story. As mentioned numerous times previously, one initially has a sense of enjoyment in being single, the 'singularity'. Then a desire arises—a sense that life could be more wonderful, adventurous, meaningful, and full of Sha'ashuim—if only there were another to share it with. As mentioned, this is the source of Tzimtzum, the contraction of self, the carving out space for the other.

---

[*] לויתן זה־יצרת לשחק־בו / "The Leviathan that You formed to sport (laugh) with it": Tehilim, 104:26. רביעיות יושב ומשחק עם לויתן / "During the fourth (three hours) Hashem sits and plays with the Leviathan": *Avodah Zarah*, 3b. And at times, this laughter serves a higher purpose — to guide us toward reflection, correction, and ultimately, Tikun: see *Sanhedrin*, 39a.

Love involves making space within oneself for the otherness of another person.

But now, with the understanding of Sha'ashuim, we can observe that creating this space is just the first step. The intention behind the Tzimtzum is to cultivate enjoyment in experiencing life with another person, much like the microcosm reflecting the macrocosm of the 'talking bird', the playful enjoyment of novelty, the novelty of the relationship itself. The very foundation of all relationships stems from this sense of Sha'ashuim.

Sha'ashuim is the foundation of the entire construct of relationships. Those who are in the life-long relationship of marriage are asked to ensure that Sha'ashuim permeate every single aspect of that relationship, bringing continuous joy, novelty, and the pleasure of friendship. The enjoyment of each other's presence as friends is a vital ingredient for a strong, healthy relationship and rooted marriage.

FRIENDSHIP MEANS ALSO BEING THERE DURING THE HARD TIMES

It is generally understood that a good friend, distinct from a mere acquaintance, is someone who stands by another in times of need, offering support and assistance. This kind of friend is ready to lend a hand, both literally and figuratively, when someone requires it. The word for 'hand' in Hebrew is יד / Yad, and one of the words for friend in Hebrew is ידיד / Yedid which is spelled as Yad-Yad. This fact is a hint at the essence of friendship: a friend is someone who

Part Two | FRIENDSHIP | 211

extends their hand to someone else's hand in moments of need, when that person 'needs a hand'.

extends their hand to someone else's hand in moments of need, when that person 'needs a hand'.

Another word for friend in Hebrew is רע, as in ואהבת לרעך כמוך / "And you will love your friend (or 'another') as yourself. This is also the word for 'friendship' in the blessing for the bride and groom that we are discussing in this chapter: ריעות / *Rei'us.* Interestingly, רע / *Ra* can also mean 'bad'.*

True friendship is not measured by the ease of the 'sunny days', but by the quiet strength that shows up in a storm. A real friend stands by us not only in our 'good' moments of joy and health but also in *Ra* / רע / 'bad' times, seasons of struggle, illness, and pain. They give a hand when ours grows weary, a steady presence when life feels uncertain. Nowhere can this be more deeply expressed than within marriage. The truest indication of friendship between husband and wife is found not in grand gestures or perfect moments, but in the simple, sacred act of showing up for each other when it matters most. To stand beside our spouse in their weakness, to carry them in their sorrow, to be present 'heart, hand, and soul'. This is the quiet heroism of love and friendship at its highest form.

Still, friendship is not *only* about standing beside someone in their hour of need. That is indeed an integral part of it, but true friendship reaches far deeper, into the quiet places of the heart. The highest beauty of friendship is not only in the hand that helps you

---

* ואהבת לרעך כמוך ברור לו מיתה יפה. Even when activating punishment, for a very 'bad' person, the Torah says we need to treat them with love, as a 'friend': *Sanhedrin*, 52a.

rise, but in the person who *believes* in you even when you falter. This is a friendship that is found not only in presence during hard times, but in the trust that says: I see you, not only as you are right now, but as you are able and meant to be.

There is something profoundly healing in knowing that someone does not merely care *for* you, but believes *in* you, knowing your goodness, your strength, your becoming. That is the hidden crown of friendship: not only to love, but to entrust your heart to another and to be entrusted in return. That quiet confidence, that silent faith, this is where friendship becomes eternal.

The hallmark of true friendship in marriage is not only found in standing beside your spouse during life's storms, but in the quiet, unwavering belief that you hold in their soul. It is the act of showing up, not just with your hands, but with your heart; not just in body, but in spirit. Friendship means being a refuge in moments of struggle, a steady presence when the world feels unkind, and a source of strength when their strength runs low. But beyond all this, perhaps a deeper gift you can offer your spouse is your faith in them, to see their hidden greatness even when they cannot see it themselves. To believe in their talents, their dreams, their goodness, their infinite worth. To remind them, simply by the way you love them, and see them, of who they truly are and who they are destined to become. This is the quiet power of friendship in marriage, not only to stand beside each other in every season, but to see one another with eyes of faith, and to love each other into the fullness of who you were always meant to be.

REAL FRIENDSHIP ALSO MEANS BEING THERE DURING THE GOOD TIMES

Beyond standing together in hardship, beyond believing in one another's hidden greatness, the highest and most luminous expression of friendship may be found in sharing and celebrating each other's joy. As a Chassidic Rebbe once said, "To feel someone else's pain is human; to feel joy in another person's happiness is Divine." True friendship is about finding genuine happiness in the successes and joys of your friend, experiencing their happiness as if it were your own.

Rebbe Shlomo of Radomsk, a great spiritual teacher, once recounted a profound lesson on true love and friendship that he learned from a drunken peasant in a tavern. During one of his travels, he stopped by a *Kretchme /* tavern for a rest and a drink. While there, he overheard a heartfelt conversation between two peasants. Ivan, inebriated but earnest, told his drinking partner, Igor, "I love you! And the proof is, whenever you are having a tough day and feeling down, I am there for you. I sympathize with you and share your pain." Igor thought for a moment and responded: "Yeah, that's true… But Ivan, when I am happy, are you genuinely happy for me?"

This simple yet profound exchange struck a chord with Rebbe Shlomo. It made him realize that true friendship goes beyond shared struggles and pain; it is equally about sharing in another's joy, celebrating their successes, and finding *Nachas /* satisfaction in another's Nachas.

Interestingly, when people hear tragic news, they perk up, and sometimes much more than when hearing good news. Yet, whether it is curiosity or an irrational touch of morbid fascination, they also demonstrate emotions of distress and a desire to help. This compassionate response may be beautiful and heartwarming; however, there can be an underlying or unconscious element at play: hearing about another person's misfortune can make a person feel better about their own life. While a person may genuinely sympathize with someone else's predicament, it can also trigger a subtle selfish tendency to compare one's own circumstances with that predicament. This can give one a perverse sense of relief in suffering less than the other. This reaction is not always a deliberate thought, but it can be especially pronounced when the person who is struggling is your so-called friend.

This phenomenon is particularly evident when we are in a position to offer tangible help, whether physically or financially; the other person's tragedy can, perhaps against your will, boost your own sense of well-being. This is especially true when the person going through the difficulty is someone we know well.

We might feel our friend's pain, but can we feel and share in their happiness? Feeling good for the other's well-being and success, without a trace of jealousy or envy, is the truest mark of friendship.

Of course, this is true in marriage as well. We should ensure that we are there for our spouse when they are not feeling well or struggling, but also, and wholeheartedly, when they are happy or experiencing success, even that which does not directly benefit us. For instance, if one's spouse closes a big business deal, and we are happy for them, our happiness may not be entirely pure, as it is also tied to the financial benefits it brings to us and the family. However, true joy for our spouse's achievements comes when they succeed in ways that have little effect upon us, like reconnecting with a long-lost friend or receiving a compliment from an employer without a pay increase.

FARGIN

A Yiddish word has made its way into modern Hebrew: *Fargin*. It is not easy to translate this in one word, but it means to be happy for another person's happiness and to only want their success. To Fargin is to recognize that success is not a zero-sum game; your wins do not equate to my losses, nor my wins to your losses. A true friend is someone who can Fargin the other their blessings, fully and wholeheartedly. How much more should this be our way of being with your spouse and family, always Fargining, always celebrating the success of our spouse, and always feeling their joy as our own. When we Fargin, we all win.

HAPPINESS FOR ANOTHER WITHOUT JEALOUSY

There is a sentiment that people may experience, that is literally the opposite of Fargining: an envy, sarcasm, or even anger that rises up when hearing of someone else's success. When a friend succeeds, it is not unusual to feel a little pang of jealousy or a twinge of frustration. Although this feeling is quite common, it is hard to admit. It often has to do with one's lack of self-confidence, or trust in one's highest destiny.

Sometimes, when old friends see each other after many years, one friend tells the other how successful he is, how he is happily married, doing well financially, and has lots of Nachas and pleasure from his children. The listening friend smiles outwardly, and may say something to the effect of 'That's great, I'm so happy for you!' Yet, deep down, emotions churn within, as he compares his challenges with this person's perhaps "unearned" ease and success. Conversely, if the old friend tells him of plans that did not work out and of personal struggles, he might sigh and show a 'mask' of distress on his face, while secretly, deep down, he feels better about his own life.

Someone who has a hard time Fargining feels subtly diminished when their friend receives public recognition and honor; he had always felt that this person was an equal, and now they have been placed on a pedestal. This spiritual and emotional immaturity needs to be corrected if and when it arises.

An illustrious Eighteenth Century rabbi of Prague, Rebbe Yonasan Eibeschutz, illustrates this point. Somebody came to him with a question whether or not a certain food in his possession was Kosher, and he ruled that it was not Kosher. The individual readily accepted the decision, discarded the food, and bore a financial loss that was significant for him without much complaint. However, that same person reacted very differently when he came to Rebbe Eibeschutz to resolve a monetary dispute with a neighbor. He ruled in favor of the other party, compelling him to reimburse them, and he fumed with rage. This shows that if you forfeit or throw away money, you might feel fine, but if you lose the same amount of money to another person, and they gain from your loss, it might disturb you.[*]

This is the opposite sentiment of Fargining, and it is Fargining that we should aspire to, especially in marriage. We should strive to celebrate our spouse's joy, success, and wellbeing with a full heart, without hesitation, without comparison, and without even the faintest shadow of envy. Their light does not dim ours; to the contrary, it only makes our shared world shine brighter.

FRIENDSHIP IS LOYALTY

Friendship is built on loyalty and commitment; this means that we will always have our spouse's back. Betrayals of one's spouse need not be grand and life-altering, they can be small, and still be insidious. Imagine, for instance, a couple standing at an airport check-in counter or a store cashier. One spouse fumbles nervously, unable to find a wallet or a ticket. If the other spouse rolls their eyes in frustration or flashes an embarrassed glance to the stranger behind the counter, this is not merely impatience; it is, in that fragile moment, a quiet betrayal. It says, 'I care more about the approval of this stranger, someone I may never see again, than about protecting you, my life partner.'

---

[*] Note the language of the sages (*Sifri*, Devarim, 12:1. *Rashi*, ad loc) "אחד מהם רואה שני נוצח בדין אומר יש לי עדים להביא יש לי ראיות להביא / If two people are engaged in litigation and one sees that his opponent is about to prevail, he quickly interjects: "I have witnesses yet to summon, and further proof to present…" In other words, it is not the prospect of his own loss that troubles him, but rather the thought of his opponent's impending victory.

True loyalty means standing by our spouse, always, even in the face of minor inconveniences or embarrassments. Clearly, when zooming out on this type of scenario, it is obvious to us that this is more important than seeking the approval of a stranger—or even a relative, friend, or acquaintance—outside the marriage.

KEEP TALKING.
NEVER GO SILENT WITHOUT EXPLANATION

Good friends talk and communicate continuously. When communication breaks down, so does the opportunity to reconcile and repair. The Sages definition of enemies are those who do not talk to each other for three days.[*]

In dealing with conflicts or moments of anger, it is essential not to resort to 'the silent treatment', or resign ourselves to not being on speaking terms with our spouse. Instead of shutting down, openly address the reason for the hurt or dismay. While it may be tempting at times to retreat into silence by shutting down and avoiding all communication, this just creates a domino effect of further harm and ill feelings as it reinforces a sense of isolation and misunderstanding.

It is wise to always begin by expressing one's emotions and the reasons behind them in a calm and respectful manner. Beginning with statements like "I feel hurt because…" or "I am upset because…" helps our spouse understand the root of our feelings

---

[*] שונא כל שלא עמו דבר שלשה ימים באיבה. Mishnah, Sanhedrin, 27b.

without feeling attacked. During these, sometimes difficult, conversations, we strive to focus on the specific issues that we are dealing with right now, rather than bringing up past grievances. Staying focused on what is bothering us right now, means that in the right time, when the possibility of calm conversation is present, we can bring up the other things in a way that will be constructive and not critical.

When dealing with difficult issues, it may be challenging to keep the conversation productive. While not retreating into silence, it may still be helpful to take breaks when and if the conversation becomes heated, and return to address the issue once emotions have settled.

If we can keep in mind that our goal is not to win the argument, but to find a solution that respects both of our feelings and needs, we can maintain open and honest communication, and then there is *always* a possibility for resolution.

There is a caveat to this, though. While we should never stop speaking and communicating, we can also determine when something needs or does not need to be said. Simply venting, just exacerbates anger and makes both partners feel even worse. Instead, we strive to simply share the deeper hurt that is fueling our negative emotions, while always being mindful not to frame our emotions as accusations or blame, and implying that what we are feeling now is our spouse's fault. We can always take ownership of our feelings and recognize that they stem from our own thoughts, interpretations, or past experiences. For instance, rather than attacking, we can focus on expressing our inner experience, communicating to our spouse the simple essence of why we believe we are feeling anger. For example, a wife becomes upset at her husband for forgetting her birthday. She calms herself down and then tells him, 'I feel hurt that you forgot my birthday, and I have a belief that this means you don't care about me.' She chooses not to say, 'I feel hurt because you never remember anything about me, and in fact, last year you also forgot our anniversary, so you obviously don't care about me!'

When we do not address our emotions, they can build up over time and eventually explode, seemingly out of nowhere, triggered by the slightest perception of insult. But if we make our feelings and reactions out to be our spouse's fault, we may never be able to resolve the issue, for it will trigger defensiveness and hurt in our spouse and leave the underlying issue unresolved. By speaking of our feelings and addressing their cause—thoughts, beliefs and conditioning that have been activated—we can prevent misunderstandings and maintain open communication.

While communication is key, sometimes the best response for the moment is to remain silent. This can be done sensitively, by communicating our need for space or silence. We include our spouse in this choice by saying, 'I need some time alone to gather my thoughts. Let's talk in a few minutes,' or 'I value our communication, but right now I need a break in order to settle myself and recover my ability to communicate well.' In this way, the silence is not breaking the connection, but becomes a vital part of staying connected.

When we are feeling overwhelmed, irritable, or simply low on energy, we can take a moment to gently communicate this to our spouse. Rather than having them guess the reason as to our withdrawal or silence, we might say, "I'm feeling really stressed right now. It's not about you, but I just need a little space to reset." By preempting misunderstandings, expressing our needs clearly and without blame, we help our spouse understand that our quiet or distance is not a rejection and not personal. This prevents unnecessary hurt and builds trust.

The need to take care of one's self when physically tired or emotionally drained is more than valid, it is a vital aspect of increasing Shalom Bayis. Something to keep in mind is "Do not martyr yourself, master yourself." This means we give ourselves permission to step back when needed, and always communicate our needs with kindness and clarity.

Effective communication is kindness, as it allows our spouse to support us better. By communicating our need for space and silence, we can prevent misunderstandings and always keep the channel of the relationship open and free-flowing.

ALWAYS RESPECT EACH OTHER WHILE COMMUNICATING & EVEN WHILE ARGUING

The power of speech is the quintessential expression of our humanity; the human being is called *Medaber* / a speaking creature. In the creation of the human being, Adam was given a "living soul."*According to the *Targum* / ancient Aramaic translation of the Torah, this is called *Ruach Memalela* / a speaking spirit.

---

* Bereishis, 2:7. נשמת חיים.

Perhaps the human capacity to think, analyze, anticipate is greater than any other form of life, but what defines the human being as *human* is the ability to articulate thoughts and feelings *to others*. Speech has the unique power to reveal the hidden depths of the soul to another person. For the listener, it offers the chance to enter the speaker's inner world. Communication, therefore, stands as the deepest spiritual tool we possess.* While physicality is defined by time and space and the divisions of past, present, and future, here and there, and you and me, speech transcends all these divisions and boundaries. Through speech, two separate individuals can merge into one, as the depth of the speaker's soul can become part of the listener's inner world. When we truly listen, we allow the words spoken from the depths of another's soul to resonate within us. Parenthetically, this is the reason that speech and communication is sometimes used as the euphemism for intimacy.**

Either way, speech is a very powerful tool and should be used appropriately, with wisdom and compassion. Even arguments can be healthy when done constructively, which means without personal attacks or excavating past grievances. Arguing can show that the other is an Eizer, a helpmate that is indeed Kenegdo, with their own opinions and perspectives.

A good rule of thumb would be that every argument should be "for the sake of Heaven." That is to say, aiming for resolution rather than merely perpetuating conflict. Chazal say, "Every argument for the sake of Heaven is destined to endure."*** How do we know if an

---

* *Likutei Sichos* 6, Yisro 1.

** ראוה מדברת עם אחר בשוק: *Kesuvos*, 1:8. מתייחדת: *Bartenura*, ad loc.

*** *Avos*, 5:17.

argument is for the sake of Heaven, namely, for a higher purpose? If its goal is to reach an enduring resolution, this is proof that it is a holy, or, 'Heavenly' argument. An argument, by contrast, whose purpose is for the sake of conflict itself, or to prove a point and win, or even worse, to make one's spouse feel diminished or small, G-d forbid, is clearly not for the sake of Heaven, and quite the opposite.

For this reason, when disagreements do arise between spouses, we strive to ensure that they are for the sake of clarity and resolution. We avoid making the discussion personal or allowing past issues to surface. A helpful practice during an argument is to consciously refrain from language such as "you always" or "you never." Statements like, "You are always late," or "I've been dealing with this for five (or ten, or twenty) years!" can be deeply painful. They shift the conversation from the specific concern at hand to an attack on the person, which is devastating and makes reconciliation even more difficult.

Try to keep the conversation anchored in the present concern, and never allow it to become personal.

Approaching disagreements with the intention of creating resolution and growth can actually strengthen the relationship and promote deeper understanding, leading to a greater unity.

Maintaining honor and respect in moments of disagreement is crucial. Not every thought needs to be voiced, but when it does need to be said, it can be done with respect. The other person is carrying the Divine image, which calls for reverence. Respectful speech and action during disagreements foster understanding, forgiveness, peace, and harmony.

Here's an example to consider: One of the partners in the marriage usually wakes up early, while their spouse (and perhaps the children) are still asleep, and enjoys those quiet moments to themselves as a way to start their day. If something changes and the night owl spouse begins waking earlier, the early riser might feel that their personal space is being encroached upon. Initially, the early bird spouse might think that telling their spouse that they are missing their morning space will be hurtful. So they keep it inside, and it builds up into a resentment that eventually erupts forcefully, and to the newly early-rising spouse seems completely out of the blue. Since there is no context in their mind for this outburst, this will feel personal and hurtful.

A peaceful approach would be to gently bring these feelings to light as soon as they are noticed. Expressing one's feelings with kindness and compassion, allows our spouse to understand our perspective without feeling hurt. Perhaps the early riser might say, "It's so nice that we are on a similar schedule now, but I am struggling with not having the quiet time in the morning that I have gotten used to. I feel like I needed that space to get my day started right. How can we make this work?" By acknowledging these emotions and communicating openly, the connection is nurtured, and a deeper understanding of our spouse is revealed.

CRITICISM VS. CONSTRUCTIVE CRITIQUE

We should refrain from criticizing our spouse. However, at times, and only with great care, we may be able to offer critique. Criticism is negative feedback directed at the person, attacking who they are.

Critique, by contrast, is a calm, thoughtful reflection on a situation or behavior, without emotional charge or judgment of character. Even critique should be offered sparingly and only when we sense that our spouse is receptive, ready, and willing to change the thing or do it differently and would welcome our honest and loving critique.

The focus of critique is never the person themselves. It is always about the action, the moment, the pattern.

What's more, when giving feedback, avoid sentences that begin with "Why are you so…" or "Why did you…?" These questions are accusatory, personal, and often trigger defensiveness. Instead, speak from the heart, in the language of feelings, replace "Why do you…?" with "I feel hurt when…." This shift turns a confrontation into a conversation.

Healthy critique arises from *Kedusha*, the holy, a place of sincerity, care, and a desire to build. Criticism, by contrast, emerges from the *Sitra Achra*, the unholy, the reactive, ego-driven impulse. One of the essential distinctions between the holy and the unholy is this: Kedusha involves effort, responsibility, and the willingness to do the work of relationship; the Sitra Achra seeks ease, control, and change without effort. So we must ask ourselves: Is what we are offering rooted in a genuine wish to engage, repair, and grow together? Or is it an attempt to release frustration, assert power, or force another into our will?

True critique is never one-sided. The one offering it is prepared to do the *mirror-work* within themselves.

Before speaking, consider: Is what I am about to say focused on behavior, not identity? And, am I prepared to help resolve this? If the answer to any of these is "no," then it is better to stay quiet, breathe, and return to the conversation at a later time. Because the goal is not merely to correct, but to connect.

OUR SPOUSE IS OUR MIRROR

Our experience of life is a mirror. Whatever quality or tendency we notice in another person is, in some way, a reflection of something within ourselves. If we perceive a 'shortcoming' in our spouse, it is a signal that this same shortcoming is somewhere within ourself, and it is something that probably needs work, or attention. Our reflection in them is showing us precisely what we need to do to make our Tikun. If we see a weakness or hangup in them, it is a message for us, revealing what we need to heal or change.

On a deeper level, we are actually the ones creating the reality which we perceive. We create our reality through our thoughts, words, and actions. Our thoughts influence our children, our words influence our spouse, and our actions, our most external self-expressions, influence our co-workers or colleagues. Thus, the Baal Shem Tov teaches that the negative words you speak create issues or difficulties with your spouse. If we see something in our spouse that we think needs correction, the first thing to do is to correct our own speech.

AFFIRMATIONS AND POSITIVE SPEECH

Any kind of criticism, even when it is completely non-judgmental critique is best not done at all, and positive speech and connective affirmations is always the most powerful tool. In marriage, (as in all relationships), it is vital to speak positively and offer words of praise and positive reinforcement. Just as the Creator brought the world into being through speech and continues to affirm creation through speech as well, we too create our reality through our words. Speech is a form of intimacy, and the way we use our words with our spouse shapes our shared home and reality. By contextualizing and verbalizing our thoughts, we bring them to life. What we speak of, and the way we speak the words, becomes our lived experience. Positive affirmations are not just kind words, they are acts of generosity that can significantly nourish our relationship.

When we think of something, it may not seem real to us, and certainly not to others. It is not until we verbalize our thoughts that they become real to us and others. When we notice a positive quality in our spouse, or something that we find attractive, it is integral that we express it in words. Words have the power to create and shape our reality, so it is essential for the growth of the relationship to make sure to always voice our appreciation and admiration.

AS IN PRAYER: ACKNOWLEDGE BEFORE REQUEST

Communication in marriage can be understood through the lens of *Tefilah* / prayer. In Tefilah, our words are arranged in a meaningful order: first praise, then requests, and finally gratitude. While the essential definition of Tefilah is indeed to make requests of the Creator, we do not begin with requests. We first acknowledge and appreciate the One to Whom we are speaking, only then do we ask, and afterward we express thanks.

So too in marriage, and in any deep relationship. Our interactions should never be purely functional or transactional. There must be warmth, presence, and emotional closeness woven into even the simplest exchanges. When we need something from our spouse, something as ordinary as, "Can you pick me up from the airport?" We should remember the order of prayer: acknowledgment of the other before the request, and always gratitude afterward.

Before asking, look inward and see if we are perhaps reducing the relationship to a transaction. When a request arises from a foundation of appreciation, the relationship remains intimate rather than utilitarian. On a deeper level, when we ask from a place of valuing who they are, not merely what they do, we preserve the sanctity and tenderness of the bond and ensure that it does not become merely transactional.

WORDS CREATE WORLDS

Our words carry immense power. They shape the emotional climate of the relationship and can gently guide how our spouse comes to see themselves. When we speak to the beauty, nobility, kindness, and strength we perceive in them, we create a space where those qualities can blossom. In such an atmosphere of warmth, love, and mutual respect, any request we make arises naturally and is received with an open heart.

The more we genuinely believe in our spouse's goodness and express it, the more they will recognize it and live from that goodness. People are most deeply affected by how they are seen by those closest to them. This is especially true in marriage, where each partner holds the heart of the other. To the extent that our spouse feels safe to be vulnerable, open, and real with us, our praise becomes not just pleasant, it becomes healing. It affirms their spirit and strengthens their sense of self.

When we consistently highlight our spouse's positive qualities, we nurture their self-esteem and encourage them to act in alignment with those virtues. When we frequently point out faults, weaknesses, or shortcomings, the other may begin to internalize those messages, leading to insecurity, withdrawal, defensiveness, or diminished joy.

Positive speech builds connection, closeness, and friendship. Negative speech erodes them. Therefore, speak with love, and speak toward the goodness we wish to see. Remember, what we articulate becomes the world we live in.

AFFIRMATION OF YOUR SPOUSE AND OF YOURSELF

Also vital to the relationship is to project positive, life-affirming feelings about yourself to your spouse. 'Self-affirmation' is communicated both verbally and non-verbally, including how you stand, walk, and speak. Without arrogance or comparison, rather with playful, innocent joy and a sense of gratitude to the Creator, we can verbalize our positive qualities by sharing with our spouse how nice we look today, how smart we are, or how we were successful in solving a particular problem. Self-affirmation and self-appreciation do not come naturally to many people, but when they are learned, these skills help fill the relationship with positivity. In this way both spouses are empowered to see and manifest our gifts and strengths.

Just as putting our spouse down is devastating, it can equally damage our marriage to put ourselves down. Saying, 'I look ugly,' 'I am stupid,' or 'I am such a mess' is detrimental to intimacy and connection. Words have power and become reality. Over time, negative self-talk will influence, even if it is subconsciously, how our spouse sees us. Show up in the same way we wish to be viewed and avoid ever demeaning oneself, especially in front of or to our spouse.

In truth, part of affirming our spouse is affirming ourselves. Our spouse feels affirmed by having married a person with so many good attributes and skills; and by pointing out our good points, we make our spouse more aware of the value of the marriage. Of course, expressing confidence and positive sentiments about ourselves in front of our spouse must be done tastefully and appropriately, in the right time and place. Sometimes we should only praise them, but other times we should include ourselves as well.

Using Tefilah as a guide, we find an interesting example that will help us illustrate this point. In the middle of the first blessing of the Amidah, one of the three passages of *Shevach* / praise, in which we praise Hashem, we say, ‏גומל חסדים טובים, קונה הכל, וזוכר חסדי אבות / "(Hashem) bestows bountiful kindness, creates all things, and re-members the piety of the *Avos* / Patriarchs." Why do we mention "the piety of the Avos" amid praising Hashem? These words seem to include a measure of self-praise and pride in our holy lineage. The lesson is that every relationship, whether between spouses or between us and the Divine, requires a sense of 'equality', so-to-speak.

A marriage cannot thrive if one person idolizes the other while simultaneously harboring negative opinions about him or her-self. There need to be two confident people coming together as one. Both spouses need to feel worthy and capable regarding their unique attributes and gifts. This means that not only must one appreciate their spouse, but to transmit a sense of self-appreciation, and gratitude for the way they themselves were created and formed.

When we project positive sentiments about ourselves to our spouse, we are helping them see us this way. When we do need to admit failure or a need to grow, this can also be done in a positive way, showing our belief that we can improve. This form of positive self-regard will also help our spouse see the beauty of our soul, in a way that uplifts and affirms them.

MEN AS *MASHPIA* / GIVER, WOMEN AS *MEKABEL* / CHERISHED

Broadly speaking, there are differences between affirmations that a husband desires to hear from his wife, and affirmations that a wife desires to hear from her husband. Not only socially, but spiritually, intellectually, emotionally, biologically, men and women are generally from different paradigms. A man predominantly represents the *Mashpia* / giver and influencer in a relationship, and a woman predominantly represents the *Mekabel* / receiver and nurturer. Both literally and metaphorically, the woman receives the seed and articulates it and develops it within her womb.

Therefore, men are often empowered by affirmations of their intelligence, kindness, and success. They specifically appreciate feeling needed. For a relationship to flourish, it is essential for the man—whether he is the primary financial provider or serving in another capacity—to feel that he is contributing, that he is a *Mashpia* / a giver. He needs to feel that what he does matters, that his contributions to the relationship and to life are real, valued, and genuinely making a meaningful difference. Women, on the other hand, who represent Malchus, the receiver, generally need to feel that they are cherished, loved, and deeply heard.

Insofar as a husband thrives on feeling needed, respected and valued as a contributor, the wife needs to compliment him on his wisdom, good deeds, and generosity. Insofar as a wife thrives on feeling appreciated, cherished, attractive, and understood, the husband should express his appreciation for her virtues, efforts, and attractiveness, and attentively cherish her for who she is.

The Torah's first description of marriage, the marriage between Rivka and Yitzchak, illustrates this beautifully. When Rivka first sees Yitzchak, she shows him tremendous honor and even reverence. A man's most profound desire is for his wife to view him with *Kavod* / honor.[*]

---

[*] The Rambam writes, וכן צוו על האשה שתהיה מכבדת את בעלה ביותר מדאי / "And thus (the Sages) advised a woman to honor her husband exceedingly": *Hilchos Ishus,*

Men crave love as much as women, but they usually do not *doubt* the love of their spouse. What men do often feel though, is uncertainty about their success in their capacity as the giver, the provider, and being a good person for their family. For a man to feel content and have a healthy self-worth, he needs a wife who will convey to him that she is proud of him, respects him, honors him, and is deeply grateful for the husband and father he is and/or is striving to become. And it is crucial that these words come from the heart, so that he won't doubt their authenticity. By affirming these particular qualities, she will connect with the core of his being and masculinity.

Women certainly require respect, as well. They, too, need to hear affirmations of their worth and contributions, and to know that their efforts, both seen and unseen, are recognized and valued. However even more than this Kavod, is their desire to be cherished, loved, and heard. A wife wants to be understood for who she is, and know that her husband admires her on all levels. For a woman to be happy and content in her marriage, she needs her husband to show her that her presence in his life is a blessing, and that her love and dedication, beauty and virtues, do not go unnoticed.

15:20. Women of course also need Kavod, honor, and indeed, וכן צוו חכמים שיהיה אדם מכבד את אשתו יותר מגופו / "Similarly, our Sages commanded that a man honor his wife more than himself": *ibid*, 15:19. But "exceedingly" is what a man needs. The Rambam also writes, ויהיה בעיניה כמו שר או מלך / "And he should be in her eyes like a minister or king." Not that he should be a ruler in his own eyes, rather, he should behave in a way that allows her to see him as noble and honorable, and she should give him the feeling that this is the way she feels about him.

By doing so, he will connect with the core of her being and femininity, and uplift and empower her.

LISTENING AS COMMUNICATION

Communication is the cornerstone of *Rei'us* / friendship and effective communication goes beyond speaking, offering constructive criticism, or providing positive and tailored affirmations; it also fundamentally involves listening. Listening effectively asks us to master the art of *Tzimtzum* / self-limitation to create a space for the other person, wherein we value and internalize their words.

Listening goes far beyond merely hearing words; it requires the individual to avoid projecting his or her own opinions, ideas, prejudices, and inclinations onto the person speaking. Mostly, when people are hearing others speak, they are bringing their own background, knowledge, experiences, cognitive biases, and expectations into the words they hear. This unconscious bias prevents them from truly listening to the other, and instead, they are simply projecting their own thoughts onto the other's words. To listen means to be as devoid of your own internal image and speech as possible, in complete openness to the other person and their story.

In a marriage which aspires to the highest form of friendship, it is essential to speak and share our world, and to listen and receive our spouse's world. Listening gives our sacred 'other' space to exist and be known, not just as part of *our* story, but as the center of their own story.

To truly listen is to be fully present, nonjudgmentally and unconditionally. Listening is not about finding answers or solutions to our spouse's questions, dilemmas, or issues raised, but about simply being there to listen. This involves setting aside our own self, our prejudices, and our preconceptions, and being fully present for them. Imagine yourself in their shoes and open yourself up to understand, as much as possible, how it is to have their imaginative background, and live inside their 'inner citadel'.

To truly listen to our spouse is to follow the rhythms of their silence, to be fully present in the moment, with the subtext, subtle gestures, energies, and emotions, and ultimately, with their deeper being, their soul.

FOUR LAYERS OF DEEP LISTENING

Listening is a profound art, subtle, delicate, and multilayered. There are many levels of truly hearing another, which ranges from simple attentiveness to a deep, unified listening of the heart.

1. REMOVING OUR OWN STORY

The first level of genuine listening is to listen without mental noise, that is to say, without self-projection, and avoiding the need to shape or steer the conversation in any particular direction. To truly listen is to be fully present and receptive, open to what is being said, and sincerely attempting to absorb what our spouse is expressing, both in the words they are saying, and in the quiet spaces between them.

2. LISTENING WITH EMPATHY

An even deeper form of listening is empathetic listening. In this mode, not only do we hear the words our spouse is speaking, but we also open ourselves to the whole person, their uniqueness and inner world. This form of listening attunes us to the subtle layers of communication: the tone of voice, the cadence, the pauses, the gestures and the emotion behind the words. Through this, we begin to truly sense where they are coming from and what they are experiencing. In empathetic listening, we are not merely receiving information, we are entering into a relationship with another's inner life.

These two forms of listening awaken the "I–You" relationship. In this dynamic, we step aside from our own preoccupations and make room to truly receive the inner world of our spouse. This is the beginning of deep relational listening, where the listener creates a safe, spacious, and non-judgmental environment in which the speaker can share openly. In such a space, the heart naturally relaxes. Our spouse has the experience of being seen, held, and understood and feels safe to be vulnerable.

Listening in this way is a profound offering. Simply being present with openness and care lightens the emotional weight they may be carrying. The act of listening itself becomes its own form of healing, supporting their journey of growth, integration, and Tikun.

3. LISTENING TO EMPOWER

The third stage of deeper listening takes us to a place of empowerment of the one whom we are listening to. This is an even higher and more expansive form of presence. Through carefully attentive and empathetic listening, we help to reveal and strengthen our spouse's potential: physical, emotional, mental, and spiritual. When we know that our spouse is not merely venting or releasing emotion, but is seeking clarity or guidance by speaking with us, we can listen with the trust that the wisdom they need already resides within them. Rather than rushing to offer solutions or advice, we create the conditions in which their own inner knowing can surface. In doing so, we help them access their higher intuition and deeper clarity. In this form of communication, both spouses feel the profound soul-bond that exists between them. The conversation becomes a shared space of growth, empowerment, and connection.

4. LISTENING TO UNITE

Unifying listening is the deepest and most intimate level of listening. At this stage, listening becomes a transformative and spiritually unifying experience. When we listen from this place, all the inner strength, clarity, or wisdom that we possess—earned through age, experience, maturity, or inner work—can be shared and felt by our spouse. Our presence itself becomes healing. For example, when we are calm and grounded, and our spouse expresses anger or distress, our steady and peaceful presence can gently flow into them through this deep listening. Without saying a word, our calm becomes their calm; our inner equilibrium becomes a resource they can draw upon. This occurs not through advice or explanation, but through soul-identification, recognizing and meeting the other at the level of essence.

At this depth, listening is no longer two separate selves interacting. It arises from the awareness that there is, in truth, one unified soul, shining through two expressions. When each spouse sees the other as part of their own deepest self, listening becomes an act of union.

Although our spouse may feel empowered and may even arrive at the insight or solution they are seeking, we ourselves are not offering advice if we are truly listening. Listening means listening. Even when we are empathizing, the focus remains on receiving, not directing. Giving advice too quickly shifts the dynamic and closes the space of openness. It subtly suggests that the answer lies outside of the one who is asking, when in truth, deep listening encourages the one speaking to discover the answer that already resides within. In this kind of listening, the act of speaking itself becomes clarifying. As our spouse articulates their concern, the fog begins to lift, and their own inner wisdom starts to emerge. At times, they may draw upon our presence, our calm, our steadiness, our faith, and use that as a mirror to find their own strength. Throughout, our role remains the same: to be present, receptive, compassionate, and supportive.

If our spouse truly asks for advice, genuinely and clearly, then we pause. We listen again, deeply, on all levels. We let their words settle in the heart. Only then, after a moment of quiet reflection, do we respond.

At its core, empowering and unifying listening operates within an "I–I" paradigm of relationship, one that transcends the ordinary notion of "two separate people relating." In this deeper mode, we experience oneness with our spouse, while still retaining our own wholeness and clarity. As discussed earlier, the union of two complete souls forms a greater symmetry, not the erasure of individuality. If we were to lose ourselves entirely, we would not be able to receive our spouse, reflect them, or support them in any real or grounded way. Yet, at the same time, this level of listening requires us to gently step beyond our lower, ego-bound self. Otherwise, we would hear only our projections, assumptions, and interpretations, not our spouse's truth. In the "I–I" paradigm, both spouses sense their shared essence: the unity of the soul, the underlying Oneness of the Divine flowing through and between them. This is the essence of true listening and deep relationships.

Practical Takeaways

WEEKLY OR DAILY *SHALOM BAYIS* / 'MARITAL PEACE' CONVERSATIONS:

To nurture a healthy and thriving relationship, spouses should make a habit of scheduling regular Shalom Bayis conversations. These conversations provide a dedicated time for discussing any issues or concerns in a constructive manner, focusing on solutions that honor both perspectives. This practice encourages open communication. True, most people think that spontaneous acts of affection and love, and open communication, are more powerful than scheduled acts of love and communication, but the truth is that for healthy relationships to thrive, most people need to schedule times and pencil in times during the week. Not everything that isn't spontaneous is fake or inauthentic. Spouses need to create 'rituals of communication', designated times every day to connect and talk.

DAILY CHECK-INS:

Make it a priority to set aside time each day for genuine and meaningful conversations, even if it is just for a few moments. Do not let a day pass without truly connecting, whether you are home or traveling. These conversations should go beyond the mundane, utilitarian communication, such as 'Did you do this,' or 'Did you go there' questions. Instead, focus on heartfelt exchanges like 'How are you feeling,' and 'How is your day going?' This habit of daily check-ins fosters emotional intimacy and keeps the lines of communication open. The (Lubavitcher) Rebbe once shared with his doctor that enjoying an afternoon tea with his wife and their daily conversation was as valuable to him as the daily Mitzvah of putting on Tefillin (so-to-speak).

SPENDING WEEKLY QUALITY TIME TOGETHER:

Dedicate one evening a week, or a few hours, or at least some quality time, to spend time together talking without distractions. During this time, eliminate all distractions, no phones, no emails, just the two of you, sitting and having a conversation.

SEEK OUT NEW EXPERIENCES:

Just as the creation of the entire world involves novelty and joy, incorporating new activities and adventures into a marriage keeps it vibrant, alive, and engaging.

SURPRISE EACH OTHER:

Small surprises and gestures, whether it is a thoughtful note or a spontaneous gift, can bring joy and excitement to your relationship.

NEVER GO TO SLEEP ANGRY:

It is very important to resolve any conflict or issues before going to bed. Allowing anger to linger overnight can have negative effects on both emotional and physical well-being. Unresolved anger can disrupt sleep patterns, create disturbing dreams, leading to restless nights and fatigue. Moreover, harboring negative emotions over-night, and maybe even subconsciously dreaming about these issues, can cause resentment to build, making it much harder to openly communicate and resolve these issues in the future.

POSITIVE BEDTIME MINDSET:

Never go to sleep with negative thoughts like fear, anxiety, ap-prehension, or worry on your mind. These negative disquieting thoughts, images, and emotions can, and probably will, seep into your dreams, resulting in restless and troubling nights filled with nightmares and devastating images. Waking up after a night filled with negative dreams can leave you feeling agitated, upset, and fear-ful in the morning, and it could take hours, perhaps until midday to finally get back your equilibrium. Your sleep state will cast long shadows over your coming day. Instead, make it a priority to go to bed in a joyful state. Embrace happiness and positivity before sleep, perhaps even with a light-hearted joke or uplifting thought, or read something that brings a smile to your face. This practice can help ensure you have pleasant dreams and wake up feeling refreshed, content, and poised to greet and embrace the day and all that the day will bring, and do so with unwavering confidence.[*]

DO NOT ARGUE OR THINK ABOUT YOUR RELATIONSHIP WHEN HUNGRY OR TIRED:

Often, when someone is experiencing a physical discomfort, deficiency or ailment, the mind and ego strive to make sense of these sensations. This can lead to the creation of narratives that justify these sensations, even though they are completely unrelated. For instance, your body might simply be hungry, or you might simply have a headache coming on, but the mind convinces you that your spouse is irritating or upsetting you, and that is why you are agitated. This phenomenon occurs because the mind seeks to explain and rationalize the discomfort, even though it is merely a physical deficiency. And so, it is essential to recognize that the true cause of the agitation is the physical need or discomfort, not your spouse's behaviour. By addressing the physical experience — such as eating if you are hungry — you can prevent unnecessary misunderstandings. So if you find yourself arguing or being irritated, make sure you first take care of your body, and understand that your irritation is not primarily emotional or psychological; rather, there is a simple physical need calling for your attention.

---

[*] Rashi writes, אם בא לישן מתוך שמחה (מילי דבדיחותא) מראין לו חלום טוב / "If one goes to sleep with joy (through humor), they will be shown a good dream": Rashi, *Shabbos*, 30b.

Similarly, it is unwise to discuss marriage or other significant matters when we are tired or depleted. When the body is exhausted, the mind can easily mistake physical fatigue for emotional or relational strain. We should therefore avoid, at all costs, evaluating life, relationships, or work while lying in bed exhausted. Such conversations require clarity and presence. It is best to wait until we are well rested and physically comfortable before engaging in them, whether with one another or within ourselves.

NEVER WALK INTO YOUR HOME HUNGRY:

On a practical and preventive level, one wise habit can make a world of difference: never walk into your home hungry. Especially after a long and stressful day, hunger can amplify irritation and make even the smallest things feel overwhelming.

Instead, take a few moments before you come into the door to nourish yourself, just enough to take the edge off.

This small act of self-care creates a buffer, softens the edges, and allows you to enter your home with a calmer mind and a gentler heart. Rather than bringing tension into your home, you arrive more relaxed, centered, ready to connect, to give, and to receive.

WHEN NEEDED, EXPRESS YOUR NEED TO BE ALONE:

One should always be communicative to their spouse and never shut them out or give them the silent treatment. Even if we are not in the mood to speak, we can tell them that. Let your spouse know gently: 'I am feeling stressed out, and it has nothing to do with you. I just need a little space to reset.' This way, your spouse understands that your need for space is not a reflection of your feelings toward them, but a necessary step for you to regain your balance.

Appendix

FREQUENTLY ASKED QUESTIONS & ANSWERS ON SOULMATES AND MARRIAGE

Q) *Does every person have only one perfect match or true soulmate?*

A) Yes. Every soul has both a masculine and feminine dynamic. Your perfect soulmate is your other half, complementing and completing you in a unique way, although your soul is also 'complete' and 'whole' on its own.

Q) *Does every* Gilgul */ reincarnation have a different soulmate?*

A) Yes. This is because in each incarnation, different aspects of our soul become more dominant and revealed, and each soul dimension embodies both masculine and feminine qualities. To simplify, each dimension of soul represents another quality. For example, if in a past life we have activated the element of Chesed / loving kindness, in this life we may be called to activate the element of Gevurah / discipline and order. In one incarnation, we may have been wealthier and we learned lessons about giving, while in another life, we may have been poorer and learned lessons about receiving.

Q) *If every soul has a counterpart in their soulmate, does that mean the two souls always reincarnate together to meet and marry?*

A) Not necessarily.

Q) *If one half of a soulmate-pair reincarnates, what happens to that half? Do they still marry?*

A) Yes, it is possible for them to marry and live happily. They may marry other souls that share a common root soul, even if not their 'perfect other half'. Adam, as the physical parent of humanity as well as its spiritual primogenitor, has a soul from which all other souls emanate.* Souls rooted in different parts of Adam's 'body' — for example, the head, hands, heart, or feet — exhibit different inclinations. 'Head souls' lean towards intellectual pursuits, 'hand souls' show physical dexterity, 'heart souls' brim with emotions, and 'feet souls' are action-oriented. Souls with a shared root often gravitate towards each other and can even marry and have happy marriages.

Q) *Can a person marry the wrong person for them?*

A) Yes. A person has free will and may sometimes choose to marry someone who is not truly right for them, and may do so for the wrong reasons.** A person may be drawn to marry for superficial reasons, the allure of beauty, wealth, or status. Yet rather than elevating or inspiring them to grow into their highest potential,

---

* Adam is the parent of humanity and the soul: *Sanhedrin*, 38a. *Sha'ar HaGilgulim*, Hakdamah 12. Ramak, *Shiur Komah*, Chap 2. See also *Medrash Rabbah*, Shemos, 40:3. *Tanchumah*, Ki Tissa, 12. *Tanya, Igeres HaKodesh*, 7.
** *Kiddushin*, 70a.

such a marriage can have the opposite effect. Their spouse may, consciously or not, pull them downward, physically, mentally, emotionally, or spiritually, draining rather than uplifting them.

Q) *If a person can really marry the wrong person, does that mean that every bad marriage was a waste?*

A) No. Perhaps it was the wrong person, not your soulmate, nor someone who lifted you or activated your Tikun. Yet, from the bigger picture of *Yediah* / Divine Knowing and Providence, everything in life, even our mistakes, carry meaning and purpose. Nothing is mere happenstance or accidental. Perhaps a certain child needed to come into this world through your relationship, or there were important lessons about yourself that you could only learn by marrying that person. Either way, it was part of the Divine plan.

There are no missteps or errors in Divine Providence. If a wedding took place and you entered into marriage, it was ordained from Above. You might look back and feel that your union was rushed, or perhaps born of deep but fleeting emotions, and therefore conclude that it must have been a mistake. You may tell yourself you should not have yielded to the pressure and rushed into the marriage. Yet perhaps the opposite is true: that inescapable sense of urgency was itself proof that it was the Divine will, showing that you did not truly have a choice. You were destined to marry at that moment, for a Tikun to be created, lessons to be learned, transformations to unfold, and perhaps new life to be welcomed into the world. In retrospect, this marriage had to occur. At this point, all you can and should do is release any anger, guilt, or shame you are still holding onto, and move forward.

Q) *What if a couple was happily married for many years and then grew apart and divorced? Does that imply that their bond as spouses was never real? Or does it mean that the love and connection that they felt for each other during their closer years was just an illusion?*

A) Here, we need to understand 'soulmates' on a deeper, more nuanced level.

Souls are multifaceted, and have multiple layers and dimensions that play out in different time periods. Sometimes, a particular aspect of a soul is connected to a specific person for a certain period, and this connection can be profound and real. That connection may serve its purpose for a season or stage in life, and then evolve or shift.

In some cases, another aspect of the soul is set aside for another person at a different stage of life. This does not diminish the significance of the first connection, nor does it invalidate the previous marriage. It simply reflects the complexity of human soul connections, that one person may be meant to play a crucial role in their life at one point, and another person may be called into that role at a later stage.

Q) *During the time someone is married to the 'wrong' person, what happens to their soulmate?*

A) Either he or she never gets married, or they find another soul that shares the same root as their own and marry them, and maybe even have a happy marriage. In this way, it is possible

that your soulmate is married to someone else.* It is also possible, although less likely, that for the purpose of Tikun, soul
correction, the other soul did not incarnate in this lifetime.

Q) *Will soulmates always eventually end up together in
each incarnation?*

A) If they are *Zocheh* / meritorious, they will end up together.**
Finding your Bashert requires merit, and yet, *Bashert* means
'destined one'. You need merit to find your destined one. Our
sages say, "Finding one's soul-mate is as great a miracle as the
splitting of the sea." The Sea of Reeds was created solely on
the condition that it would part for Klal Yisrael, the People
of Israel, as they were escaping their enslavement in Egypt.
As the pre-destined time approached and they stood on the
shore of the sea, the waters refused to part. The sea only split
for them once their true nature was revealed through a heroic
act of ultimate faith. As the Egyptian army was approaching
from behind, and the sea remained in front of them, blocking their way to freedom, Nachshon, a member of the tribe
of Yehudah, walked straight into the sea. The waters finally
parted as they reached his nose. This is a beautiful example of
a 'Divinely decreed' event occurring in the *Zechus*, the merit
of one's actions.

Q) *Our sages teach that, on the one hand, we are paired with our spouse
based on our deeds, and on the other hand, forty days before the creation of a child, a Heavenly Voice issues forth and proclaims: 'The*

* As our sages teach, שמא יקדמנו אחר ברחמים: *Moed Katan,* 18b.
** *Zohar* 1, 229a.

daughter of so-and-so is destined to marry so-and-so'. Furthermore, these two statements are not contradictory, rather, the latter teaching refers to a 'first match,' and the former to a 'second match'. In other words, the first person we marry (and hopefully the only one) is Divinely orchestrated and our soulmate. And the 'second match' — supposing a person marries a second time — is based on merit. So, the question is, if I seem to find my true happiness and companionship in my second marriage, and did not find it in my first, does this still mean that my spouse in the second marriage was not destined for me and is not my soulmate?

First, let us clarify a subtle point often misunderstood: the Heavenly proclamation is said to occur forty days 'before the *formation* of the fetus', not 'before its creation'. In other words, it takes place forty days before the child is *formed*, which means at the moment of conception, since the full formation of the fetus occurs forty days after conception.

Secondly, it is vital to understand that the terms "first match" and "second match" do not necessarily correspond to the chronological order of one's relationships, such as a first or second spouse. Rather, they refer to an ontological order, a hierarchy of soul connection. The 'first' relationship is ordained by Heavenly decree, while the 'second' relationship arises from a person's choices and decisions.* Indeed, a person can marry his or her 'first' match in a second or even later marriage, and be married in his first marriage to his 'second' match. This is precisely why our Sages do not speak in terms of a "first or second spouse," but rather of

---

* *Shevilei Emunah,* Nesiv 3:1.

a "first or second match." It is not a matter of sequence, but of essence.

On a deeper level, we can understand the concept of 'first' and 'second' matches and how these archetypes can both manifest within a single marriage. Each of us has a first match, a soulmate, who we ideally marry the first time around. This soulmate is intrinsically connected to our own soul. However, to truly 'receive' our soulmate and live together in happiness and harmony, we must 'deserve' them; they must *become* our second match. We 'earn' and merit our rightful soulmate by doing the internal work necessary to recognize them as our soulmate. Happy marriages involve more than simply 'finding the right person'; to marry, one must actually *be* the right person in order for both spouses to recognize and be recognized as soulmates.

Another, perhaps, even deeper perspective is that while we hopefully marry our soulmate, our 'first' match, the soul gifted to us by the Heavenly Voice — yet over time, our spouse becomes a reflection of who we are, our 'second' match, the one based on our deeds. Our spouse mirrors our actions and behaviour. In simple terms, you get what you deserve, for better or for worse. If you consistently act with kindness, compassion, and sensitivity towards your spouse, they will respond in kind, and you will find yourself in a loving, caring, kind relationship. Conversely, negative behaviour will also be mirrored back to you. If you find yourself in a difficult marriage (and assuming your spouse is an emotionally healthy person, and was at one time a loving spouse), you need to ask yourself the question of what am I putting into the marriage? Am I being the 'kind self' that

I was when we were married? Usually, when you are married to your first match, what you put in is what you take out, and your marriage is your reflection. In simple terms, you get what you give. Your relationship, like a mirror, reflects your own inner world back to you.

If you have a second match, they too, with time, become a reflection of your actions, 'according to your deeds'. Ideally, you come to mirror each other in the most beautiful and elevated way, so that you can honestly say: 'At first, I married the person I "needed," the one who was sent to challenge me, refine me, and help me with my inward Tikun. But now, I am married to the person I truly 'want' — not out of need, but out of choice, from a place of love and openness.'

Q) If a person has been married twice or even multiple times, in the time of Moshiach and Techiyas HaMeisim / *the Resurrection, with which spouse will that individual be married to and reunited?*

A) At the time of the resurrection, every individual will be reunited with their true soulmate, their 'first match' (whether that was their first marriage or not). Souls that share the same primordial root will remain eternally connected.[*] For those who have remarried, such as after the loss of a spouse, they will return to their first wife, their 'first match'.[**]

Again, if their first spouse was not their true soulmate or 'first match', the situation may be different.[***]

[*] *Sha'ar HaGilgulim*, Hakdamah 10.

[**] *Zohar* 1, 61b. Ben Ish Chai *Rav Poalim*, Part 2, Sod Yesharim 2. *Matzav Ha-Yashar*, Teshuvah 7. *Ma'avar Yavok*, Ma'amar 2, Chap. 7.

[***] *Zera Emes*, Part 2, Siman 146. See *Yabia Omer 7*, Yoreh Deah, Siman 40.

Q) As mentioned, every soul has both a masculine and feminine dynamic, and your soulmate is the masculine to the feminine and the feminine to the masculine, the other half that complements and completes you. But if every Neshamah / *soul is also 'complete' and 'whole' on its own, would it be correct to say that each soul is made up of the Ten Sefiros, and these already encompass both their masculine and feminine qualities?*

A) Yes. In general, there are the Ten Cosmic Sefiros, and there are the Ten Sefiros within our own consciousness as well. In short the ten are as follows; Chochmah / Wisdom and Intuition, Binah / Reason and Cognition, Da'as / Knowledge and Awareness, Chesed / Lovingkindness & Expansion, Gevurah / Strength and Restriction, Tiferes / Compassion and Balance, Netzach / Victory and Ambition, Hod / Humility and Gratitude, Yesod / Focus & Relationship, Malchus / Nobility and Receptivity. Each 'half' of Neshamah, so to speak, comprises ten dimensions, which collectively form a whole that includes both the feminine and masculine aspects. For example, there is both a masculine dimension of Binah (reason and cognition) and a feminine quality of Binah, and the same is true with all the Sefiros.

For this reason, the Tzemach Tzedek wanted to stop giving advice after the passing of his Rebbetzin, because he sensed that without his wife, he lacked, perhaps, the feminine intelligence essential for guiding his disciples. This is in line with what our sages say, "any man whose (first) wife dies…his ability to offer counsel diminishes."*

---

*כל אדם שמתה אשתו בימיו...עצתו נופלת :Sanhedrin, 22a. Here is an essential teaching

Q) In light of the above, what is the relationship between the two souls before their marriage and their eventual reunion? Are there two separate people, each with their own Bechirah Chofshis */ free choice, and thus subject to two separate and entirely different experiences of* Din *and* Cheshbon */ accounting and judgment?*

A) Yes. Each soul retains its own Bechirah, free choice, and is individually accountable. Every person is fully responsible for their own life and actions.

Q) Do any actions of one spouse, even before they marry, affect the other spouse?

A) Yes, but only *L'Zechus* / for merit. The Mitzvos, the positive deeds done by one spouse can have a positive effect on the other, even before marriage.*

---

from the Zohar 1, Lech Lecha: בההיא שעתא דאפיק קודשא בריך הוא נשמתין לעלמא, כל
אנון רוחין ונשמתין כלהו כליל דכר ונוקבא דמתחברן כחדא....וכד (מחא) מטא עידן דזווגא דלהון.
קודשא בריך הוא דידע אנון רוחין ונשמתין מחבר לון כדבקדמיתא... וכד אתחברן אתעבידו חד גופא חד
נשמתא ימינא ושמאלא כדקא חזי... דאי זכי ועובדוי אתכשרן, זכי להההוא דיליה לאתחברא ביה כמה
דנפיק / "At that moment when the Holy One, blessed be He, brings souls into the world, all these spirits and souls are combined as male and female, and they are united as one…And when the time comes for their union, the Holy One, blessed be He, Who knows those spirits and souls, unites them as they were at the beginning…. And when they are united, they become one body, one soul, right and left as they should be… If they are meritorious and their deeds are proper, they merit that which is theirs to unite with as it was in the beginning".

* An example of this is regarding the male's Mitzvah of *Bris* / circumcision. The Bris of the male affects his female soulmate, hence, a woman, even a single woman, can say in *Birkas HaMazon* / Grace after Eating, the words על בריתך שחתמת בבשרנו / "for the Bris which You signed upon *our* flesh…"

Q) Can there be deep 'soul connections' on different levels of relationship, such as between male or female friends, teachers and students, or even parents and children or grandchildren?

A) Yes. As explained, souls that share a common root within the great primordial soul of Adam will be connected to each on a very deep level. At times, the bond and sense of closeness can be extraordinary between souls that are not 'partners'. This connection, deeply rooted in the essence of their souls, often transcends the ties of blood relationships, as well. The feelings of closeness between souls that share a common root is even more powerful, at least on a revealed level, than between siblings. In the words of the great Moroccan Sage, the Ohr HaChayim HaKadosh, "There are some siblings whose minds are distant from each other, yet with others, not related by blood, they will share a profound love. This stems from the root of their souls, for there are souls that are close in their origin and are drawn to each other despite physical distance. Conversely, there are souls that are distant in their origin but come together closely in birth. The souls that are close in their origin will have a deeper love than those close by birth."*

In fact, when two souls that 'literally' share a common root meet each other for the first time, they will experience an almost unavoidable and reflexive attraction and magnetic pull towards each other. Although, this attraction is not always positive.**

When similar souls encounter each other for the first time,

---

* In the words of the Ohr HaChayim, שיש כמה אחים שדעתם מרוחקת זה מזה ועם אנשים אחרים לא קרובים המה להם יאהבו אהבה נפש וזה ימשך משורש הנשמות כי יש נשמות שקרובים בשורשם ונמשכים בריחוק מולידים, ויש נשמות שהם מרוחקים בשורשם ובאים בקירוב מוליד ויותר יאהבו הקרובים בקורבת השורש מהקרובים בבחינת מוליד: *Ohr HaChayim,* Shemos, 32:27.
** *Sha'ar HaGilgulim,* 20.

there may even be aversion. Their internal chemistry could be 'too alike', similar to two objects with identical magnetic energy fields trying to fuse. These two souls may feel challenged by each other, if not consciously, then on a deeper level. A 'spiritual' type of jealousy may arise, pinning one soul against the next, vying for more energy from their Source. If, however, these two individuals attain a more evolved measure of spiritual maturity and they are highly developed individuals who experience a level of *Ruach HaKodesh* / Divine intuition, then instead of an abhorrence and dislike, a beautiful love can be nurtured and flourish between them.*

Supposing these two powerful energy sources do in fact coalesce and manage to resonate with each other, the vibrations that are created would be eminently more powerful. Similarly, light that is generated through friction and discord can be stronger than light that is produced in harmony and uniformity.

There is also another phenomenon, and that is that souls that experienced a closeness on higher dimensions of reality, souls that were connected in the world of Gan Eden, Paradise, will be attracted to each other in the physical universe as well. "It is stated in the holy books that the reason we sometimes see two people who deeply love each other, even though they were not acquainted before, but have recently met and come together, and both cling to each other with great love, is because they were neighbors in their dwelling in the Garden of Eden. Now, upon

---

* Ibid. *Pri Eitz Chayim*, Sha'ar Hanhagos HaLimud. *Kehilas Yaakov*, Machlokes.

meeting each other again, the old love that existed between them in the Garden of Eden is rekindled."*

Q) If I am married to my soulmate, then why is it so difficult? Why do I find that my marriage has so many challenges? Does this maybe mean I am not married to my soulmate? Shouldn't everything be much easier if I were truly married to my soulmate?

A) Just because something is challenging does not mean it is not true or worth it. Our sages teach that it would have been *Noach* / easier for a human not to have been created, but that certainly does not mean not being created is better; it is just easier.** It is easier for the soul to remain in a spiritual realm and not descend into this world. However, it is certainly worth it to come down and create a dwelling place in this world for the Divine Presence through our refined consciousness, beneficial actions and Mitzvos.

This is also true of marriage. No one guarantees that marriage will be easy. Just because you married your Bashert, it does not mean that your marriage will always feel easy, smooth or effortless. Even your relationship with your own self may not always be settling.

---

* In the words of the Noam Elimelech, ואיתא בספרים הטעם שאנו רואים שלפעמים באים שני בני אדם ואוהבים זה את זה מאוד גם שלא היו מכירים זה את זה מקודם כי אם עתה מקרוב באו ונתוועדו יחד ושניהם דבקו יחדיו באהבה רבה, והטעם מחמת שהיו שכנים זה אצל זה בישיבתם בגן עדן יחד ועתה בבואם להדדי נתעורר בהם אהבה הישנה שהיתה בהם בגן עדן: *Noam Elimelech*, Vayechi. *Ohr HaGanuz LaTzadikim*, Bo. See also, Rebbe Eliezer of Worms, *Sodei Razya, Chochmas HaNefesh*, p. 382, regarding soulmates.

** *Eiruvin*, 13b. *Nishmas Chayim*, Ma'amar 2:6. *Likutei Torah*.

The assumption that being with a soulmate means everything should be effortless is a misconception. In reality, marriage — especially to one's true soulmate — is the arena in which a person is refined, challenged, and given the opportunity to fulfill their ultimate purpose and Tikun.

Your soulmate is not just a perfect match who makes your life happy or less lonely; rather, they are the person through whom one can reach their highest potential. That includes working through challenges, healing the past and childhood wounds, and transforming difficult patterns into opportunities for growth. The purpose of marrying your soulmate is achieving your Tikun, soul elevation, correction, and perfection.

Beyond all the external concerns that accompany marriage and parenthood, health challenges, educational responsibilities and financial pressures, there lies a deeper challenge, the challenge of truly sharing your life with another person. Yet, it is precisely within this sacred union that we come to know ourselves and blossom into the person we desire to be and are destined to become. In marriage, every hidden facet of our character is revealed, inviting us to grow in ways we never could alone. Marriage is the crucible in which *Emunah* / faith is directly tested; our belief in Hashem and in our own potential is forged within its fires. Indeed, it is 'easier' to be alone. When we are single, interpersonal disagreements can often be sidestepped and solitude can offer a retreat; in marriage, there is no running away. You are called to face your spouse, to navigate life's trials side by side, and to transform each challenge into an opportunity for shared growth and deeper connection. It is precisely in marriage that people attain their Tikun, soul elevation and correction.

Each spouse helps the other attain the exact Tikun they need. As explained earlier, sometimes people marry the person similar to the parent they had a challenge with, and one of the functions of the marriage is to recreate that scenario or sense of challenge in some, perhaps subtler, way, in order to overcome it and move on.

Each spouse has to recognize the specific Tikunim of their spouse and take responsibility to support their healing. These can be emotional wounds or even spiritual wounds that they need to heal, caused by emotional trauma, and sometimes 'religious trauma' associated with the way Torah and Mitzvos were presented to them in their youth. However, your own personal Tikun is not actually accomplished by having your spouse heal you; rather, your Tikun is supporting your spouse in *their* healing. This orientation requires creativity, mindfulness and compassion, and steering clear of reactivity, and automatic and unconscious behaviors in relation to your spouse's incomplete Tikun, especially avoiding negative or hurtful responses to their current state. It also helps you avoid frustrations in the marriage, so you can be radically present for your spouse.

It is also important to recognize that your Tikun may change during the time period of your marriage. For example, a person may go through a life-altering experience — such as illness, job loss, or a significant personal loss, a 'death' of sorts, and when they emerge from these experiences, they might find that their Tikun has shifted, and now, even within the marriage, they have a new Tikun moving forward. We see an example of this with Yaakov in the Torah. He was destined to marry Rochel, yet his inner transformation while working for Lavan led him to embody some of the positive qualities of his wilder brother Eisav. Having integrated the *Tohu* / 'chaos' of the man of the field, Yaakov became outgoing and wealthy. As a result, he also married Leah, who our sages say was "an outgoing one." This scenario is with two separate people, but the same can also occur within the same marriage.

Q) Should I point out faults in my spouse to help them reach their Tikun?

A) No, absolutely not. Your *Avodah*, your spiritual, mental, emotional and physical work in this world, is only to work on *yourself*. Of course, there might be times when offering 'constructive criticism' to your spouse is appropriate, especially if it can be done with honor and humble kindness. But as a rule, it's important to respect each other's paths and focus only on improving oneself. Your life and Tikun is your business, and your spouse's life and Tikun is their business. Stay in your lane and remain focused on your business.

In fact, the Chidah teaches that a person's behaviour towards Hashem is reflected in how their spouse will treat them. If you feel your spouse is doing something against your will, look and reflect on your own actions and consider whether, on some level, you are doing something against Hashem's will.

In a similar vein, the Baal Shem Tov teaches[*] that your spouse corresponds to your 'words.' If you are not careful with your

---

[*] *Ben Poras Yoseph,* in the end. *Toldos Yaakov Yoseph*, Lech Lecha.

words, the negative effects of your speech may be mirrored in your spouse's behavior. Similarly, any mental, emotional, or spiritual defects in your thoughts may influence how your children relate to you, and your negative actions will impact how your co-workers or acquaintances interact with you.

In other words, everything happening around you, in the 'outer world', is a reflection of your 'inner self.' If you notice something seemingly amiss in others, know that you are seeing this because you are dealing with these very same issues within yourself, even if in a subtle way. Not only do you have the same faults — otherwise you wouldn't have noticed them within others — but in a sense, you are also the orchestrator and the creator of what you see in them. This is why it is best to always keep to your business and just focus on how you can change *yourself*.

Q) What if I am growing, changing, and evolving, but I feel like my spouse isn't, what should I do?

A) This is one of the most painful and challenging dynamics that can arise in a marriage. You are on a path of deep inner work, transforming, evolving spiritually, mentally, emotionally, becoming more committed to growth and Yiddishkeit, and you look at your spouse and feel they are stuck in their status quo. What then? Do you try to push them to grow? Do you wait? What is your role?

There is no one-size-fits-all answer, because every relationship is unique and complex. But there *are* a few guiding principles that can help you navigate this.

First of all, it is important to understand that if you have done deep, honest work, then some of that should have naturally manifested or reflected within your spouse. Maybe the change in them is not the same as the change in you, but *something* should have shifted within your spouse as well, at least through osmosis, assuming they are receptive on some level. If absolutely nothing shifts on your spouse's end, then it may be that the issue is not only about different trajectories in life, but something more fundamental, that there is something flawed in the relationship itself.

Let's assume otherwise, and that you are generally in a positive relationship, other than this issue. Then you need to go a little deeper. You need to double down, even more, on your own inner work. Not out of frustration, but with humility. It is not your job to change your spouse. That is *their* journey. Your work is to become the best version of yourself: more compassionate, more open, more loving, more grounded. That kind of inner clarity and presence has a quiet power; it invites others to shift, gently, without pressure.

Also understand that your spouse is your perfect mirror. In a healthy relationship, your spouse reflects back aspects of your own inner state. If you feel like you are being open and giving, but your spouse is closed and stagnant, ask yourself honestly: *"Is there a place where I am still closed off? Where I am being rigid, or judgmental, or subtly superior?"* Sometimes, the very thing we feel is missing in the other is the next frontier in our own growth.

Often couples may think or even say, "This isn't the person I married," and they are probably right. People change, and so do you. Take ownership and know that your behavior, your presence, your words, all have an effect. Your spouse becomes, in many ways, a reflection of who you have been to them. If your spouse has grown distant or disinterested, the first question is not "What happened to them?" but "What have I contributed to this dynamic?" This does not mean self-blame, it means ownership. Ownership is the opposite of the scenario in the Garden of Eden, where Adam blames Chava, and Chava, in turn, blames the Snake. Pointing the finger and passing responsibility onto others is the beginning of exile. A truly healthy mind asks: "What's my part in this?"

Always, always remember that real change takes time. We live in a culture of instant gratification, but true growth does not work that way; it is a process, so be patient.

People grow in surprising ways, especially when they feel loved and seen, rather than judged. You may discover that, in time, your spouse begins to evolve in their own unique way, not by your prompts, but through the quiet support and presence you provide.

Basically, distinguish your business from your spouse's business. Your growth is your responsibility, and their growth is theirs. Stay in your lane, be an example, and do so with love and compassion.

Q) OK, got it, so my business is my business, my life is my Tikun, and I need to take full responsibility for my thoughts, words, and actions, but what happens if I mess up, should I tell my spouse what I have done? In the name of honesty, should I always share my faults with my spouse?

A) No, certainly not "always." Honesty is a sacred value, but that doesn't mean you must always share everything, especially when doing so may cause unnecessary harm. Suppose you have made a serious mistake that does not directly impact your spouse, yet they don't know about it and probably never will. Before disclosing it, ask yourself: What purpose would it serve?

It is a sign of integrity that you feel remorse and are committed to Teshuvah, taking responsibility and doing the inner work to repair what's been damaged. But while honesty is vital in a relationship, it doesn't always require full disclosure of every fault or misstep, especially when sharing it would only cause your spouse unnecessary pain.

Sometimes, the urge to confess is more about relieving your own guilt than it is about serving the other person. What may seem like an act of transparency or love, in truth, is merely a form of emotional dumping, unloading your pain onto your spouse in order to feel lighter yourself.

In such cases, unburdening yourself is not an act of selflessness, but rather selfishness, cloaked in the language of intimacy and transparency.

Your Teshuvah is your task. Your inner healing is your responsibility. This is your work, not theirs. Turn to Hashem in private. Pour out your heart in prayer. Seek guidance from a trusted spiritual mentor or counselor. All of this allows you to process your mistake in a way that brings true and inner transformation, without compromising your spouse's peace or stability.

Q) A general question about soulmates and Basherts: Do opposites attract? Or are people drawn to those who are similar to themselves?

A) Actually, both scenarios are possible. The debate about whether opposites attract or if similarity draws people together has intrigued humanity for millennia. Some argue that opposites are naturally drawn to each other, much like the earth craves water. Others believe that like attracts like, that shared character traits create the strongest attraction.*

However, the deeper answer transcends these binary arguments. The root of truly wholesome attraction, whether it is between opposite or similar individuals, is the soul's yearning to reunite and become one again with its 'other half'. When this soul-level connection manifests in a relationship between 'opposites', it can become a harmonizing of diversity, and a unity within multiplicity. When it manifests in matches where similarities spark the initial attraction, it can become a more seamless and effortless unity. The Zohar** speaks of spouses as variations on the same quality, with one embodying a harsher aspect and the other a gentler aspect of that quality.

When differences between marriage partners are more pronounced, for example, when an extroverted individual is drawn to an introverted person, an assertive individual to a more passive counterpart, a rigid person to a free-flowing person, or a ce-

---

* *Akeidas Yitzchak*, Sha'ar 8:2, 4. R. Yehudah Abarbanel, *Vikuach Al HaAhavah*.
** Zohar 1, p. 137a.

rebral individual to an emotional one, it suggests that Supernal orchestration is at work. Only a Higher force could cause such opposites to dwell together on a long-term basis. Such spouses were clearly brought together by a Divine declaration at the moments of their conceptions, that 'So-and-so is destined to marry so-and-so.'

Each spouse seeks to find and unite with someone who is 'created in their own image,' so to speak. When the marriage is a union of opposites, 'their own image' in the other may be more hidden, but this image was certainly seen and identified when they 'found' each other. During their life together, their differences may seem to become more pronounced, but if they are true soulmates, they will continue to be drawn and attracted to outwardly revealing their symmetrical equilibrium and their singular 'image'. They may need to actively *create* this balance of energies and capacities, allowing each other to complement their unique character traits. This can, of course, be a challenging process if their interests are very different, but it helps if they can recognize that they do come from the same soul root and image, and that their Creator, as their 'Shadchan', deemed their differences compatible. On the other hand, such marriages can be more passionate, as the other's differences are intriguing and 'out of the ordinary'.

In this type of marriage, soulmates naturally challenge one another to grow and evolve by providing each other with a countervailing force to wrestle against and align with. Each spouse highlights and calls forth the unique talents of the other, while also illuminating the darker areas where support and encouragement are needed, to become the best versions of themselves.

Marriages between *outwardly similar* people function through symmetrical equilibrium. When both parties share common interests, activities, and approaches to life, they reflect each other's qualities rather than balancing each other out through challenging and complementing. They function in a mirroring capacity. This reinforces the other's current level and perspective. Such a marriage will also foster growth, but the spouses may grow together in similar ways, rather than growing in opposing ways together.

Both types of relationship hold the infinite potential to provide each spouse with the conditions and consciousness necessary to evolve into the person they were meant to become. What is more, within a single marriage itself, it is possible for both these dynamics to manifest at different times, depending on the particular circumstances and stages of the marriage. Sometimes the dynamic of opposites comes to the forefront, and sometimes the element of sameness.

It is also important to keep in mind that whether you marry someone who feels very similar to you or someone whose way of being is entirely different, both are possible and meaningful paths. On the other hand, one should not marry someone simply *because* of their difference or sameness. If you are marrying them because they resemble yourself, then you are marrying those similarities, not the entirety of the person. Similarly, if you are drawn to them because they are different, you are captivated by the contrast, not by the essence and the fullness of who they are. The fullness of you needs to be married to the fullness of the other.

Our sages say, "It is forbidden for a man to betroth a woman until he sees her, lest he see something that he finds repulsive in her after the betrothal, and she will become repugnant to him, which will cause him not to like her, and the Torah says, 'And you shall love your neighbor as yourself'."* "Seeing" your future spouse, as our sages teach, is not speaking only of physical sight. It also means seeing the whole person; their presence, their essence. The Torah instructs us to truly "see" before we commit, not so that we can fall in love with what we see, but to make sure that we do not perceive traits within the other that may *prevent* us from loving them. If there is something physical, emotional, or behavioural that you see and you sense that it will cause aversion or annoyance, this is a sign to pause and contemplate your trajectory. Since marriage is about choosing the entirety of the person, a real aversion will become a barrier to your ability to love them fully. Similarly, when you marry someone for their beauty, wealth, status, or even their brilliance or creativity, you are not truly choosing *them*; you are choosing a trait, a facet of who they are.

Q) *Before discovering their Bashert, people often go through a dating process, which means they will have met and connected with other people before they have met and connected with their actual spouse. The question arises: why do some people need to date other people before finding their soulmate?*

A) Every person you date brings you one step closer to your Bashert. The Chassidic Rebbe, Reb Chayim of Tzanz, was known for

---

* *Kiddushin*, 41a.

his meticulous practice of offering *Shadchanus* / match-making money, a fee or gift given to the one who introduced the couple, even if the couple only met once or even the idea was only discussed and they did not marry. He would explain that forty days before the creation of a child, a Heavenly Voice issues forth, proclaiming, "The daughter of so-and-so is destined to marry so-and-so." However, initially, this is posed as a question: "Is the daughter of so-and-so destined to marry so-and-so?" Many souls are then suggested and brought before the Heavenly tribunal until it is finally proclaimed, "Yes, this is in fact the one — so-and-so is destined to marry so-and-so." All the suggested matches are the souls first proposed in Heaven but subsequently passed over, as they were not yet the perfect match. In this way, every suggestion here on earth brings one closer to their true soulmate.

On a more practical level, every person you date allows you to learn something new about yourself, who you are, and what you are seeking in a spouse. Sometimes, people need to make adjustments and refinements in themselves until they truly understand who they are. Then, based on that, they can pinpoint what qualities they desire in a spouse, and what type of person will be the companion who will help them live their optimal life, physically, emotionally, mentally, and spiritually. This process may take time, but the more self-awareness you have, the quicker it can unfold.

Q) How does one go about finding their Bashert?

A) You need to find your own self, your own *soul*, before you can find your soul-*mate*. Without self-awareness, it is entirely possible that your Bashert would be standing right in front of you for years, and you would never know. Recognizing them begins with self-recognition. If you do not yet know who you are, how will you know who is meant for you?

In this way, the first step to finding your Bashert is to more deeply discover your true self, and your unique set of values, strengths, deficiencies, shadows, and callings. Only then can you begin the second step: discerning who will help you grow. Sometimes a potential match mirrors your qualities, and would probably harmonize with your purpose and reinforce your path. Another potential match might present as your opposite, and would probably challenge, and complement you through counterbalancing your qualities, refining you in ways that only contrast can. The journey to marrying one's Bashert is ultimately a journey toward one's true self and one's essential wholeness. For only when you are whole enough to give and humble enough to receive, can you truly recognize and be recognized by the one who was meant for you all along.

Now, once you have this self-knowledge and a clear sense of who you are and what you seek, it is important to 'dream' it and create a mental and inner space within yourself for that person to be able to enter.

In the original story of Adam and Eve, the Torah says, "So Hashem cast a deep sleep upon Adam; and, while he slept, took one of his sides and closed up the flesh at that site. And Hashem fashioned the side that had been taken from Adam into a woman, bringing her to Adam." Adam (who was at this point a composite of a male self and a female self, as explained in great length above), was put to sleep and within his 'dream', his *Tzeil* / 'shadow' or imagination, Chava, his wife was created.

Earlier in that story, Hashem "created Adam in His own image, in the image of Elokim He created; male *and* female He created them." But what is the Divine image? And what does "Male and female He created them" mean? 'image' can also be understood as 'imagination'. For instance, when a person daydreams on a Monday morning at work, imagining himself on vacation, this is his 'image'. Similarly, he may envision himself at a later point in life, retired and enjoying, with his wife, the fruits of his labor. Coming back to the present moment, he goes back to working hard and long hours to reach his envisioned 'images'.

Hashem had an 'image' (as it were) of a world, and then created it. This image was to create the space for something 'other' than Himself to emerge. The Infinite Light desired a finite world in which to have a relationship, so to speak, with us, His creation. This is the Divine image within the Creator, so to speak, and we too are created in this Divine image, hence, with the power to create life through our own 'image'.

Let's delve a little deeper. The Torah states, "In the image of Elokim He created them; male and female He created them." This signifies that within the Infinite Light itself (so to speak), there exists (the potential for both) the 'male' giver and creator, and the 'female' receiver and creation. In this way, Adam, who embodied both male and female aspects, was created in the Divine image, and we too possess these dual qualities.

The male aspect represents our creative power and active imagination, while the female aspect is the vessel that receives, holds and nurtures our imagination. In simple terms, to find your Bashert and have a healthy marriage, you need to envision and create the space within yourself for your soulmate — the 'female to your male' (whether you are a man or woman) — to enter. Otherwise, there is no room within yourself for the other. Once you imagine and create that space through your own 'image', your intended spouse will appear.

Yet, to properly envision your life and your future spouse, you must first have a clear understanding of your own self-image. Finding your Bashert is a natural outcome of finding yourself. You need to have a healthy self-image, feel comfortable with yourself, recognize your special qualities, your unique intelligences, and where you excel. You enter the path of your personal Tikun when you pursue and follow your positive traits, while refraining from activating your weakness and negative traits. You need to first step into your path of Tikun and your reason for being in this life, and then you can more easily recognize the individual who will help you achieve that Tikun.

When considering a potential match, it is natural to ask, "Is this person right for me?" Perhaps a more mature question is, "Am I right for them?" Too often, one's focus is inward, centered on their own needs, desires, and satisfaction. But love calls you to go beyond yourself and your own wants, and to ask, "Can I be a source of goodness, growth, and support for this person?"

More than just compatibility, the real question is whether you are good for each other, whether the relationship can become a shared sacred space for growth, in which both individuals are challenged, refined, and elevated. A healthy relationship is not defined by comfort alone, but by mutual potential for courageous self-transformation. Marriage is a partnership in becoming, in which each spouse unselfconsciously serves as a mirror and catalyst for the other.

Also, if you truly want to form a deeper connection with someone whom you intuit could be your soulmate, but you are not yet sure how to 'break the ice' and bridge the divide between your two inner worlds, you need to understand the interpersonal dynamics of *Makif* / 'surrounding light' and *Penimi* / 'internal light'. A Makif is a passageway that allows two people to encounter each other. If someone is entirely Penimi, inward and self-contained, with no projection outward, they are not at that moment open to your approach. A true meeting of selves cannot begin while the other is closed off to you. But when a person radiates openness, warmth, and receptivity, a welcoming Makif, 'surrounding light', it may be an invitation to relate. When we approach, perhaps with a greeting, or a lighthearted or humorous word, we are extending our Makif. When laughter is shared, an interface between two Makifim, a shared space of mutuality, may be formed. Then an honest encounter or conversation may arise.

You cannot simply walk up to someone and begin discussing existential matters. First, you need to detect whether the person is projecting a Makif, a sense of openness, and an outer expression of receptivity. If that is present, you can begin to project your own Makif. If your Makif is received and a shared space is created, the discussion you want to have might then be possible. Even then, it might take time for a true deep dialogue and relationship to emerge. Depth takes time to unfold. You need to consistently and with full permission step into their space, invite them to step into yours, and through the subtle interplay of these Makifim, a doorway to genuine connection may open.

Q) In addition to the specific qualities that will help me grow, what general qualities should a person seek when looking for a spouse?

A) The number one quality should be kindness; a generous, open person that you feel you can connect with.

Yet, before delving any further, it would do us well to understand that individuals always possess *Bechirah* / free choice, even when seeking their 'destined' spouse. One can act contrary to the Heavenly voice that declared "so-and-so is destined for so-and-so" and alter their destiny.

On a deeper level, 'destiny', more accurately called *Yedia* / Divine foreknowledge, does not actually contradict Bechirah. Paradoxically, both realities exist at once, at every moment. Absolute *Yedia* and *Hashgacha Peratiyus* / 'orchestration through Divine Providence' coexist with absolute *Bechirah* / Free Choice in all details of creation. As Rebbe Akiva so eloquently said, הכל צפוי, והרשות נתונה / "Everything is foreseen *and* permission is granted."*

---

* *Avos*, 3:15. Hashem can be revealed in opposites, as in the Aron in the *Kodesh HaKodashim* / Holy of Holies: *Yuma*, 21a. Maharal, *Gevuras Hashem,* Hakdama, 2. See also the Rebbe Rashab, *Sefer HaMa'amarim,* 5649, p. 274. Predicated on this idea of revelation in opposites, there is the reconciliation of *Yedia* / Divine Knowing and Providence and Bechirah, free choice — this idea is first explained by the Mahara M'panu: *Asara Ma'amaros*, Ma'amar Chikur Din, 4, 9. The idea of

Of course, Bechirah plays a vital role from our perspective, and it is paramount that we approach such decisions with the utmost seriousness and mindfulness.

A tradition tells us that if you wish to understand an issue well, look in the Torah where the idea first appears. Regarding the idea of Shidduchim, one could look at the Pesukim, verses mentioning the qualities of Rivkah, when she was chosen for Yitzchak. This is the first recorded Shidduch in the Torah, although marriage was mentioned earlier. In this story, Avraham, Yitzchak's father, sends his servant Eliezer on a mission to find a suitable wife for his son. Eliezer soon encounters Rivkah at a well, a symbol of flowing water representing nurturing and giving (Later on, Yaakov and Moshe, too, find their spouses at a well). Rivkah prominently demonstrates generosity and kindness when she offers to give water to Eliezer and his animals.

Hashgacha / providence and *Hashgacha Peratiyus* / specific Divine Providence *in every detail of Creation* was only revealed recently in history, through the teachings of the Baal Shem Tov. As time advances away from the dawn of Creation, the gift of Bechirah expands ever more, becoming more and more available. The absolute Oneness of Hashem's Providence and the power of free choice arise simultaneously. Just as Hashgacha Peratiyus was only revealed recently, individual freedom of choice is also a truth that is becoming more and more revealed with the passage of time. ובאמת בדורות הראשונים היה להם כחות ודעות גדולות, רק כח בחירה לא היה להם. יען שהיה תיכף אחר בריאת עולם, לכן היה בקושי גדול... בדורות הראשונים שהיו קרובים לקודם בריאת העולם, שאז לא היה כל הבריאה הוי' בפני עצמה לכן לא היה להם בחירה, ובכל דור יש להם בחירה יותר / "And truly, the early generations possessed great intellectual and spiritual capacities, yet they lacked true free choice. This was because they lived soon after the creation of the world, and therefore, the distinction between existence and its Creator was not yet fully established. Thus, free will was limited. But as the generations progressed, growing further from the moment of creation, the sense of existence as something distinct became stronger, and with it, the capacity for free choice increased": *Beis Yaakov*, Bereishis, 10.

Eliezer is the servant of Avraham, and he knows that the bride chosen for Yitzchak must carry forward the legacy of Avraham and Sarah; she must be a beacon of monotheism and help continue to spread recognition of the Oneness of Hashem. Yet, he does not approach Rivkah to discuss with her lofty doctrines of Divine Unity to see if she understands or appreciates them. He seeks the sign of a tender, compassionate heart. In Rivkah he beholds someone with boundless generosity, a person of character, unmarred by selfishness and self-centeredness. This is how he recognizes that she is perfectly suited for Yitzchak, and that she will humbly learn from her husband and join him in the mission to magnify Hashem's Presence in the world.

Rivkah clearly has a wonderful character trait of compassion, yet she also shows signs of strength and confidence. When she is asked her opinion regarding the marriage proposal, she accepts it simply and with conviction, demonstrating that she is not passive or resigned to 'fate'. She is fully willing to leave her home behind to embark on a new life, ready to move away from the past and embrace the future. She chooses to move away from her parents, meaning that she does not bring her parents into the marriage, which is a difficult issue that many contemporary marriages struggle with. The Torah presents these traits as praiseworthy for a Shidduch, and we can understand each of them as praiseworthy for both a woman and for a man.

Like all things in life, especially impactful endeavors like choosing the person you hope to spend the rest of your life with, it is not merely a process of effort, but one of faith. One must have *Emunah* / deep trust that Hashem will guide you to the person who is truly meant for Tefilah / prayer is also always essential. One should pray not only to find the right person, but to gain the clarity of mind and heart to recognize them when they do appear. Pray for insight, for inner stillness, and for the awareness to see beyond superficial levels of 'attraction'.

Also, even when and if you feel an initial spark, a magnetic pull, it is important to pause and practice *Hashkata* / quieting of mind and heart. Give yourself some time for calm reflection on both the objective details of the potential match and the spiritual sensations within you. If the sense of connection and happiness remains, if there is still a Mashichas HaLev / pull of the heart, *Daven* / pray again for clarity. If there is clarity, then jump in with all your heart and without hesitation, and don't look back.

Q) *This is more of a theoretical question, but it can also be a practical one as well: who finds whom?*

As a man, should I actively seek my partner, or will she find me? Conversely, if I were a woman, would the approach change?

A) In general, Chazal tell us, "It is the way of a man to pursue a woman." * Yet, the Arizal speaks of the two days of Rosh Ha-shanah in relation to Leah and Rochel, the two wives of Yaakov. Leah represents the inner 'world of thought', the first day of Rosh Hashanah, and Rochel the outer 'world of speech' and physicality, the second day of Rosh Hashanah. All *Zivugim /* matches and marriages that will be formed in the coming year are drawn down during the time of judgment on Rosh Ha-

---

* In the words of our sages, מפני שדרכו של איש לחזר על אשה... בעל אבידה מחזר על אבידה בעל אבידתו: *Kiddushin*, 2b.

shanah (which is the day on which Adam and Chava became physically separate in order that they could come together face to face). In general, there are two types of matches: either the male goes out and finds the female, or the female goes toward the male.* Yaakov ventured out and found Rochel at the well, whereas Leah went toward Yaakov.**

When a match begins with the female identifying or approaching her Bashert, it suggests that the judgment predicting their meeting occurred on the first day of Rosh Hashanah, the day of inner, spiritual blessings. This reflects the paradigm of Leah, representing spirituality and *Penimiyus* / inwardness, as Leah is the one who approached Yaakov. Conversely, if the male seeks out and finds the female, it indicates that the match was made on the second day of Rosh Hashanah, the day of outer, physical blessings. This aligns with the paradigm of Rochel, symbolizing physicality and *Chitzoniyus* / externality, as it was Yaakov who went out and identified Rochel.***

Since both approaches are possible, we can understand that there are diverse paths that can lead to uniting with your Bashert. Indeed, the dance between the masculine and feminine is not linear, but circular; sometimes you seek, and sometimes you are found, and often, both are happening at once.

Additionally, in connection to the archetypes of Leah and Rochel, and as a summation of a core truth explored throughout

---

* *Medrash Rabbah*, Bereishis, 63:3.
** Similarly, Rivkah went to encounter Yitzchak, as the Medrash above writes. See also, *Ohr haTorah*, Bereishis, 864.
*** *Bnei Yissaschar*, Tishrei Ma'amar 2:15.

this work, every marriage contains two simultaneous dynamics: a Leah dynamic and a Rochel dynamic.

When Adam sees Chava emerge as a separate being, he exclaims, "This one is bone of my bones and flesh of my flesh…" "Bone of my bone" corresponds to Leah, "flesh of my flesh" corresponds to Rochel."*

The word *Etzem* / bone also means essence. There is an 'essence' connection between spouses, and this is the paradigm of Leah. There is also an 'external' connection between spouses, and this is the paradigm of Rochel.

On an external, Chitzoniyus level, marriage is a relationship between two individuals who meet, choose one another, and build a life together. This is the world of effort, of decision, of creating a bond through will and commitment. Rochel represents the Chitzoniyus, the outer world. Here, marriage is a conscious decision, an act of choosing. The connection is based in flesh, the outer part of the body, not bone / essence; the external rather than the internal. It is more relational than essential.

Yet, on the deeper Penimiyus / inner level, two souls are not separate beings who happened to find each other, they are, in truth, parts of a single greater soul. Their union is not merely formed, it is remembered, rediscovered, a reunion of essence with essence. This connection is intrinsic, eternal, and unbreakable. It is beyond choice, as it were.

---

* *Likutei Torah*, Bereishis. *Sha'ar Ma'amrei Rashbi*, Bereishis. *Ra'maz*, Zohar 1, Bereishis, 26:1.

Leah represents the Penimiyus, the inner world, the hidden dimension. In this realm, there is an almost organic attraction between the feminine and the masculine because they are, in truth, already one. The bond is essential and inevitable. The bond is not constructed, rather revealed.*

Both aspects of marriage are real, vital, and profound. For a marriage to be whole and mature, it must weave together two dimensions: The inner, soul-level bond, symbolized by Leah, a connection that feels destined, beyond words, as if the souls themselves are already intertwined. And the outer, choice-based relationship, represented by Rochel, where the relationship is consciously chosen, nurtured, and expressed through daily acts of kindness, presence, patience, devotion, and commitment.

A true and lasting marriage must hold both: the mystery and the choice, the stillness of being and the movement of becoming.

Leah is the silent, inner knowing; Rochel is the open-eyed, engaged devotion. One is rooted in essence, the other in effort. When these two dimensions are lived simultaneously, marriage becomes a sacred space, a union of destiny and choice, soul and body, inner and outer, spiritual and physical. And ultimately, it becomes a meeting point between Heaven and Earth, between that which is Eternal and that which is lovingly remade anew, day by day.

---

* Hence, even though marriage requires mutual consent, there is an element of positivity, reflecting a place that is 'beyond choice'. In the words of the Ran, *Nedarim*, 30a, אצל נפשה ומשוי ורצונה דעתה מבטלת היא האיש לקדושי מסכמת שהיא מכיון אלא הפקר של כדבר הבעל.

Other Books by Rav Pinson

Rav Pinson on the Torah

Awakenings:

Drawing Life from the Weekly Torah Reading

The deeper teachings of the Torah reveal to us that the weekly Torah reading is connected to the unique energetic properties of that week. Every Torah portion, and thus every week, radiates with a particular quality, a distinct energy that, when understood and received, can bring tremendous guidance and assistance to every facet of our lives.

Delving into the weekly Torah reading and uncovering its overarching theme allows us to apply the power available on that week in our practical life.

We can learn how to harness the Ko'ach, power, of each unique Torah reading to expand consciousness, overcome challenges, gain control of our lives, and come to learn how to serve Hashem, self and others more mindfully, productively and effectively.

Weaving together the various facets of Torah interpretation, from the most esoteric (Kabbalah) and mystical (Chassidus) to the straightforward literal meaning (Peshat), this book is a multi-dimensional tapestry of practical, allegorical, philosophical, and mystical ideas and implications.

Rav Pinson on the Life Cycle

A BOND FOR ETERNITY
Understanding the Bris Milah

What is the Bris Milah – the covenant of circumcision? What does it repre-sent, symbolize and signify? This book provides an in depth and sensitive review of this fundamental Mitzvah. In this little masterpiece of wisdom – profound yet accessible —the deeper meaning of this essential rite of passage and its eter-nal link to the Jewish people, is revealed and explored.

UPSHERNISH: THE FIRST HAIRCUT
Exploring the Laws, Customs & Meanings
of a Boy's First Haircut

What is the meaning of Upsherin, the traditional celebration of a boy's first haircut at the age of three? Why is a boy's hair allowed to grow freely for his first three years? What is the deeper import of hair in all its lengths and variet-ies? What is the meaning of hair coverings? Includes a guide to conducting an Upsherin ceremony.

THE JEWISH WEDDING:
A Guide to the Rituals and Traditions
of the Wedding Ceremony

The Jewish Wedding: A Guide to the Rituals and Traditions of the Wedding Ceremony.

This guide is based on the teachings of Torah, Talmud, Medrash, Zohar, Halacha, Poskim, Kabbalah and Chassidus. By quoting these teachings, we actively draw down the 'presence' of these holy souls who revealed these teachings, thus extending blessings to the bride and groom and all in attendance at the Chupa.

THE MYSTERY OF KADDISH
Understanding the Mourner's Kaddish

The Mystery of Kaddish is an in-depth exploration into the Mourner's Prayer. Throughout Jewish history, there have been many rites and rituals associated with loss and mourning, yet none have prevailed quite like the Mourner's Kaddish Prayer, which has become the definitive ritual of mourning. The book explores the source of this prayer and deconstructs the meaning to better understand the grieving process and how the Kaddish prayer supports and uplifts the bereaved through their own personal journey to healing.

THE BOOK OF LIFE AFTER LIFE

What is a soul? What happens to us after we physically die? What is consciousness, and can it survive without a physical brain? Can we remember our past lives? Do near-death experiences prove immortality?

What is Gan Eden? Resurrection?

Exploring the possibility of surviving death, the near-death experience and a glimpse into what awaits us after this life.

(This book is an updated and expanded version of the book; Jewish Wisdom of the Afterlife)

Rav Pinson on Kabbalah

REINCARNATION AND JUDAISM
The Journey of the Soul

A fascinating analysis of the concept of Gilgul / Reincarnation. Dipping into the fountain of ancient wisdom and modern understanding, this book addresses and answers such basic questions as: What is reincarnation? Why does it occur? And how does it affect us personally?

INNER RHYTHMS
The Kabbalah of Music

Exploring the inner dimension of sound and music, and particularly, how music permeates all aspects of life. The topics range from Deveikus/Unity and Yichudim/Unifications, to the more personal issues, such as Simcha/Happiness and Marirus/ sadness.

THIRTY-TWO GATES OF WISDOM
Into the Heart of Kabbalah & Chassidus

What is Kabbalah? And what are the differences between the theoretical, meditative, magical and personal Kabbalistic teachings? What are the four paths of interpreting the teachings of the ARIzal? What did Chassidus teach? These are some of the fundamental issues expanded upon in this text. And then, more specifically, why are there so many names of G-d and what do they represent? What are the key concepts of these deeper teachings?

The book explores the grand narrative of the great chain of reality, how there was and is a movement from the Infinite Oneness of Hashem to a world of (apparent) duality and multiplicity.

PASSPORT TO KABBALAH
A Journey of Inner Transformation

Life is a journey full of ups and downs, inside-outs, and unexpected detours. There are times when we think we know exactly where we want to be headed, and other times when we are so lost we don't even know where we are. This slim book provides readers with a passport of sorts to help them through any obstacles along their path of self-refinement, reflection, and self-transformation.

THE SEVEN PRINCIPLES:
Towards a Life of Meaning and Purpose
A book on the Seven Mitzvos of Noach

These seven principles will open you up to a new and empowering way of thinking and being in this world.

It will inspire you to engage in life proactively with openness, care, clarity of consciousness and attachment to the Source of life and fulfillment. Overflowing with thought provoking insights, Divine guidance and practical exercises, The Seven Principles is a manual to leading a life of purpose and joy.

THE GARDEN OF PARADOX:
The Essence of Non - Dual Kabbalah

This book is a Primer on the Essential Philosophy of Kabbalah presented as a series of 3 conversations, revealing the mysteries of Creator, Creation and Consciousness. With three representational students, embodying respectively, the philosopher, the activist and the mystic, the book tackles the larger questions of life. Who is G-d? Who am I? Why do I exist? What is my purpose in this life? Written in clear and concise prose, the text, gently guides the reader towards making sense of life's paradoxes and living meaningfully.

THE POWER OF CHOICE:
A Practical Guide to Conscious Living

It is the essential premise of this book that we hold the key to unlock many of the gates that seem closed to us and keep us from living our fullest life. That key we all hold is the power to choose. The Power of Choice is the primary tool that we have at our disposal to impact the world and effect change within our own lives. We often give up this power to outside forces such as the market, media, politicians or peer pressure; or to internal forces that often function beyond our conscious control such as ego, anger, lust, greed or jealousy. Making conscious, compassionate and creative decisions is the cornerstone of living a mature and meaningful life.

MYSTIC TALES FROM THE EMEK HAMELECH

Mystic Tales of the Emek HaMelech, is a wondrous and inspiring collection of stories culled from the Emek HaMelech. Emek HaMelech, from which these stories have been taken, (as well as its author) is a bit of a mystery. But like all good mysteries, it is one worth investigating. In this spirit the present volume is being offered to the general public in the merit and memory of its saintly author, as well as in the hopes of introducing a vital voice of deeper Torah teaching and tradition to a contemporary English speaking audience

————

Rav Pinson on Meditation

————

MEDITATION AND JUDAISM
Exploring the Jewish Meditative Paths

A comprehensive work encompassing the entire spectrum of Jewish thought, from the sages of the Talmud and the early Kabbalists to the modern philosophers and Chassidic masters. This book is both a scholarly, in-depth study of meditative practices, and a practical, easy to follow guide for any person interested in meditating the Jewish way.

————

TOWARD THE INFINITE

A book focusing exclusively on the Chassidic approach to meditation known as Hisbonenus. Encompassing the entire meditative experience, it takes the reader on a comprehensive and engaging journey through this unique practice. The book explores the various states of consciousness that a person encounters in the course of the meditation, beginning at a level of extreme self-awareness and concluding with a state of total non-awareness.

_____

BREATHING & QUIETING THE MIND

Achieving a sense of self-mastery and inner freedom demands that we gain a measure of hegemony over our thoughts. We learn to choose out thoughts so that we are not at the mercy of whatever belches up to the mind. Through quieting the mind and conscious breathing we can slow the onrush of anxious, scattered thinking and come to a deeper awareness of the interconnectedness of all of life.

Source texts are included in translation, with how-to-guides for the various practices.

_____

SOUND AND VIBRATION:
Tuning into the Echoes of Creation

Through our perception of sound and vibration we internalize the world around us. What we hear, and how we process that hearing, has a profound impact on how we experience life. What we hear can empower us or harm us. A defining human capacity is to harness the power sound -- through speech, dialogue, and song, and through listening to others. Hearing is primary dimension of our existence. In fact, as a fetus our ears were the first fully operating sensory organs to develop.

This book will guide you in methods of utilizing the power of sound and vibration to heal and maintain mental, emotional and spiritual health, to fine-tune your Midos and even to guide you into deeper levels of Deveikus / conscious unity with Hashem. The vibratory patterns of the Aleph-Beis are particularly useful portals into our deeper conscious selves. Through chanting and deep listening, we can use the letters and sounds to shift our very mindset, to induce us into a state of presence and spiritual elevation.

———————

VISUALIZATION AND IMAGERY:
Harnessing the Power of our Mind's Eye

We assume that what we see with our eyes is absolute. Yet, beyond our ability to choose what we see, we have the ability to choose how we see. This directly translates into how we experience life. In a world saturated with visual imagery, our senses are continuously assaulted with Kelipa/empty/fantasy imagery that we would not necessarily choose. These images can negatively affect our relationship with ourselves, with the world around us, and with the Divine. This volume seeks to show us how we can alter that which we observe through harnessing the power of our mind's eye, the inner sanctum of our imagination. We thus create a new way to see and experience the world. This book teaches us how to utilize visualization and imagery as a way to develop our spiritual sensitivity and higher intuition, and ultimately achieve Deveikus/Unity with Hashem.

CONTEMPLATING AND TRANSCENDING MIND
Hisbonenus: The Meditative Path of Chabad

What is Hisbonenus / meditative contemplation? And how is it actually practiced? The illustrious first Rebbe of Chabad, the Alter Rebbe, aimed for the deepest teachings of the Torah and Chassidus to be internalized and deeply contemplated. Hisbonenus, the process of focused contemplation, begins by training your mind to dwell, for example, on the unity of Hashem, for extended periods. This practice engages the entire spectrum of your intellect-your Chochmah (wisdom or spark of intuition), Binah (analysis and understanding), and Da'as (knowledge and integration). As you progress, your thoughts will naturally stir your heart and emotions. When your mind contemplates lofty concepts such as the unity of the Creator with all of Creation, emotions of profound love for Hashem and a deep sense of wonder will arise. These emotions become more refined and subtle as you delve deeper, eventually leading to Ayin (transparency of self) and Deveikus ('conscious' unity with the Divine).

When the mind reaches its full potential for concentration and contemplation, it may 'implode' from exhaustion, so to speak, leading to a state of Ayin. This phenomenon shows that we don't have to circumvent or invalidate the intellect to transcend it. Rather, we can use the mind itself as a bridge to the Beyond.

Achieving 'intellectual exhaustion' allows us to transition into a state of Ayin-consciousness and mystical union more easily than trying to leap over the mind or stop thinking entirely. This advanced stage of Hisbonenus involves moving from Binah (understanding) back to Chochmah (supra-rational wisdom), and beyond.

Rav Pinson on The Holidays

THE HAGGADAH:
Pathways to Pesach and the Haggadah

"In every generation a person must regard oneself as having gone out of Mitzrayim / Egypt." This means that when recalling the Exodus, which occurred thousands of years ago, we also need to envision ourselves as being taken out of Mitzrayim and freed from enslavement.

Introducing the Haggadah and the themes of Pesach, this book delves into the greater context of the Festival and the Seder, allowing us to tap into the profound inspiration and Koach / power that Pesach and Seder Night offers.

EIGHT LIGHTS
8 Meditations for Chanukah

What is the meaning and message of Chanukah? What is the spiritual significance of the Lights of the Menorah? What are the Lights telling us? What is the deeper dimension of the Dreidel? Rav Pinson, with his trademark deep learning and spiritual sensitivity guides us through eight meditations relating to the Lights of the Menorah, the eight days of Chanukah, and a fascinating exploration of the symbolism and structure of the Dreidel. Includes a detailed how-to guide for lighting the Chanukah Menorah.

THE PURIM READER
The Holiday of Purim Explored

With a Persian name, a masquerade dress code and a woman as the heroine, Purim is certainly unusual amongst the Jewish holidays. Most people are very familiar with the costumes, Megilah and revelry, but are mystified by their significance. This book offers a glimpse into the hidden world of Purim, uncovering these mysteries and offering a deeper understanding of this unique holiday.

The High Holiday Series:

A CALL TO MAJESTY:
The Mysteries of Shofar & Rosh Hashanah

The Shofar is the preeminent symbol of Rosh Hashanah, waking us up to a time of deep introspection and celebration. But why do we blow the Shofar on this most special of days? While the Torah decrees that the Shofar must be blown, it does not provide a reason. On the deepest level, the Shofar is of course beyond reason altogether, and yet, from within its shape, sound and story, a constellation of "reasons" emerge. Rebirth. Responsibility. Radical Amazement. On a primal vibrational level, the Shofar calls each of us to a place of deeper consciousness and community as we crown the King of All Creation.

A CALL TO MAJESTY delves deeply into the world of Rosh Hashanah and its primary Mitzvah, the sound of the Shofar. Weaving together a multi-dimensional tapestry of practical, allegorical, philosophical, and mystical ideas and implications, the teachings collected herein empower us all to answer the higher calling of the Shofar.

————————

A LIGHTNESS OF BEING:
Your Guide to Yom Kippur

Yom Kippur is unabashedly transformative; the power of the day beckons us to work toward fundamental transformation and Teshuvah / return to who we really are. Often, the word Teshuvah is unfortunately translated as 'repentance'. It is more accurately rendered as 'return', meaning both a return 'from' our states of spiritual alienation and exile, as well as a 'turning to' experiencing our deepest selves. Yom Kippur empowers us to return to our essence, reclaim who we truly are, and live from that place.

A LIGHTNESS OF BEING delves into the powerful and transformative day of Yom Kippur. Weaving together a multi-dimensional tapestry of practical, allegorical, philosophical and mystical ideas and implications, the teachings gathered herein empower us all to enter Yom Kippur and truly feel enlightened, elevated, lighter and transformed.

_____

EMBRACED IN DIVINE SPACE:
The Festivals of Sukkos, Hoshana Rabba
& Simchas Torah

From among all the Yamim Tovim, Sukkos stands out as one of the most elusive and mysterious. While Sukkos is called "the Season of our Joy" - and it is a very joyful time indeed, replete with singing, celebrating, and dancing - it may not be so clear what we are celebrating and why joy is so central to the Yom Tov. Weaving together the various threads of Torah interpretation, from the most esoteric and mystical (Sod / Kabbalah / Chassidus) to the straightforward literal meaning (Peshat), as well as the allegorical (Remez) and homiletical (Derush), this book is a multi-dimensional tapestry of practical, philosophical, and mystical ideas and implications. The graceful interaction of all these elements reveals profound insights which will greatly enrich one's experience of Sukkos.

_____

THE FOUR SPECIES
The Symbolism of the Lulav & Esrog

The Four Species have inspired countless commentaries and traditions and intrigued scholars and mystics alike. In this little masterpiece of wisdom both profound and practical - the deep symbolic roots and nature of the Four Species are explored. The Na'anuim, or ritual of the Lulav movement, is meticulously detailed and Kavanos,, are offered for use with the practice. Includes an illustrated guide to the Lulav Movements.

Rav Pinson on Prayer

INNER WORLDS OF JEWISH PRAYER
A Guide to Develop and Deepen
the Prayer Experience

While much attention has been paid to the poetry, history, theology and contextual meaning of the prayers, the intention of this work is to provide a guide to finding meaning and effecting transformation through the prayer experience itself.

Explore: *What happens when we pray? *How do we enter the mind-state of prayer? *Learning to incorporate the body into the prayers. *Discover techniques to enhance and deepen prayer and make it a transformative experience.

This empowering and inspiring text, demonstrates how through proper mindset, preparation and dedication, the experience of prayer can be deeply transformative and ultimately, life-altering.

ILLUMINATED SOUND:
The Baal Shem Tov on Prayer

In the year 1698 a great light was revealed to the world with the descent of the holy soul of the Baal Shem Tov. In time, the Baal Shem Tov became one of the most important and influential teachers of Torah in all of history, and the founder of Chassidus.

Amongst the vast repository of profound and revolutionary teachings of the holy Baal Shem Tov, the teachings on the path of Tefilah / Prayer are the most elaborate. The teachings of the Baal Shem Tov on Tefilah include some of his most innovative expressions, or Chidushim. Tefilah is the essential and central tenet from which all other teachings flow.

In this masterful and practical text, Rav Pinson revives the awe-inspiring and transformational teachings of the Baal Shem Tov, and illuminates his unique path to Tefilah.

Rav Pinson on Jewish Practice

RECLAIMING THE SELF
The Way of Teshuvah

Teshuvah is one of the great gifts of life. It speaks of a hope for a better today and empowers us to choose a brighter tomorrow. But what exactly is Teshuvah? How does it work? How can we undo our past and how do we deal with guilt? And what is healthy regret without eroding our self-esteem? In this fascinating and empowering book, the path for genuine transformation and a way to include all of our past in the powerful moment of the now, is explored and demonstrated.

WRAPPED IN MAJESTY
Tefillin - Exploring the Mystery

Tefillin, the black boxes and leather straps that are worn during prayer, are curiously powerful and mysterious. Within the inky black boxes lie untold secrets. In this profound, passionate and thought-provoking text, the multi-dimensional perspectives of Tefillin are explored and revealed. Magically weaving together all levels of Torah including the Peshat (literal observation), to Remez (allegorical), to Derush, (homiletic), to Sod (hidden) into one beautiful tapestry. Inspirational and instructive, Wrapped in Majesty: Tefillin, will make putting on the Tefillin more meaningful and inspiring.

SECRETS OF THE MIKVAH:
Waters of Transformation

A Mikvah is a pool of water used for the purpose of ritual immersion; a place where one moves from a state of Tumah; impurity, blockage and death—to a place of Teharah; purity, fluidity and life.

In SECRETS OF THE MIKVAH, Rav Pinson delves into the transformative powers of the Mikvah with his trademark all-encompassing perspective that ranges from the literal, Pshat observation and Halachic implications of the texts, to the allegorical, the philosophical, and finally, to the deep secrets of the Mikvah as revealed by Kabbalah and Chassidus.

This insightful and inspirational text demonstrates how immersion in a Mikvah can be a transformative and life-altering practice, and includes various Kavanos—deep intentions—for all people, through various stages of life, that empower and enrich the immersion experience.

THE MYSTERY OF SHABBOS
Shabbat Rediscovered

Delving into the transformative power of Shabbos. With an all-encompassing perspective that ranges from the literal, Pshat observation and Halachic implications of the texts, to the allegorical, the philosophical, and finally, to the deeper secrets as revealed by Kabbalah and Chassidus, creating an elegant tapestry of thought and experience. THE MYSTERY OF SHABBOS is a profound meditation on the meaning of Shabbos and demonstrates the physical, emotional, mental and spiritual possibilities available and given to us with the gift of Shabbos. Studying and contemplating this inspired text on the depths of Shabbos will unveil a redemptive light in your experience of the Seventh Day -- and by extension, every day of your life.

Rav Pinson on Time

THE SPIRAL OF TIME:
A 12 Part Series on the Months of the Year

VOL 1: THE SPIRAL OF TIME:
Unraveling the Yearly Cycle

Many centuries ago, the Sages of Israel were the foremost authority in the fields of both astronomical calculation and astrological wisdom, including the deeper interpretations of the cycles and seasons. Over time, this wisdom became hidden within the esoteric teachings of the Torah, and as a result was known only to students and scholars of the deepest depths of the tradition. More re cently, the great teachers, from R.Yitzchak Luria (the Arizal) to the Baal Shem Tov, taught that as the world approaches the Era of Redemption, it is a Mitzvah / spiritual obligation to broadly reveal this wisdom.

"The Spiral of Time" is volume 1 in a series of 12 books, and serves as an introductory book to the basic concepts and nature of the Hebrew calendar and explores the special day of Rosh Chodesh.

VOL 2: THE MONTH OF NISAN:
Miraculous Awakenings from Above

The month of NISAN is the first month of the lunar cycle of the year, a month that brings in the spring and a month of redemption. Spring represents a time of plenty, abundance, sunshine, hope, and possibility. Redemption, on whatever level, feels palpable and accessible. In spring, the world is redeemed from the cold winter, the flower is redeemed from the tree, the grass from the earth, and we too feel that redemption is possible. A whole complex of ideas, including newness, redemption, going out of Egypt, and being freed from slavery, is intricately bound with the idea of Aviv / spring and the powerful month of Nisan.

VOL 3: THE MONTH OF IYYAR:
EVOLVING THE SELF
& The Holiday of LAG B'OMER

The month of IYYAR is the second month of the spring, a month that connects the Redemption from Egypt in Nissan with the Revelation of Torah in Sivan. The Chai/ Eighteenth day of the Month is the day we celebrate the Rashbi (Rabbi Shimon Bar Yochai) and the revealing of the hidden aspects of the Torah. This is the 'Holiday' of Lag b'Omer. The book explores the unique quality of this special month, a month that has a Mitzvah of counting the Omer every day. In addition, the book explores the roots and significance of the mystical 'holiday' of Lag b'Omer. Including the customs & Practices of Lag b'Omer, such as, bonfires, bows & arrows, parades, Upsherin, and more.

VOL 4: THE MONTH OF SIVAN:
The Art of Receiving:
Shavuos and Matan Torah

Sivan is the third month of the lunar cycle. One is a singularity. Two is division. Three is harmony, a unity that synthesizes individuality and multiplicity, Heaven and Earth, Spirituality and Physicality. During this month we celebrate Shavuos and the giving of the Torah, the ultimate expression of the unity of the Above and Below and we aspire to connect with the Keser/Crown of Torah that Transcends and yet includes all Worlds. Learning how to truly receive Higher wisdom in our Lower faculties is the mental, emotional, and spiritual exercise of the month.

———————

VOL 5: THE MONTHS OF TAMUZ AND AV:
Embracing Brokenness -
17th of Tamuz, Tisha B'Av, & Tu B'Av

Each month and season of the year, radiates with distinct Divine qualities and unique opportunities for growth and Tikkun.

The summer month of Tamuz and Av contain the longest and hottest days of the year. The raised temperature is indicative of a corresponding spiritual heat, a time of harsher judgement and potential destruction, such as the destructions of the first and second Beis HaMikdash, which began on the 17th of Tamuz and culminated on the 9th and 10th of Av.

A few days later, on Tu b'Av, the darkness is transformed and reveals the greatest light and possibility for new life. During these summer months of Tamuz and Av we embrace our brokenness so that we can heal and transform darkness into light.

———————

VOL 6: THE MONTH OF ELUL:
Days of Introspection and Transformation

Each month of the year radiates with a distinct quality and provides unique opportunities for growth and personal transformation. Elul, as the final month of the spring/summer season is connected to endings. Elul gives us the strength to be able to finish strong, to end well. Elul also serves as a month of preparation for the New Year/Rosh Hashanah.

We inhale our past year, ending with wisdom and then we also gain the wisdom to begin anew and exhale a positive year into being. The mental, emotional, and spiritual objective of this month is introspection and the reclaiming of our inner purity and wholeness.

――――――

VOL 7: THE MONTH OF TISHREI:
A Time of Rebirth & Upward Movement

Each month of the year radiates with distinct Divine qualities and unique opportunities for growth and spiritual illumination. As Tishrei begins the new yearly cycle, it is an appropriate month to introspect, reflect and resolve to move forward and preserve moving forward into the more inward months of the winter. This month creates the space to unburden ourselves from our negativities, and enter a more sacred, grounded sacred space. In Tishrei we are given the gift of forgiveness and then the ability to truly regain our space and inner joy.

――――――

VOL 8: THE MONTH OF CHESHVAN:
Navigating Transitions, Elevating the Fall

Directly on the heels of the inspiring and holiday-filled month of Tishrei, Cheshvan is a month that is quiet and devoid of holidays. In the month of Cheshvan we use the stored up energies of the previous months to self-generate our inspiration and creativity and provide ourselves with the strength to rise up after a fall. In Cheshvan we are entering into a stormier, wetter and colder season. It is a month of transition. The mental, emotional and spiritual objective of this month is to weather the transitions, learn to self-generate and stand tall. And if we do fall, we use the quality of this month to get back up and do so with more conviction, strength, wisdom and clarity.

VOL 9: THE MONTH OF KISLEV:
Rekindling Hope, Dreams and Trust

Kislev is the final month of the fall. Throughout this month, daylight progressively shortens, and the temperatures drop. Towards the end of the month, at the darkest hour, the winter solstice arrives and we begin the celebration of Chanukah. We commemorate the miracle of a small jug of oil that burned for eight nights, and as we celebrate, daylight expands. In the month of Kislev-despite the darkness, or perhaps because of it-we have the ability to tap into the Ohr HaGanuz, the hidden light of hope that rekindles our dreams and aspirations.

VOL 10: THE MONTH OF TEVES:
Refining Relationships, Elevating the Body

The quality of Teves is generally harsh—much like its counterpart Tamuz in the summer, thus the tendency for many is to hunker down, retract, curl up and wait for the month to pass by, only to reemerge when the harshness has dissipated. Think for a moment about the 'easier' months of the year, which, like gentle waves in the ocean, carry us where we want to go. We can ride these energies easily and they can propel us forward effortlessly, we just need to go with the overall flow, so to speak. The harsher months, on the other hand, can be compared to the more powerful waves that emanate from the belly of the ocean, which come forcefully crashing down and can easily drown a person before they even realize what has happened. However, those who want to utilize the momentum of the powerful energy that is available during such times can, with caution and creativity, harness these intense waves and ride them higher and farther than other, more gentle circumstances may allow. However, harnessing the power of Tohu, the raw energy of the body, does in fact need to be approached with great care and attention.

VOL 11: THE MONTH OF SHEVAT: ELEVATING EATING
& The Holiday of Tu b'Shevat

Each month of the year radiates with a distinct Divine energy and thus unique opportunities for growth, *Tikkun* and illumination. According to the deeper teachings of the Torah, all of these distinct qualities, opportunities and natural phenomena correspond to a certain data set. That is, the nature of each month is elucidated by a specific letter of the Aleph Beis, a tribe, verse, human sense, and so forth. The month of Shevat is particularly connected to food and our relationship to bodily intake. During this month we celebrate Tu b'Shevat, the New Year of the Tree, and aspire to create a proper and physically/emotionally/spiritually healthy relationship with food.

VOL 12: THE MONTH OF ADAR:
Transformation Through Laughter & Holy Doubt

Each month of the year radiates with distinct Divine qualities and unique opportunities for growth and spiritual illumination. As Adar concludes the monthly cycle of the year, as well as the solar phenomena of the winter, it is an appropriate month to think about our essential identity, before moving out to meet the world come spring. This month we strive to create a healthy relationship with holy humor, unbounded joy, and a general sense of lightness of being. Through the work of Adar we transform negative, crippling doubt and uncertainties into radical wonderment and openness.

New Release!

___

PROCESS AND PRESENCE
Life in Balance

In the world of process, the self and the world are broken, and we ambitiously strive to improve and to better.
In presence reality, all is now, everything is perfect, and there is nowhere to progress and certainly no reason to fight or strive.
This book offers the gift of a balanced life, wherein the path of process and the pathless path of presence are lived in unison.

www.ingramcontent.com/pod-product-compliance
Lightning Source LLC
Chambersburg PA
CBHW041254160426
42812CB00084B/2504